The

Man

Who

Made

Lists

Pronuba ———————— a Bride maid

Avus ————— a Grandfather.
Nepos ———— a Grandson.
Juvenis ———— a Young Man.
Sponsa ————————— a Bride
Sponsus ———————— a Bridegroom
Pauper ———— a Poor Man

Agricola ————— a Country Man
Aratrum ———— a Plough.
Arator ———————— a Ploughman.
Servus ———————— a Slave.
Catena ——————— a Chain
Arcus ———————— an Arch.
Columna ————————— Columna & Pillar
Carcer ——————— a Prison

Beasts / Elephas ———————— an Elephant.
Tigris ——————— a Tiger.
Porcus ————————— a Hog
Sorex ————————— a Rat.
Pecus ————————— Cattle
Bestia ———————— a Beast
Animalia ———————— Animals
Lepus ————————— a Hare

The
Man
Who
Made
Lists

Love, Death, Madness,

and the Creation of

Roget's Thesaurus

JOSHUA KENDALL

BERKLEY BOOKS, NEW YORK

THE BERKLEY PUBLISHING GROUP
Published by the Penguin Group
Penguin Group (USA) Inc.
375 Hudson Street, New York, New York 10014, USA
Penguin Group (Canada), 90 Eglinton Avenue East, Suite 700, Toronto, Ontario M4P 2Y3, Canada
(a division of Pearson Penguin Canada Inc.)
Penguin Books Ltd., 80 Strand, London WC2R 0RL, England
Penguin Group Ireland, 25 St. Stephen's Green, Dublin 2, Ireland (a division of Penguin Books Ltd.)
Penguin Group (Australia), 250 Camberwell Road, Camberwell, Victoria 3124, Australia
(a division of Pearson Australia Group Pty. Ltd.)
Penguin Books India Pvt. Ltd., 11 Community Centre, Panchsheel Park, New Delhi—110 017, India
Penguin Group (NZ), 67 Apollo Drive, Rosedale, North Shore 0632, New Zealand
(a division of Pearson New Zealand Ltd.)
Penguin Books (South Africa) (Pty.) Ltd., 24 Sturdee Avenue, Rosebank, Johannesburg 2196,
South Africa

Penguin Books Ltd., Registered Offices: 80 Strand, London, WC2R 0RL, England

While the author has made every effort to provide accurate telephone numbers and Internet addresses at the time of publication, neither the publisher nor the author assumes any responsibility for errors, or for changes that occur after publication. Further, publisher does not have any control over and does not assume any responsibility for the website or its content.

PRINTING HISTORY
G. P. Putnam's Sons hardcover edition / March 2008
Berkley trade paperback edition / March 2009

Berkley trade paperback ISBN: 978-0-425-22589-9

The Library of Congress has cataloged the G. P. Putnam's Sons hardcover edition as follows:

Kendall, Joshua C., date.
    The man who made lists: love, death, madness, and the creation of Roget's Thesaurus /
Joshua Kendall.
    p.   cm.
    ISBN 978-0-399-15462-1
    1. Roget, Peter Mark, 1779–1869. 2. Lexicographers—Great Britain—Biography. 3. Philologists—Great Britain—Biography. 4. Physicians—Great Britain—Biography. 5. Roget, Peter Mark, 1779–1869. Thesaurus of English words and phrases. 6. English language—Synonyms and antonyms—Lexicography. 7. Great Britain—Biography. I. Title.
    CT788.R534K46   2008   2007029264
    413.092—dc22
    [B]

PRINTED IN THE UNITED STATES OF AMERICA

10 9 8 7 6 5 4 3 2 1

Most Berkley Books are available at special quantity discounts for bulk purchases for sales, promotions, premiums, fund-raising, or educational use. Special books, or book excerpts, can also be created to fit specific needs.

For details, write: Special Markets, The Berkley Publishing Group, 375 Hudson Street, New York, New York 10014.

Contents

Preface

(64) PRECURSOR, antecedent, predecessor, forerunner, van-courier, outrider, avant-courier.

Prelude, preamble, preface, prologue, avant-propos, proemium, prolusion, preludium, proem, prolepsis, prolegomena, prefix, introduction, frontispiece, groundwork.

Since first rolling off the presses of London's Longman, Brown, Green and Longmans in June 1852, *Roget's Thesaurus of English Words and Phrases* has emerged as one of the most recognizable books in the English language. A proprietary eponym like Coke or Kleenex, *Roget's* has sold nearly forty million copies.

Though nearly everyone is familiar with *Roget's*, few people know anything about Peter Mark Roget, the eminent nineteenth-century polymath—physician, physiology expert, mathematician, inventor, writer, editor, and chess whiz—and what motivated him to write this immortal book.

Obsessed with words ever since he began studying Latin as a schoolboy, Roget completed a first draft of the *Thesaurus* (the Latin word for "treasure" or "treasury") in 1805, when he was just twenty-six. Then working as a physician in Manchester, Roget managed to crank out this string of word lists in less than a year.

However, it was not until his retirement from science, in 1848, at the age of sixty-nine, that Roget took on the challenge of finishing the *Thesaurus*. The still spry Roget worked nonstop for nearly four years to prepare the book for publication. He would continue to tinker with his masterpiece until his death at the age of ninety in 1869, having watched over the publication of some twenty-eight editions.

Roget's Thesaurus of English Words and Phrases Classified and Arranged So as to Facilitate the Expression of Ideas and Assist in Literary Composition clearly bore the stamp of its creator. *Roget's* was a two-for-one: it put both a book of synonyms and a topical dictionary (a compendium of thematically arranged concepts) under one cover.

Borrowing the principles of zoological classification, Roget organized all knowledge—not just words. Just as his hero, the eighteenth-century naturalist Carl Linnaeus, divided animals into six classes, Roget divvied up his one thousand concepts as follows:

    I. Abstract Relations
   II. Space
  III. Matter
   IV. Intellect
    V. Volition
   VI. Affections

The first edition actually contains 1,002 concepts, but Roget was a stickler for symmetry. Upon discovering that he had a couple too many, he numbered "Absence of Intellect" *450a*, and "Indiscrimination" *465a*.

The one thousand headings of the 1852 edition, from which are culled the epigraphs to each chapter in this book, were arranged not alphabetically but according to where a given idea fit within Roget's classification system. In that edition, the first entry is "Existence" (which falls under the first class, Abstract Relations). The purpose: to help readers find *le mot juste* ("the right word") for a given idea—say, "being" or "reality" for "Existence." Shortly before publication, Roget decided to insert an alphabetical index as an appendix, thus enabling readers to use the *Thesaurus* as a conventional book of synonyms—without necessarily having to delve into its complex philosophical underpinnings.

Scholars immediately began fawning over his prodigious efforts. In 1853 an anonymous reviewer observed in the *Westminster Review*:

> As the words are arranged in groups, the whole Thesaurus may be read *through*, and not prove dry reading either. We have known students who had the courage to read through Latin and Greek dictionaries, but the *ideal* classification in this work renders such an exploit much more easy and pleasing than the ordinary alphabetical arrangement. . . . Roget will rank with Samuel Johnson as a literary instrument-maker of the first-class.

Generations of British writers would look up to Roget as a kindred soul who could offer both emotional as well as intellectual sustenance. In the stage directions to *Peter Pan*, J. M. Barrie includes an homage to Roget:

> The night nursery of the Darling family, which is the scene of our opening Act, is at the top of a rather depressed street in Bloomsbury. We might have a right to place it where we will, and the reason Bloomsbury is chosen is that Mr. Roget once lived there. So did we in the days when his Thesaurus was our only companion in London; and we whom he has helped to wend our way through life have always wanted to pay him a little compliment.

For Barrie, Roget's masterpiece was synonymous with virtue itself. To describe the one saving grace of the play's villain, Captain Hook, Barrie adds, "The man is not wholly evil—he has a *Thesaurus* in his cabin."

Described by one literary critic as "a horn of plenty out of which words pour for our examination and selection," *Roget's* has also served as a muse for some of the English language's most acclaimed poets. In her diary entry for February 19, 1956, the young Sylvia Plath, then a graduate student at Cambridge University, writes, "Today my thesaurus, which I would rather live with on a desert isle than a bible, as I have so often boasted cleverly, lay open after I'd written the draft of a bad, sick poem, at 545: Deception, 546: Untruth, 547: Dupe, 548: Deceiver." Plath's attachment to Roget was not merely platonic. A week later, in the same entry in which she describes her famous first kiss with "that big, dark, hunky boy"—the poet Ted Hughes, whom she would marry just four months later—Plath confesses that she already has a lover, characterizing herself as "Roget's strumpet." To compose her first collection of poems, *The Colossus*, published in 1960, Plath would frequently consult her dead-white paramour.

Plath's contemporary, the Welsh poet Dylan Thomas, also couldn't have written some of his most cherished poems without *Roget's*. The manuscript of his last poem, "Poem on his Birthday," published two years before his death in 1953, is festooned with seemingly random numbers. For a couple of decades, the meaning of these digits remained a mystery until one critic suddenly realized that they refer to concepts from *Roget's*. To revise his early drafts of the poem, to tweak an image or sound pattern he was developing, Thomas rifled through *Roget's*. A scholar who did a computer analysis of the original manuscript concludes that about thirty of the 370 different words that appear in the poem's final version can be traced back to this technique. Summing up his reading of the poem, the renowned literary critic

David Holbrook of Cambridge University observes, "[Thomas's] substitute for inspiration was Roget."

The American version of the *Thesaurus*, which came out in 1854, initially appealed mostly to scholars. But the crossword puzzle craze of the 1920s turned Roget into a celebrity on the other side of the pond as well. In a feature story, "Roget Becomes Saint of Crosswordia," appearing in February 1925, *The New York Times Magazine* reported:

> Roget. *Thesaurus*. Until the word in six letters meaning this or that . . . threw its tantalizing shadow across a hitherto tranquil land, the meaning to the layman of either Roget or Thesaurus might be described, chemically, as "a trace." . . . In homes where a few weeks ago *volume* and *compiler* were not even names, the book found a place where in the Age of Innocence the family Bible might have rested. Hand in hand, of course, went growing familiarity with its author's name. Almost unconsciously one grew away from a habit of calling him Rojjet or Rogget and imperceptibly Rozhay became as much a part of the radiator-side patter as discussion of the latest super-film or the newest wrinkle in radio.

In the days before every laptop came equipped with a thesaurus, Roget, who had the market all to himself, was an icon.

But Roget's new world of one thousand concepts was not only his monumental gift to posterity. It was, first and foremost, the primary means by which he preserved his own sanity. Overwhelmed by the early death of his father and the emotional instability of his mother, Roget was constantly burying himself in books to cope with his sadness, anxiety, and anger. As a boy, Roget kept dreaming up new worlds in the hope of escaping the dreary one in which he found himself. Commenting on his embrace of astronomy when he was twelve, his mother remarked, "Peter ever eager after new studies, has for this while left this world and lived wholly in the Starry regions."

Madness ran in the immediate family. Roget's maternal grandmother, Margaret Garnault Romilly, suffered from an unidentified mental disorder—probably severe depression or schizophrenia—that left her in an almost vegetative state for most of her life. In his memoir published in 1840, Roget's uncle, the distinguished Member of Parliament Sir Samuel Romilly, mentions that she had a nervous collapse when her parents initially objected to her marriage to his father. Romilly also reveals that he and his two siblings, Thomas and Catherine—Peter's mother—were raised jointly by an aunt, Margaret Facquier, and a nurse, Mary Evans, adding that "as for my mother, she was incapable, from the bad state of her health, of taking any part in our education."

Romilly himself would give in to his own suicidal despair at the age of sixty-one, at which time, Roget's mother, until then merely temperamental and emotionally demanding, would lapse into paranoia. For the last decade and a half of her life, Catherine Romilly Roget engaged in increasingly bizarre behavior. She would often accuse the servants of plotting against her and could sit for hours on end stone-faced. She was also prone to wander aimlessly around the Devon resort town of Ilfracombe, where she lived with Roget's sister, Annette. Like her mother, Annette would suffer frequent bouts of depression and die a lonely woman. The life of Roget's daughter, Kate, followed a similar trajectory.

Roget himself was not immune. As his uncle once wrote him, "Despondency is, I have always thought, the great defect of our family, and I do not think that you are more exempt from it than the rest." Described at fourteen by his mother as "awkwardly bashful," the young Roget was slow to make friends and felt most comfortable in his own company.

However, unlike his mother or uncle, Roget managed to stave off madness. As a boy, he stumbled upon a remarkable discovery—that compiling lists of words could provide solace, no matter what misfortunes might befall him. He was particularly fond of cataloguing the objects, both animate and inanimate, in his environment. As an adult, he kept returning to the classification of words and concepts. Immersion in the nuances of language could invariably both energize him and keep his persistent anxiety at bay.

As he grew older, though he had satisfying relationships with both his wife, Mary, and Margaret Spowers, the governess who became his unofficial second wife after Mary's early death, Roget remained more interested in words than in people. In a recent short story titled "Roget's Thesaurus," the award-winning Canadian writer Keath Fraser imagines the thoughts that must have been buzzing inside Roget's head after he published his *Thesaurus*: "Men are odd animals. I have never felt as at home around *them* as around their words; without these they're monkeys. (See TRUISM.) The other day I was going through my book and it struck me that I have more words for Disapprobation than Approbation. Why is this?"

PROLOGUE

Stained
by the
Blood of
a National
Hero

(828) PAIN, suffering, physical pain.

Grief, sorrow, distress, affliction, woe, bitterness, heartache, a heavy heart, a bleeding heart, a broken heart, heavy affliction, &c.

Unhappiness, infelicity, misery, wretchedness, desolation.

It was Monday morning, November 2, 1818, and a dense yellow fog was hanging over London. One of England's most esteemed members of Parliament was acutely ill. Sir Samuel Romilly, known as "the honestest man in the House of Commons," was bedridden with a high fever. Even more alarming, he was rapidly losing his mind.

Just five months earlier, Romilly had delivered a rousing speech before Parliament, urging repeal of the repressive laws that Great Britain had been forced to adopt in the effort to defeat Napoleon. With the "Great War" now over for more than three years, Romilly thought the time for reform had arrived. He could not understand why the government should still sanction the hanging of criminals or the beating of soldiers. On June 5, 1818, to a thunderous response of many a "Hear! Hear!" he had thus exhorted his colleagues to live up to their ideals: "Who our successors may be, I know not; but God grant that this country may never see another Parliament so regardless of the liberties and rights of the people."

But this heroic statesman, distinguished by his thin nose and his delicate lips, was now a shell of the imposing figure he had once been. His beloved wife, Anne, had just died from cancer. Exhausted from weeks of insomnia, Romilly was gaunt, his flowing mane of white hair disheveled.

He was home in his townhouse at 21 Russell Square. Like most Regency bedrooms, Romilly's was sparsely furnished. On the left side of the fireplace, across from the bed, stood his writing desk and wardrobe; on the right side were a washbasin and a full-length mirror. From his third-floor window he could peer directly into the lime trees that shrouded the square, as well as into the houses on the other side of the street.

Romilly appeared calm—so much so that his eighteen-year-old daughter, Sophia, became uneasy. Sitting in a chair next to the bed, Sophia could not make eye contact with her father, as his small brown eyes were fixed in a blank stare. His attention seemed to be focused on sensations that only he could perceive. The sixty-one-year-old barrister, who had achieved international renown for his tireless advocacy on behalf of the downtrodden, now found himself in need of urgent help.

Shortly after two o'clock that afternoon, Romilly asked Sophia to go downstairs and summon his doctor and favorite nephew, Peter Mark Roget.

Roget was then a bachelor approaching forty who also lived in

Bloomsbury, just two blocks from his uncle. His medical practice was flourishing, and three years earlier, upon his election as a fellow of the Royal Society, Roget had officially joined London's scientific elite.

But on this occasion, Romilly was not interested in Roget's ministrations. Ever since Anne's death a few days earlier, he had lost all hope. What Romilly really wanted was to be left alone so that he could bring his suffering to an end. Moments after Sophia left the room, the other family members and servants gathered downstairs heard a crash emanating from the third floor.

Minutes later, Dr. Roget pried open the bedroom door and rushed in. He found his uncle—dressed only in a shirt, and with a blanket wrapped around his waist—staggering next to the washstand. To his horror, he saw that Romilly had slit his throat with a razor.

For a moment, Roget was paralyzed. He then grabbed his uncle, who, dripping with blood, motioned for a pen and paper to be brought to him. Propped up by Roget, Romilly proceeded to scribble out a couple of words, but soon dropped to the floor. The barely legible note read: "My dear . . . I wish . . ." Roget was not sure what Romilly meant. Most commentators later concluded that Romilly was somehow trying to communicate with his late wife.

Kneeling next to his uncle on the floor, Roget, too, was now splattered with blood. He immediately began tending to Romilly's wounds and trying to revive him. An hour later, Romilly breathed his last breath in his nephew's arms.

Six weeks earlier, at Romilly's request, Roget had traveled to Cowes Castle, an elegant villa on the northernmost harbor of the Isle of Wight, to look after Romilly's wife. As Roget wrote to a friend in mid-September, Anne Romilly had had "a serious attack of illness, principally in the chest." At first, Roget thought that she was likely to recover within a couple of weeks. But it soon became clear that Anne's illness was terminal.

In early October, Samuel Romilly was still in full possession of his mental faculties, though his wife's precarious condition was the source of much discomfort. For a while, he held on to some largely illusory hopes for Anne's recovery. About ten days after Roget's arrival, in a letter to his longtime confidant Etienne Dumont, the Swiss pastor who would later achieve renown as the French translator of the philosopher Jeremy Bentham, Romilly noted that "my dear Anne is *better*, not very considerably, but she certainly is *better*."

But as her health continued to deteriorate, Romilly could no longer avoid facing reality. He began to express fears of going mad; as he was acutely aware, insanity had ravaged his late mother. On October 8, Romilly added a codicil to his will, noting that "I am at the present moment of perfectly sound mind . . . but I am labouring under a most severe affliction and I cannot but recollect that insanity is amongst the evils which unusual afflictions sometimes produce."

For Romilly, the prospect of the imminent loss of Anne, then just forty-four, was terrifying. Over the course of their twenty-one-year marriage, which had produced seven children, Anne had been his anchor—his other half. Without Anne, his rise from a humble middle-class background to the pinnacle of British politics would have been inconceivable.

Responding to Roget's reports about Romilly from Cowes Castle, Dr. Alexander Marcet, who lived next door to Romilly at 23 Russell Square, cautioned his close friend and medical colleague, "Any symptoms of declining firmness of mind is doubly alarming in a man of [Romilly's] stamp. Pray try to prevail upon him to occupy his mind, even with occasional business if the common modes of diverting one's attention fail him." But despite Marcet's prodding, Roget was oblivious to these warning signs. Though well versed in the symptoms of medical diseases, Roget was poorly attuned to the language of emotional distress.

When Anne died, on Thursday, October 29, Roget shouldered the responsibility of informing his uncle of the devastating news. Romilly quickly became unhinged. Muscles throughout his body began twitching, and nothing could be found to stop these spasms. "[Romilly] told me," Dumont, by then also at Cowes Castle, later reported, "his brains were burning hot."

Despite his uncle's expressed desire to recuperate in the country, Roget insisted on taking him back to London immediately. Roget's impulsive decision would have dire consequences. The trip turned out to be harrowing for both Romilly and his extensive retinue, which included two of his children, William and Sophia, his sister-in-law, the servants, Dumont, and Roget.

Romilly sat in the same chaise as Sophia, clutching her hand for a good part of the journey, but she was unable to calm her father down. As the horses continued to slosh through the muddy turf, Romilly's anxiety kept mounting; he repeatedly tore away at his own flesh—his fingers, hands, and nose—to the point of drawing blood. The family spent Friday night at an inn in Winchester, where Roget shared a room with Romilly to keep an eye on him. Though the coach could easily have reached London on Saturday, Romilly's distress forced the traveling party to spend another night at an inn in Miller's Green, two stages, or rest stops, from Winchester. Once again, Roget was paired with Romilly for the night.

At about five o'clock on Sunday afternoon, November 1, the carriage reached Kensington. Dumont thought it unwise to bring Romilly back to his townhouse because reminders of Anne would be everywhere. But Romilly, sensing that he would need a long time to recuperate from his illness, insisted on going home right away.

SIR SAMUEL ROMILLY, KNT.

M.P. for Westminster, Chancellor of Durham &c. &c.

Drawn by G. Bratland — Engraved by W. Freeman

Published November 19 1816 by T. Bratland, Wood St. Spa-fields.

Samuel Romilly, 1816. Today the blue plaque at 21 Russell Square reads,
"Here, Lived, Sir Samuel Romilly, Law Reformer / Born 1757 / Died 1818."

A few minutes later, the carriage pulled up to 21 Russell Square. Upon seeing his master, Romilly's footman, Bowen, remarked that he looked "better than one would have expected." But Dumont was less sanguine; as he later put it, Romilly was "in a state of delirium."

Rather than returning to his own nearby home, Roget spent another nearly sleepless night at his uncle's side. But by three o'clock the next day, Romilly was gone.

On November 4, the front page of *The Times* of London was wall-to-wall Samuel Romilly; it contained news of nothing else. This national tragedy, which put the spotlight on Roget's clinical acumen, temporarily sullied the doctor's reputation. As word of Romilly's suicide spread, both medical experts and the British public at large began second-guessing the recent decisions he had made regarding his uncle's medical care. Roget had been stained by his uncle's blood because, in the eyes of many observers, he bore considerable responsibility for his patient's demise. Though no one questioned Roget's concern for his uncle, a consensus emerged that he had failed to grasp the full extent of Romilly's emotional agony.

Romilly's spilled blood rattled Roget's soul. Roget's Bloomsbury neighbor Jane Griffin understood the depth of the blow, writing in her diary: "Dr. Roget . . . was the only one who saw his dying uncle, who supported him on the floor while his powerless hand vainly endeavoured to scrawl on the blood-stained paper his last wishes, and who received his dying breath; that Uncle too who was his pride, his treasure, his glory, who loved him as a son!" Worse even than the horror, shame, and guilt that gripped Roget was the loss. Having hardly known his long-dead father, and feeling uncomfortable around his mother, Roget had depended on Romilly's steady nurturance since infancy. The pain of having failed the person to whom he had felt more attached than to anybody else on the face of the earth was nearly unbearable.

The night of Romilly's suicide, Roget locked himself in his crepe-lined bedroom, refusing to see any visitors. As soon as he rose the next day, he wrote a letter to Dr. Alexander Marcet, which read in part, "I have had no sleep, but am calmer this morning. I perspired copiously all night. Pulse at present 80. . . . I am also anxious about the business of the day. Have you ascertained whether it is necessary for me to attend at the inquest? It would be most harrowing to my feelings." Marcet managed to have him excused from appearing that afternoon at the hearing called by the coroner. And for the last two months of 1818, Roget remained largely sequestered. Catching a brief glimpse of the doctor that November, Jane Griffin observed: "He looked like . . . an apparition."

Roget would eventually rebound, but his recovery was slow. He didn't return to work until the beginning of the following year. Once he did, he would have trouble recruiting new patients. He also underwent a midlife crisis. In June of 1821, he wrote to Etienne Dumont:

I will confide in you what I won't let anyone else know, that the experience of these last years has greatly diminished the confidence that I used to have about succeeding in my profession. I sometimes doubt if it's worth the effort to continue; but what prevents me from renouncing it is the impossibility at my age of doing anything else but pursuing the career that I began.

In this letter, Roget told Dumont of his plan to "start again at the foot of the ladder," by which he meant that, after an eight-year hiatus, he would resume giving lectures on anatomy at the Royal Institution, the scientific academy that offered a full slate of what we might today call adult education classes. He also asked his Swiss friend not to inform his mother about his "lack of success because her natural disposition to anxiety would not make the cure any easier."

But Roget's decision to go back to the Royal Institution would turn his life around. In 1822, his course on Natural Philosophy, in which he systematically reviewed the behavior of all forms of human and animal life, turned out to be a smashing success. *The Literary Gazette and Journal of Belles Lettres, Arts, Sciences, etc.*, a prominent London literary magazine, began providing detailed summaries of each of Roget's lectures, owing to "the vivid sensation produced in the scientific world" and "the intelligence which they contain and the admiration which they have excited." A few years later, Longmans, which would later publish the *Thesaurus*, put out his first book—a transcript of one of his celebrated lectures on human and comparative physiology.

Following Romilly's tragic death, Roget had been forced to accept that clinical medicine wasn't for him. His own internal radar could pick up nuances with words and concepts, but not with people. Cutting back on patient care, Roget would cement his reputation as a first-rate scientist and lecturer. He would also move in a new direction—becoming a science writer for the masses. In the 1820s and 1830s, Roget would publish three hundred thousand words in the *Encyclopaedia Britannica* and also write several lengthy review articles for the Society for the Diffusion of Useful Knowledge, the organization affiliated with the new University of London, which sought to enable the British working class to educate itself.

By 1824, while in his mid-forties, Roget would finally marry and start a family of his own. Unlike his numerous close relatives who fell prey to extended bouts of severe mental illness, Roget had found a creative outlet for his feelings of loss and despair. He would dedicate the rest of his lengthy life to disseminating abstract knowledge in a clear and useful way. As if by magic, these prodigious intellectual labors, many of which involved organizing the entirety of a given scientific discipline—say, anatomy, electricity, magnetism, physiology, or zoology—insulated him from his turbulent emotions.

His immortal *Thesaurus* was the culmination of this lifelong desire to bring order to the world, as it involved classifying everything. It also, or so Roget hoped, could advance the march of scientific progress by transforming the man in the street into a wordsmith. "It is of the utmost consequence," he wrote in the introduction, "that strict accuracy should regulate our use of language, and that every one should acquire the power and the habit of expressing his thoughts with perspicuity and correctness." Like Henry Higgins, the headstrong linguistics professor in Shaw's *Pygmalion* (and likewise, the Lerner and Loewe musical *My Fair Lady*), Roget approached the challenge of teaching the English how to speak with a missionary's zeal. But to understand fully how Roget's obsession with words and abstract knowledge managed to inoculate him against life's trials requires going back to his lonely and chaotic boyhood.

PART ONE

Formations

(1779–1808)

(129) INFANT, babe, baby.

Child, bairn, little one, youth, boy, lad, stripling, youngster, younker, whipster, whippersnapper, schoolboy, hobbarby-hoy, hobbledy-hoy, cadet, minor.

1.

The
Boy
Without
a Home

(189) PLACE OF HABITATION.

ABODE, dwelling, lodging, domicile, residence, address, habitation, berth, seat, lap, sojourn, housing, quarters, headquarters, resiance, throne, ark.

Home, household, homestall, fireside, snuggery, hearth, lares et penates, household gods, roof, household, housing.

Peter Roget was not the first Roget (derived from the French *rouge*, the name means "little red man") to have had a flair for words. Trained in the ministry in his native Switzerland, his father, Jean Roget, composed sermons, which, as Samuel Romilly later recalled, were noteworthy for their "taste and elegance."

In 1775, at the age of twenty-four, Jean Roget, whose father was a Geneva clockmaker, immigrated to London to take over as pastor at Le Quarré (The Square), a French Protestant church in Soho. That's where he met Catherine Romilly and her younger brother, Samuel, at the time a young law student. Though swept off his feet by the comely Catherine, who shared his passion for French literature,

Jean Roget was hesitant about proposing marriage. Lacking any property, he feared that Catherine's father, Peter Romilly, a prosperous jeweler then earning some 20,000 pounds a year (roughly $2 million today), would not find him suitable. But according to Samuel Romilly, Jean Roget never had any reason to be so worried:

> Upon the first mention of Roget's addresses, my father declared that if they had my sister's approbation, they had his; he had long before resolved never to resist . . . his daughter's inclinations. With respect to Roget, however, it was not a case in which my father was merely not to oppose; he could not but approve a marriage so well calculated to make a beloved child happy.

The Rogets were married on February 12, 1778, in St. Marylebone Church, a few weeks after Catherine's twenty-third birthday, and settled on Broad Street (now Broadwick Street) near Golden Square in the heart of Soho. Their first child, Peter, was born on January 18 of the following year.

The Rogets' house was situated between the two churches, one French and one English, to which the infant belonged. A few blocks to the north stood the Huguenot church on Little Dean Street where Jean Roget preached. First established in 1689, Le Quarré was one of nearly twenty French Huguenot churches then sprinkled throughout London. By 1800, the number had dwindled to ten, as Peter Roget's generation of English Huguenots loosened the ties with France. Le Quarré would shut its doors in 1853.

A few blocks to the south of the home of Jean and Catherine Roget was St. James's Anglican Church, located right around the corner from Piccadilly Circus, where it still stands. Designed roughly a century earlier by the legendary architect Sir Christopher Wren, St. James's is the largest of Wren's churches and is said to have been his favorite. Forced to work on a tight budget in the wake of the Great Fire of 1666, Wren had described it as "beautiful and convenient—as such the cheapest I could invent." Its exterior is plain, but its interior is exquisite, featuring a huge organ and elaborate wood carvings by Grinling Gibbons. It was there that the three-week-old infant was christened Peter Mark Roget on February 11, 1779.

In the eighteenth century, Soho was a middle-class neighborhood teeming with foreigners. The biggest wave of immigrants had come from France after King Louis XIV outlawed Protestantism in 1685, and the English, then fiercely anti-Catholic, had proved particularly welcoming. At the time of Peter Roget's birth, French Huguenots comprised about half of Soho's population, but many foreigners from other European countries—particularly Greece and Italy—had also ended up there.

First completed in the 1730s, Broad Street featured a little bit of everything. Its denizens consisted of the very wealthy and the very poor, as well as those in between. On its cobblestones could be found street vendors hawking their wares, beggars shouting profanities, and mourning doves making their way over from nearby Golden Square. While passers-by occasionally had to step over garbage, Broad Street was also lined with elegant small shops that specialized in various goods such as china, crystal, and engravings. The artist and poet William Blake—who, like Roget, had been christened at St. James's Church—grew up in a four-story house at 28 Broad Street; from its basement, his father and older brother ran "Blake and Son, Hosiers & Haberdashers."

In this lively strip of Soho, the Rogets were thriving. But within

just a few months of his birth, Peter's idyllic family life began to unravel. In his memoir, Samuel Romilly described the unexpected crisis
that tore it apart:

> The happiness [the Rogets] enjoyed upon their marriage was as
> pure, and as complete, as is ever the portion of human beings; but
> it was of very short duration. They were blessed with one sweet
> child to increase that happiness; but not long after the joyful event
> of his birth, in the spring of 1779, and just when I had projected to
> pass the approaching summer with them in a lodging they had
> taken at Fulham, and when we had begun to carry our project into
> execution, Roget was seized with an inflammation of the lungs, at-
> tended with a violent spitting of blood, and with other symptoms so
> alarming, that his life appeared to be in the most imminent danger.

Jean Roget had developed tuberculosis. At the urging of his doctor,
he decided to go back to Geneva in the hope of finding a rest cure.
On June 3, 1779, Peter's parents departed from London, leaving the
nearly six-month-old baby in the care of his namesake, Catherine's
father, Peter Romilly.

On the trip to Switzerland, Catherine nursed her husband, smoth-
ering him with tender affection. From Dover, she wrote her father: "I
write this while I flatter myself mon cher epoux [my dear spouse] is
enjoying a little sleep. You must not expect, my dear father, any account of the places I go through, as I never leave him, and till he gets
better mean to be his constant companion." The journey would have
many frightening moments. About two weeks later, Catherine reported from St. Dezier, "Roget has been exceedingly ill. . . . The surgeon . . . has just bled Roget. He assures me the journey is of service

to him. . . . But to be sick on a journey is a melancholy situation. . . .
What have I not suffered from those unhappy thoughts which have
haunted my mind since our leaving of Calais." Catherine's letters back
home were addressed solely to her father; her mother, Margaret
Romilly, was nearly always too incapacitated by depression to show
much interest in her daily activities. From her infancy on, Catherine
had been unable to rely on her mother for emotional support.
Throughout Catherine's childhood, Margaret Romilly had rarely been
well enough even to go on routine family outings.

Jean and Catherine Roget arrived safely in Geneva at the end of
June. According to their initial plan, they hoped to return to London
in a few months.

After his parents left for Switzerland, Peter was brought to live with
his maternal grandfather, Peter Romilly, on High Street in the exclu-
sive suburb of Marylebone. Though the tony neighborhood was a step
up from Soho, the small house—with just two tiny windows on each
floor—was "very scanty and homely," according to Samuel Romilly's
description. The Romillys were a well-known fixture in this close-knit
community, then a mile west of the city limits. In fact, just a couple of
years before Catherine dropped off the infant Peter, some eight hundred well-wishers had shown up at a celebration commemorating the
thirtieth anniversary of her parents' marriage. "In such a tittle-tattle
place," Peter Romilly once complained to his daughter, "it is hardly
possible to form any party but the whole place must know of it."

Peter Romilly's father had worked as a wax-bleacher after immi-
grating to London from the family homestead in Montpelier. As an
adolescent, Romilly had served as an apprentice for a French jeweler
named Lafosse on Broad Street before opening his own Soho shop
at 18 Frith Street. Though Peter Romilly's wife, Margaret, had given
birth to nine children, only the last three—Thomas, Catherine, and
Samuel—managed to survive past early childhood.

The Romilly children had grown up in the house above their father's jewelry shop. Both Catherine and Samuel were about the same age as the eight-year-old composer Wolfgang Amadeus Mozart—Catherine was nine and Samuel seven—who had moved next door, into 20 Frith Street, in 1764. That spring, the Romillys' neighbor, Leopold Mozart, hosted concerts nearly every afternoon between noon and three. Patrons, who paid either five shillings for admission or ten shillings for a copy of young Mozart's sonatas, had, as Leopold Mozart advertised in a local paper, "an opportunity of putting the boy's Talents to a more Particular Proof, by giving him any Thing to play at Sight, or any Music without a Bass, which he will write on the Spot." A few weeks after this run ended, the Mozarts were gone; the seamy side of Soho, which included a steady contingent of streetwalkers, had proved intolerable to the staid Leopold Mozart.

In 1769, the Romillys had been showered by good fortune when Philip de la Haize, the cousin of Roget's grandmother, Margaret Garnault Romilly, died, leaving 15,000 pounds—then a considerable sum—to the family. The inheritance paved the way for the family's move to Marylebone.

Though Peter Romilly could be moody, he was also capable of considerable warmth. In her essay "Traits and Stories of the Huguenots," published in 1853 in *Household Words*, the periodical edited by Charles Dickens, the renowned novelist Elizabeth Gaskell presented Roget's grandfather as a paragon of benevolence. Basing her characterization on her perusal of Samuel Romilly's memoir, Gaskell drew a somewhat idealized portrait:

> Most affectionate, impulsive, generous, carried away by transports
> of anger and of grief, tender and true in all his relationships—the
> reader does not easily forget the father of Sir Samuel Romilly, with

his fond adoption of Montaigne's idea, "playing on a flute by the side of his daughter's bed, in order to waken her in the morning." . . . There was much more demonstration of affection in all these French households, if what I have gathered from their descendants be correct, than we English should ever dare to manifest.

Though deprived of his parents' presence, the infant Peter was still showered with some amount of familial affection. Peter Romilly also hired a nursemaid, known as Miss Bell, to help take care of his grandson.

Peter Roget's godmother was Miss Margaret Facquier, a cousin of his grandmother Margaret, who had moved in with the Romillys upon their marriage. Given Margaret Romilly's chronic mental instability, Miss Facquier, who along with the nursemaid Mary Evans had helped raise the three Romilly children, was used to being the stand-in. But Miss Facquier, then in her early sixties, had some serious health problems of her own, and she died in 1781, leaving her two-year-old godson fifty pounds in her will.

Roget's grandmother would remain a nonentity in his life, though she lived until 1796 and cast a long shadow. In his memoir, Sir Samuel originally had written several pages about his parents' odd marriage, but he later crossed them out. While family members avoided talking much about Margaret Romilly, her mental illness, exacerbated by the early deaths of six of her children, would have reverberations on generations of Rogets and Romillys. Like Catherine Roget, Samuel Romilly was also forever haunted by having being denied a normal relationship with his own mother.

Whatever the nature of her troubles, Margaret Garnault Romilly also came from a distinguished Huguenot family. The Garnaults had immigrated to England from Poitou, France, in the late seventeenth and early eighteenth centuries. By the early 1800s, the family had amassed a considerable fortune as governors of the New River Company, a highly successful firm that was responsible for cleaning up the river water from the Thames. Though the last male heir died in the mid-1800s, the Garnault women have married into some of Britain's most prominent families, such as Ouvry, Treacher, Collins, and Bowles. (In the late twentieth century, Bowles would emerge as a household name around the globe after one Camilla Shand married into the family. Camilla Parker Bowles, as every tabloid reader knows, has since remarried her first love, Prince Charles.)

After being untimely ripped from his Broad Street home, Peter would not see his father and mother for more than two years. In the meantime, his parents would move back and forth between Geneva and Lausanne a couple of times before finally settling in Lausanne. In 1781, with his health still languishing, Jean Roget resigned from his position at his church on Little Dean Street: he realized he would probably never make it back to England.

That spring, the two-year-old Peter was taken to live in Switzerland with his parents. Assigned the task of transporting the toddler was Catherine's brother Samuel Romilly, then studying for admission to the bar. The trip did not seem to faze Peter. Upon arriving in Ostend, Romilly, who was accompanied by Peter's nursery maid, reported to his sister:

Your dear little boy . . . is in perfect health and in excellent spirits. He is quite delighted with his journey; he plays till he is tired and then sleeps for two or three hours together upon the road. Of all the passengers, he was the only one who was not sick upon our little voyage and the only one who could sleep well. His sleep was quite as sound the whole night as if he had been on shore.

The picture that Romilly paints of Peter's imperviousness to stress during this trip is consistent with the myth that the family created about his entire childhood. Though Peter would also come to believe that he was not scarred by the trauma of his father's early death and the shuttling around between temporary homes, the truth appears to lie elsewhere. The lack of stability in his early years no doubt contributed to his extreme shyness and to what family members referred to as his "melancholy temperament."

After the birth of her second child, christened Ann Susanne Louise—and called Annette—in April 1783, Catherine fell into a deep depression. Jean Roget's sudden death a month later threatened to push her over the edge. "Never did any woman," Samuel Romilly observed, "adore a husband with more passionate fondness than she did hers. . . . And never was affliction greater than that which she now endured."

Samuel shared her profound grief. The two men had kept up their deep friendship by exchanging frequent letters during the four years the Rogets had spent in Switzerland. In June, Samuel wrote Catherine, "I have lost the best and dearest friend I ever had, a better and a deeper one than I ever shall have again." In another letter a few days later, he acknowledged just how much he had looked up to Jean Roget: "I reflect that . . . he will still be the guardian and director of my conduct and whenever I am doubtful how to act, I will consider how he would have acted in such a situation and I shall then be certain to determine what is just and virtuous." Eager to repay Jean Roget's kindness, Romilly readily assumed many paternal responsibilities for Peter.

That September, Romilly rushed to Lausanne to help his sister take Peter and Annette back to London. He was worried lest Catherine fall apart. As Romilly later recalled, he decided to take a circuitous route, "avoiding any of the places, through which my sister passed with her husband when she left the country, and which she thought would be attended with remembrances too painful for her to endure."

But Samuel's fears were unwarranted. During the twenty-four-day return trip from Switzerland, Catherine seemed calm. Throughout Peter's boyhood, Catherine would be fraught with intense anxiety and would often find much to complain about. But in the immediate aftermath of her husband's death, she remained remarkably easygoing. Apparently, the horror had yet to fully register, and she was temporarily numb.

Rather than being paralyzed by sadness, Catherine eagerly explored the various cities they passed through. She also kept a detailed diary. Her observations tended to focus on physical descriptions of the landscape and the quality of their lodgings. Cleanliness was often on her mind. Of Bern, she wrote:

[It] is a very beautiful city, the streets wide, regularly built and with arches, that you may walk all around the town in bad weather without being wet; under these arches are the shops; in the middle of the street runs a small stream of water, which with the well-built fountains and the cleanliness of the whole is very agreeable. The streets are kept clean by the criminals. . . . Everything appeared very clean and the people very cheerful, which shows that their taskmasters were not severe.

A couple of weeks later, as they arrived in the Netherlands, Catherine described the town of Breda as "pretty." In an entry dated October 10, she added a telling prophecy in parentheses, "Peter will remember the Dutch cleanliness." Like his mother, Peter would wage a lifelong battle against dirt and disorder.

The Rogets arrived in London at six o'clock on the night of October 18, 1783. Living with Peter and Annette in temporary lodgings in Paddington that fall, Catherine had to start facing life without her husband. In Georgian England, widowhood—at any age, particularly Catherine's relatively young twenty-eight—posed enormous challenges. The economic ramifications alone were staggering. For the rest of her life, Catherine would have to fall back on family— first, on her brother Samuel, and then on her son, Peter—for the money to get by. Widows also instantly lost their social status, and they could do little to recapture it, as remarriage—except for the most alluring—was relatively rare. In Catherine Roget's day, the odds that an English woman widowed at thirty might remarry were just one in a hundred.

After the shock and the disbelief passed, despair set in quickly enough. Catherine would always feel as if she had been prematurely expelled from the Garden of Eden. In a letter congratulating Samuel on his marriage, written some fifteen years after her husband's death, she lamented, "You cannot think the pleasure I received when I reflect that you are now a married man—enjoying the perfect happiness which was once my lot." But Catherine rarely expressed any anger about her fate, not even to her brother. With social convention leaving her little choice but to bottle it up, she often felt depressed and listless.

Jean Roget's early death had equally profound effects on his son. Though the young boy would keep his feelings to himself, loss, and the fear of loss, were to shape the way Peter saw the world. The adult Roget would reveal this lifelong struggle in a poignant list, "Dates of Deaths," which he appended to the front of his "List of Principal Events," a telegraphic rendering of the major milestones of his life. (Many entries are just a few syllables; for example, next to November 2, 1818, Roget wrote: "Sir S. R. d.") Before he got around to recording

Dates of Deaths

1783	John Roget
84	Peter Romilly
	Jane Romilly
1802	David Chauvet
03	
18	Rachel Rede
—	Sir Samuel Romilly
19	Catherine Hunter
22	Thomas Smith
	Ann Fisher
	John Reid
	Alexr. Marcet
27	Sarah Ingram
28	Thos. Peter Romilly
29	E. L. Dumont — Davy
	Lady Scarlett
31	Caroline Allen
33	Jonathan Hobson
	Mary J. Roget
34	Samuel Romilly
35	Catherine Roget
37	Cuthbert Romilly
40	John Whishaw
44	John Hewlett
	Bostock

The Dates of Deaths list is revealing of the young
Peter's attachments—only one of his four
grandparents made the cut.

the events themselves—the text begins in 1787, when Roget was eight
and ends in 1857 when he was seventy-eight—Roget completed
"Dates of Deaths." Included are the names of about thirty people—
those family members and friends who meant the most to him. Its

first two entries are "Jean Roget, 1783" and "Peter Romilly, 1784." By the time he was five, Peter was forced to cope with the unexpected deaths of both his beloved father and his doting grandfather.

These two sudden losses also dramatically altered the way in which his mother related to him. Without a husband and father to lean on, Catherine became excessively dependent on Peter—so much so that she almost began living through him. This extreme method of dulling emotional pain was common among the English widows of her day. "I now live on in the life of others," one despondent widow put it, "waiting on, hoping on, for them, and praying for blessings to come." In Catherine's case, she would measure the value of her own life by Peter's achievements. Forced into the role of the man of the house, Peter also had to put up with Catherine's attempts to seek from him the love and protection that she might otherwise have received from her husband.

By contrast, Annette and Catherine had a very different type of relationship. Catherine did not focus the same attention on Annette, nor did she saddle her daughter with the same emotional demands. Catherine rarely mentioned Annette in her letters except to comment on whether she was eating enough. Catherine seemed relatively unconcerned about Annette's future. Brother and sister moved in separate orbits.

Monitoring Peter's education became Catherine's biggest concern. Despite her various psychological quirks—indecisiveness, a tendency to wallow in self-pity, and an inability to differentiate her own needs from those of others—Catherine handled this challenge with considerable aplomb. She grew up writing both English and French, but mastered neither. In both languages, her spelling was bad, her grammar atrocious. Peter Romilly had also made sure that she learned how to speak French: on Sundays, no English was spoken at home. Though Catherine had received little formal education, she was an avid reader who tried hard to stay abreast of the latest developments in politics and culture. Above all, Catherine possessed genuine street smarts and resourcefulness.

Gradually his mother would proceed to turn the traditional parent-child relationship upside down, leaning on Peter to help her regulate her anxiety and distress, rather than the other way around. And the more she smothered Peter, the more he turned away both from her and from people in general. Catherine tended to judge Peter's activities by their impact on *her* feelings rather than on his. For example, when Peter took horseback riding lessons as a teenager, she was particularly pleased because it reduced her "timidity when a [riding] party is proposed." Catherine typically encouraged Peter to do whatever made her less anxious.

After Jean Roget's death, the overbearing Catherine Roget also became increasingly unpredictable. Her internal anguish would propel her to move the family around constantly. Catherine rationalized her failure to lay down roots: her love and concern for her children, she believed, were the cause. As she saw it, she never provided a stable home because she was unable to locate the ideal place to raise her children. But introspection was not her forte.

Catherine was miserable, no matter where she happened to be. She considered Bloomsbury unsuitable because "the air is not so good. Near Frith Street it is still worse. . . . I have too many good reasons to not foresee unhappiness—therefore what is to be done?" Catherine was also worried that if she stayed in London too long, she would eventually have to accede to her mother's wish to move in with her and the children. And she didn't want to be weighed down by any additional caretaking responsibilities. Catherine also detested country towns because of the summer tourists. "A crowd of stares is my aversion," she once confessed.

During Peter's childhood, his mother took the family to live at a host of cities outside London, including Chichester and Southampton on the Sussex coast, as well as Gloucester and Worcester. As Catherine herself put it, she was a "country rambler." The family moved at least two or three times a year, sometimes even more frequently than that. Almost all the childhood events that Roget recorded in his "List of Principal Events" relate to these family peregrinations. For example, Roget summed up 1789 as follows: "Mar. 24 Abergavenny, June Malvern and Sept. Worcester."

These constant dislocations compounded the sense of angst caused by Peter's early losses and his mother's intrusions. The young Peter felt insecure about his station in life. Always uncertain about what tomorrow would bring, he had a hard time developing trust. His sense of connection with the people and places in his environment was tenuous.

To feel rooted and connected, Peter turned inward—away from the real world. He became a daydreamer who easily got lost in the contents of his own mind. He kept imagining other worlds, such as the world of the stars and the world of the ancient Romans. And of these alternate worlds, his favorite would be that of words.

Despite all the moves, there was one place where Peter found a modicum of continuity—Kensington Square, then a leafy suburb on the outskirts of London. While in Kensington, the family would either rent rooms on a temporary basis or stay, typically as a paying guest, with David Chauvet, a family friend who had known Jean Roget in Geneva.

Chauvet was a teacher who ran a small school in his home based on an elaborate system of education that he had devised. The curriculum emphasized a classical education with intensive instruction in Latin and Greek, modern languages, and all branches of science.

But the primary focus was on immersing his select group of young charges in the art of the written word. Chauvet noted in a school brochure: "As the perfect and grammatical knowledge of the English language is absolutely necessary in the instruction of British youth, great attention is paid to that part of their education." Roget spent the equivalent of about six full years under Chauvet's tutelage, no doubt relishing his lessons.

Chauvet, like Samuel Romilly, was one of a handful of surrogate fathers in Peter's life. Another was the Swiss preacher Etienne Dumont, who had been introduced to Samuel Romilly by Jean Roget in Geneva in 1781. Dumont—who a few years later would write speeches for the Comte de Mirabeau, a political leader in Paris during the French Revolution—and Romilly eventually became life-long friends.

Heavyset, Dumont had bushy eyebrows and a large, round face. His temperament was effusive and energetic. Dumont felt compassion for the struggling widow of his close friend, and he kept sending Catherine letters to boost her spirits. He may also have harbored a romantic interest in Catherine, but if so, he never chose to act on it. These avuncular missives, which he kept writing for more than twenty years, typically attempted to allay Catherine's excessive fears about her children's well-being. In one letter, written when Peter was eight, he reassured her that "idleness is not at all dangerous at his age." But, like Catherine, Dumont was also worried about Peter's inability to mingle with other children. As he wrote in the same letter, "I'm still surprised that he hasn't found a friend to enliven his activities."

Even by the age of eight, Peter had already begun to escape into words. Dumont may well have been responsible for nudging him in that direction. At the end of a letter written to Catherine in Southampton during the summer of 1787, Dumont addressed a note to Peter himself:

> I hope, my dear Peter, that you had a lot of fun in Southampton. . . . I await from you a description of the town and its environment with a little detail about your other activities, in particular Latin and geography. You have no doubt observed the eclipse of the sun as is to be expected from an apprentice astronomer and good almanac maker. . . . Explain to me, if you will, how you understand that eclipses take place.

Thrilled to be recognized as a separate person in his own right—and as a budding scientist no less—Peter took these words to heart. He would spend the next several months figuring out how to respond. Dumont inadvertently became the muse who would inspire Peter's creative outpourings.

Peter's response to Dumont's questions about his scientific interests eventually came not in a letter, but in the form of entries in the notebook that he began keeping later that year. A couple of months after moving with his mother and sister to new quarters on Sloane Street in London, he took out his pen and wrote on the front cover of his notebook: "Peter, Mark, Roget. His Book. Thursday, Nov. the 21st. 1787."

Before his acquisition of this notebook, the shy and lonely Peter often didn't know what to do with himself. Playing with the other boys on Sloane Street never held much appeal. Neither did spending time with his mother or sister; they didn't understand him. But suddenly everything changed.

Once Peter began recording his scientific musings in his notebook, he could hardly stop. He felt invigorated because he now always had something interesting to occupy his mind. His feelings of loneliness started to dissipate. On words he could always rely; unlike people, they could be counted on not to disappear like his father or intrude upon him like his mother. Peter could study the contents of his notebook any time he wanted. For the rest of his life, words would remain Peter's favorite playmates.

It is fitting that Peter Roget should have begun his career as an organizer of words and concepts while living on Sloane Street. Constructed in 1780 by Henry Holland—who later served as King George IV's personal architect—it paid tribute to the physician and naturalist Hans Sloane. Upon Sloane's death in 1753, his private collection of plants, animals, coins, antiquities, and manuscripts would form the basis of the British Museum. Peter Roget's life was to take many of the same turns as the man on whose street he lived for this six-month stint in 1787 and 1788. Buried at Chelsea Old Church exactly twenty-six years to the day before Roget's birth, Hans Sloane had set up shop as a Bloomsbury doctor in 1695. In a long and distinguished scientific career, Sloane would, like Roget after him, also serve as secretary to the Royal Society and write thick tomes on plant and animal physiology. As an adult, Roget was proud of this association: Sloane Street is the only street name that appears in his account of his childhood wanderings in his "List of Principal Events."

To respond to Dumont's queries, Peter began filling up his notebook with diagrams and mathematical drawings. He tried to answer the question about how eclipses occur with a diagram containing a sun projecting light on about a dozen circles—presumably meant to designate planets and moons. Some circles blocked the sun's light from reaching other circles. However, Peter appears to have been confused about the difference between the words *eclipse* and *ellipsis* (denoting an oval-shaped geometric figure). On account of this mix-up, which would not be uncommon in a schoolboy—even one as intellectually precocious as Peter—he also drew, on the facing page, a picture of an ellipse.

Peter also demonstrated his qualifications as an "apprentice astronomer" by providing what he called "An Account of the Ptolomaic, Tychonic and Copernican Systems." Even in his Sloane Street days, Roget was well aware that some scientists could offer much more convincing portraits of the world than others. Of Ptolemy, he wrote, "The system of the famous Egyptian astronomer was the most gross and vulgar: He supposed the Earth possessed the center of the world."

Among his mathematical drawings was a series of geometric figures. Peter started with triangles—namely, a scalene triangle (one with three unequal sides) and an equilateral triangle, or triagon (one with three equal sides)—before moving on to a tetragon (a figure with four sides), a pentagon (five sides), and a hexagon (six sides), right up to a dodecagon (twelve sides). Though many schoolboys can draw triangles, few get around to churning out dodecagons.

This boyhood interest in geometry and algebra was no passing fancy, as Roget would return to mathematical problems throughout his life. In some respects, mathematics proved even more alluring to Roget than verbal communication because he saw it as a pure form of language, one that addresses directly the relationship between abstract concepts.

At the heart of Peter's childhood notebook are his word lists, written in a neat hand and consisting of Latin words juxtaposed with their English meanings, grouped under categories such as "Beasts," "People," "Parts of the Body," "Of Writing, Reading, etc.," "In the

Garden," "Of the Weather," as well as a miscellaneous category, "Other Things." In each list, Roget provided a catalogue of the key concepts. For example, "Beasts" started off with:

Elephas	*an Elephant*
Tigris	*a Tiger*
Porcus	*a Hog*
Sorex	*a Rat*

Likewise, the first few entries of "In the Garden" were:

Folium	*a Leaf*
Arbor	*a Tree*
Lignum	*Wood*
Lactuca	*a Lettuce*

Peter's word lists reveal not just how he learned Latin; more significantly, they also reflect how he learned about the world outside himself. While most children acquaint themselves with animals and plants by using all of their senses—by looking, listening, sniffing, and touching—and by accessing their emotions, Peter, by contrast, relied exclusively on his mind. With neither parent available to help him process all the potentially confusing and frightening stimuli— say, the snorting of a hog, or even the descent of a leaf in autumn— Peter was forced to limit how much of the external environment he took in. Rather than experiencing the contents of the world in all their wonder, he took a shortcut powered by his keen intellect: he classified them.

To reduce his anxiety about exploring the environment and to feel a sense of mastery, no matter how illusory, Peter completed an inventory of the world. Organizing these items in his notebook quickly

Pages from the notebook Peter used to organize the world around him.

became an obsession; day after day, he would spend hours making new lists and combing over old ones.

Putting everything in its proper category also relieved Peter's existential anxiety. Classifying made Dumont's eight-year-old scientist feel both more real and more alive. "I classify, therefore, I am," would emerge as the guiding principle of Roget's life. As long as he understood how all these abstractions related to one another, he felt that he had nothing to fear. At least on the pages of his notebook, everything was in order. No longer was he so upset by the chaos in his own family circumstances.

With his word lists, Peter simultaneously created both a replica of the real world as well as a private imaginary world—what

contemporary psychologists call a "paracosm." The defining character-
istics of a paracosm are that the child sustains interest in it over a considerable period of time—typically between the ages of eight and
twelve—and that he or she has an intense emotional investment in its
contents. By providing a stable reference point, paracosms can help
children cope with stressful situations such as loneliness and emotional
abuse. As children, many famous artists and writers—including W. H.
Auden, the Brontë sisters, C. S. Lewis, and Friedrich Nietzsche—
developed a paracosm, which, in its pure form, features a variety of
imaginary people and places. Roget's substitute universe, however, was
just two-dimensional, consisting solely of concepts. Yet Roget could
still turn to his paracosm for the soothing that he wasn't able to receive
from either of his parents.

Though inspired by Dumont, Peter's Latin word lists also reflected
his time and place. In eighteenth-century England, lexicographers
were constantly publishing Latin–English dictionaries, which had practically the same status as encyclopedias; a few bore the title that Roget
would latch on to some sixty-odd years later: *Thesaurus*. For example,
Robert Ainsworth's *Thesaurus Linguae Latinae: Or, A Compendious Dictionary of the Latin Tongue*, first published in 1736, contained a series of
appendixes on various topics—such as one on proper names and another one on places—that consisted of Latin words followed by their
English equivalents. Likewise, a late-eighteenth-century volume by
John Entick, with the long-winded title *Tyronis Thesaurus; or Entick's
New Latin-English Dictionary, Designed for the Use of Grammar Schools
and Private Education: Containing All the Words and Phrases Proper for
Reading the Classic Authors in Both Languages*, also featured a slew of
Latin word lists opposite their English equivalents.

Peter may have seen one or both of these books in London (say, at

Chauvet's school), or perhaps Dumont introduced him to them. Though the correspondence does not contain any references to Latin dictionaries as far back as 1787, Dumont refers to sending Peter a book of Latin synonyms in a letter written in 1794, informing Catherine that "he must choose the most used words because all words are not of the same importance, and that would fill his head with useless stuff to take note of all these subtle distinctions in a dead language."

Just as the child is the father to the man—to cite the poet William Wordsworth, whom the adolescent Roget would meet a decade later—Peter's notebook is clearly the urtext—or blueprint—of *Roget's Thesaurus*. However, the word lists of the eight-year-old Peter and those of the adult Roget go about classifying the world in slightly different ways. Unlike his childhood notebook, Roget's handy reference work would end up focusing on the general rather than the particular. For example, the entry for "Animal" 366 refers to animals generally and consists of synonyms such as "the animal kingdom," "a beast," "brute," and "creature"; likewise, the book leaves out the names of specific plants and animals such as "hog" and "tiger," featured in the notebook's list of "Beasts." Though "hog" and "tiger" are to be found in the index to the *Thesaurus*, readers are referred back only to terms reflecting what these animals symbolize—gluttony, or courage, as the case may be. Roget describes this editorial decision in the introduction to his *Thesaurus*:

> There are a multitude of words of a specific character, which, although they properly occupy places in the columns of a dictionary, yet, having no relation to general ideas, do not come within the scope of this compilation and are consequently omitted. . . . Exceptions must, however, be made in favour of such words as admit of metaphorical signification to general subjects.

But Peter's childhood lists are even more closely related to another magnum opus that he would write as an adult. Over the course of his scientific career, Roget would specialize in physiology, and in 1834 he would publish the two-volume *Animal and Vegetable Physiology, Considered with Reference to Natural Theology*. Also known as his *Bridgewater Treatise*, this work, held in the highest esteem by nineteenth-century academics, consists of nothing but a catalogue of specific plants and animals. In the preface to the fourth and final edition, published in 1867, some eighty years after he scribbled down his first word lists, Roget defines physiology as "a science of vast and almost boundless extent, since it comprehends within its range all the animal and vegetable beings on the globe."

Roget's childhood notebook turned out to be a dry run for both his scientific as well as his linguistic masterpiece. While Roget's *Bridgewater Treatise* organizes nature, and his *Thesaurus* all of human knowledge, *Peter, Mark, Roget: His Book* constitutes an ambitious attempt by an avid eight-year-old list maker to categorize both the animate and inanimate world.

But even while jotting down his word lists, Peter could not entirely escape his mother's close scrutiny. As a boy, Peter was rarely afforded the opportunity to breathe apart from her, much less to have a notebook of his own. On the backs of the pages of her son's notebook, Catherine had translated a long pedagogical essay from the French, "Advice from a Mother to Her Daughter," which gave tips on how to raise children. For Catherine, this text was invaluable as it substituted for the real thing—namely, guidance from a flesh-and-blood mother, her own mother having been too ill to do any parenting. Unfortunately, Catherine saw wisdom in the cruel parental maxims contained therein, such as the following: "You should not always threaten without punishing lest your threats become contemptible." Though Catherine felt proud of herself whenever she could back up her threats with action, such behavior filled her son with abject terror.

With his mother granting herself permission to inspect his notebook at will, Peter's possibilities for self-expression were limited. His notebook included no statements of his own thoughts and feelings about his daily life. However, Peter did appear to entertain—albeit just briefly—the notion of opening up his soul on these pages. Right above a list of the Latin and English words for the four elements, he wrote the following heading: "On the Loss of Friends," a reference to how lonely he felt on Sloane Street.

But these words (as well as the phrase "That it is vain to shrink from," printed just below, which also apparently reflected his distress) were crossed out. With Catherine hovering over him, Peter did not feel safe writing anything but the abstractions that he could easily insert into one of his categories. As an adult, Peter would internalize Catherine's censorship and rarely express his feelings, either with others or on paper. Like his childhood notebook, nearly all of his academic work—and even his stabs at autobiography—would essentially involve organizing and describing lists of abstractions.

As a young boy, Peter was not in a position to raise any objections to his mother's incursions into his personal space. But, surprisingly, as a parent, he ended up imitating her. Deeply attached to this book of lists, the adult Roget passed it on to his own son, John, when he turned seven in 1835. John then put his name on the notebook's title page. But John also could hardly have felt that it was truly his book as both his father's and grandmother's musings were strewn all over it.

The notebook meant so much to the adult Roget because it represented his discovery as a boy of eight what was to be *his* calling. He

had stumbled upon an all-encompassing intellectual pursuit: classifying the world, an obsession that would preoccupy him for the rest
of his life. As a boy, Roget was compelled to crank out his word lists.
Without this outlet, he may well have lapsed into the madness that
gripped numerous family members, including his grandmother,
mother, and uncle.

Only a few generations after Roget's death did psychiatrists begin
to understand how obsessions can dominate the inner lives of children. In a 1913 paper, "Predisposition to Obsessional Neurosis,"
Sigmund Freud argued that obsessions, which tend to first appear
between the ages of six and eight, serve the function of helping people ward off intense and painful emotions such as anxiety and hate.
Freud also noted that obsessionality—in contrast with most other
psychiatric ailments—is remarkably consistent over the life span.
This was certainly the case for Roget; some eighty years after he
started his notebook, he was harnessing the same obsessive energy
to churn out new editions of his *Thesaurus*. Summing up Freud's key
insights, a recent psychoanalytic handbook asserts, "Most obsessive
thoughts and compulsive actions involve efforts to undo or counter-
act impulses toward destructiveness, greed and messiness."

Though Roget's obsessions did help him cope with his stressful
early life, they came at a cost. Categorizing rather than experiencing
the world has its limits. Like his mother, Peter was incapable of looking inward. Immersed in his own analytical observations, he was not
particularly attuned to what others were feeling. Not understanding
what a healthy connection—one that involved mutual give-and-take—
might feel like, he also had trouble making friends. At the age of
twelve, he was wont to bore his mother and sister with three-hour so-
liloquies on astronomy.

But whatever the drawbacks of Roget's obsessive personality, it may well have been instrumental to the success of his *Thesaurus*. After all, obsessive-compulsive people, particularly those who are driven to engage in painstaking intellectual labor, are well suited to the challenges of lexicography. Consider Samuel Johnson, whose *Dictionary of the English Language*, first published in 1755, roughly a century before the *Thesaurus*, set the standard for literary excellence. Roget's obsessions and compulsions actually pale in comparison to Johnson's.

Johnson's nervous disposition, like Roget's, also dated back to a dreary childhood. Johnson had been born blind in one eye, and partially deaf. As an infant, he was also scarred by the glandular disease known as scrofula, which he got because his wet nurse had tuberculosis. And life on the home front was far from peaceful. His father was prone to melancholy, and his parents argued constantly. Johnson's definition of a family as "a little kingdom, torn with factions and exposed to revolutions" no doubt reflects his own experience early in life.

As an adult, Johnson lived in thrall to the troubling thoughts that would constantly torment him. To fend them off, he would engage in odd compulsions, such as pausing to touch every lamppost as he walked down Fleet Street. Another "superstitious habit" as described by his biographer, James Boswell, was:

> his anxious care to go out or in at a door or passage, by a certain number of steps from a certain point, or at least so as that either his right or his left foot, (I am not certain which), should constantly make the first actual movement when he came close to the door or passage . . . for I have, upon innumerable occasions, observed him suddenly stop, and then seem to count his steps with a deep earnestness.

Johnson also suffered from disabling physical symptoms—namely, tics and convulsions. Both his arms and legs were prone to jerk involuntarily.

To relieve his constant anxiety, Johnson was always looking for ways to distract himself from his innermost thoughts and feelings. As his close friend Sir Joshua Reynolds, the renowned artist, put it, "the great business of his life was to escape from his mind." The company of friends, Johnson found, could help him relax. But his scholarly labors also proved critical to maintaining his sanity. Johnson summed up his approach to life in one of his famous maxims: "Be not solitary, be not idle." Cut from the same cloth, Roget also saw in cleaning up the English language both a moral calling and a welcome distraction from his turbulent inner world. Perhaps the main difference between these two great dictionary men is that Roget was not afraid of solitude. Unlike Johnson, who enlisted six assistants to help him edit his dictionary out of his Gough Square study, Roget preferred to do his list making by himself. *Roget's Thesaurus*, in contrast with Johnson's *Dictionary*, was a one-man operation.

Despite the considerable ingenuity that Roget displayed all over his notebook, his mother kept despairing that he would never amount to much. When Peter was twelve, she wrote to her brother Samuel, "He is still often trifling in his pursuits. . . . You will be surprised when I tell you that he promises less than he did a year ago." Catherine's high degree of free-floating anxiety often clouded her judgment. Neither Romilly nor Dumont was ever so pessimistic about the boy's future.

Catherine was determined to steer Peter toward a promising career. However, the two most prestigious professions of his era were the church and the law—the paths chosen by his father and uncle, respectively—and neither one seemed a good fit for him. A British native, Peter would, unlike his father, be expected to make his mark in the Church of England, where he may not have felt entirely at home, given his Huguenot descent. While growing up in Marylebone, his mother had attended services on Sundays at both the French church in Soho and the neighborhood branch of the Church of England. But as a boy, Roget had little to do with the French church and attended Anglican services only infrequently.

But even more important, Peter seemed to lack an interest in reading and writing—a critical ingredient for success in both fields. Though Peter was studious, his boyhood pursuits involved immersing himself in abstract knowledge such as astronomy, chemistry, mathematics, and his Latin word lists. In 1791, his mother remarked to her brother, "He does not promise to have that goût for the Belles Lettres as we might wish or expect. Everything is Calculation, and a desire to know more." As Roget himself later acknowledged, he felt compelled to come up with his 1805 draft of the *Thesaurus* to compensate for his relative absence of innate literary talent.

Peter would never show evidence of a literary sensibility. Those who love literature typically are fascinated with stories and storytelling. But that's not how Roget's mind worked. Lacking a vivid imagination, he was a practical person. Since boyhood, words always constituted the means to an end. All of his scholarly publications, including the *Thesaurus*, were directed toward disseminating scientific knowledge that ultimately had some useful purpose.

Other possibilities for Peter's future were business and the military. His schoolteacher, Chauvet, made the case for business, but Catherine ruled that out because he was too shy and seemed to require a lot of solitude. "I sometimes fancy," she once observed, "Peter is aspiring to a vocation which does not suit a small fortune. . . . His mind will, I see, never bend to business." Having already lost her husband, Catherine was too terrified to give the military much thought. Peter's frailty also made a military career impossible. As a boy, he was both exceptionally thin and prone to coming down with various minor ailments such as coughs and fevers. Catherine was constantly worrying about the state of his health. In the hope of inoculating Peter against illness, she gave him all kinds of curious concoctions, including ass's milk.

Despite his thinness—he was then well below his adult weight of about 125 pounds—Peter cut an imposing figure as he entered adolescence. He was slightly taller than average, and with his dark eyes, long angular face, firm jaw, and brown hair, he came across as particularly handsome. However, he tended to stoop—a habit he would give up as he grew older and became more confident of his appeal to the fairer sex.

After conducting long discussions about Peter's future with a few of his surrogate fathers, namely Romilly, Dumont, and Chauvet, Catherine decided to enroll him at the University of Edinburgh. She figured his scientific interests suited him for a career in medicine. In the late eighteenth century, a medical education required constant perusing of classical Latin and Greek medical texts; with little contemporary empirical literature to go by, physicians often found themselves consulting Aristotle or Galen. (Until 1750, all classes at the University of Edinburgh were conducted in Latin.) According to King Henry VIII's dictum, the practice of "physic" was limited to "those persons that be profound, sad and discreet, groundedly learned and deeply studied." For a melancholy boy who loved tinkering with Latin concepts, medicine appeared to be the best path to a stable income.

Roget was not slated to be an ordinary doctor, but a physician. In the late 1700s, physicians, who were the only doctors to receive extensive university training, constituted a small elite—just ten percent of all doctors. Throughout the eighteenth and nineteenth centuries, English medicine was a so-called tripartite profession, consisting of physicians, surgeons, and apothecaries. While physicians treated internal diseases (say, a fever), surgeons treated exclusively external disorders (say, a broken bone). Apothecaries, in turn, both provided medical consultations (typically for less well-to-do patients) and prescribed medications. Both apothecaries and surgeons occupied a rung beneath doctors. In fact, until 1745, when the Company of Surgeons was established, surgeons had been allied with barbers. (The red stripe of the barber's pole—symbolizing blood—can be traced to this age-old connection.) Considered technicians rather than men of science, surgeons were addressed as "Mister" rather than "Doctor"—a custom that continues to this day throughout the United Kingdom.

The surviving correspondence does not contain any explanation for why Catherine chose Edinburgh. She may have preferred living there with her daughter, Annette, rather than in Oxford or Cambridge, which were, at the time, still the only two universities in all of England. Religion may have played a part. In the late 1700s, Oxford and Cambridge were limited to Church of England members. It is not clear whether this stipulation disqualified her son. The "godless institution of Gower Street," the University of London, where Roget was later to serve as an Examiner in Physiology, did not begin taking students until 1828. Roget's son, John Lewis, would start at the University of London before attending Cambridge.

But when it came to this move, Catherine was not acting rashly. During the late eighteenth century, the University of Edinburgh's faculty was second to none. It was where the Scottish Enlightenment, which was to have vast repercussions for academics all over

the world, was born. During a visit in 1775, America's first polymath, Benjamin Franklin, observed "[At Edinburgh] at this time
there happen to be collected a set of as truly great men, professors of
the several branches of knowledge, as have ever appeared in any age
or country."

Scotland—and Edinburgh in particular—was also the center of
medical education in the English-speaking world. Of the roughly 3,050
medical school graduates in Great Britain between 1750 and 1800,
some 2,600 had done their medical studies at one of the four universities in Scotland—Edinburgh, Aberdeen, Glasgow, and St. Andrews—
as compared with just 250 at Oxford and Cambridge. (The other 200
or so were educated in Continental Europe). And most of the major
nineteenth-century scientific heavyweights, such as Erasmus Darwin
and his more famous grandson, Charles, along with Thomas Hodgkin
and Thomas Addison, both of whom would later give their names to
diseases, would attend Edinburgh. The first university to combine
medical education with a teaching hospital, Edinburgh was also the
model for the first U.S. medical school, established in Philadelphia, at
the University of Pennsylvania, in 1765.

Yet Catherine also had her own personal reasons for steering her
son toward medicine in Edinburgh. This career formalized the family
role that she had already assigned Peter—that of her caretaker. Long
before he ever began medical school, Peter already was busily engaged in tending to the health of his mother, whose fragile sense of
self was continually causing her to unravel. Not shy about expressing
her expectations of her son, Catherine had family friends seeing
things her way. In a letter to her, written when Peter was just beginning medical school, Dumont notes that "In four or five years, you
will have a doctor who will take care of you."

In Edinburgh, Peter would finally begin to come out from under his mother's shadow and form his own identity as a brilliant young physician. However, Catherine's emotional neediness had left an indelible mark. For the rest of his life, he would turn to his word lists for comfort.

2.

The Brilliant Student

(5 4 1) L E A R N E R , scholar, student, disciple, pupil, eleve, schoolboy, beginner, tyro, abecedarian, novice, neophyte, inceptor, probationer, apprentice, condisciple, freshman, freshwater sailor.

I n the summer of 1793, before heading off to Edinburgh, Catherine took Peter and Annette to the Chauvets in Kensington for what would be the last time. As was frequently the case, Catherine was filled with worries about Peter. In August, she wrote her brother Samuel, then in Edinburgh making some inquiries on her behalf, "Peter looks yellow and very thin, not half so well as when we arrived, that is another reason for me to wish changed air. . . . He is so awkwardly bashful. . . . And in the country he takes more exercise than he does here, which I am persuaded is good for him. I never came to Kensington that I did not find . . . that Peter looked worse." Catherine was eager to leave Kensington as soon as possible.

Samuel's positive reports about their destination also provided a spur for Catherine to make the move. Though already a major international city with some 80,000 inhabitants, Edinburgh possessed many of the advantages of the country, which Catherine considered so vital to her own mental health. Romilly provided a glowing assessment, "Nothing is wanting in Edinburgh but a fine climate to make it the place in which I should prefer, before any that I have seen, to pass my life, if I were obliged to pass it in any town. Nothing can surpass the beauty of the country around it, which is rich, highly cultivated, well wooded, well peopled and bounded on the different sides with the sea or with mountains." While in Edinburgh, Romilly stayed at the Canongate Street home of Dugald Stewart, the world-renowned professor of moral philosophy. Like Romilly, Stewart was interested in infusing British politics with the ideals of the French Revolution (but without any of the violence). Of his longtime friend, Romilly observed, "The more I know, the more I esteem for the qualities of his heart, and the more I admire and respect for his knowledge and his talents." At Romilly's prodding, Stewart was both to welcome the Rogets upon their arrival and take a personal interest in Peter's welfare.

In early September, Catherine took a brief trip to Dover to make the final travel arrangements. She was feeling frustrated. As she wrote Samuel, injecting her characteristic dose of self-pity, "My young children are eager to be on the road as well as their old mother, who feels herself wearing away to the size of a thread-paper from these repeated delays and unsettled stage projects." Catherine was then thirty-eight and in excellent health, and her fears of withering away reflected little more than the brittle state of her psyche.

Though she was easily flappable, on this occasion, Catherine had some good reasons to be nervous. Planning the four-hundred-mile journey was daunting. The main sticking point: the farthest any mail coach or post chaise (a small, enclosed carriage) went was about two hundred miles, and booking one was no easy matter. Besides working out the connections between the various stages of the trip, she also had to figure out a way to send their belongings. During the war with France, which began that February, a month after King Louis XVI met his end on the guillotine, few commercial ships left from Dover. As a result, travel by land was much more expensive, and customs agents were opening everything, both at Dover and at London. (In the end, Catherine opted to send the luggage by ship, and some items would be lost.) Added to these problems was that her budget did not allow her to book a post chaise for the whole journey, and travel by mail coach meant mixing with "the vulgar," as she put it.

At eight o'clock on the evening of September 18, Catherine, Peter, and Annette boarded a hackney coach from Kensington to the Bull and Mouth Inn in Aldersgate Street. Upon their arrival, they began the wait for the mail coach to York. Catherine soon became antsy. As she later recalled, "We felt ourselves awkward doing nothing, when every mouth in the room besides ours was employed with eating, so we called for a tumbler of negus and a few biscuits." Her pangs of hunger soothed, Catherine suddenly became lost in reverie. She kept thinking about the friends in London whom she was leaving behind. Though Catherine and the children had moved many times, she had never taken them outside England. She was not looking forward to spending several years in unfamiliar territory.

Fortunately, Peter was used to Catherine's mental lapses, and he was prepared to take on the parental role at a moment's notice. Without his vigilance, the family might never have made it out of London. An hour later, Peter alerted his mother and sister that someone was calling for the Edinburgh and York Mail papers. This was the sign that their coach was ready to set off, and they rushed to find it and get on board.

Seated next to a stranger later characterized by Catherine as "a lusty middle-aged man," the Roget trio began heading toward York, located halfway between London and Edinburgh. The man was very talkative, and Catherine soon was filled with dread, lest she have to listen to his "clack" for some two hundred miles. But to her great relief, he stopped telling stories about his family after half an hour. That's when he put on a large fur cap—one whose odd appearance startled the ten-year-old Annette. The two Roget children soon made their own preparations for the night—Peter tying a handkerchief around his head because he had forgotten his nightcap, and Annette putting on her white French coat. And then the four passengers all went to sleep.

At eleven o'clock that night, the Rogets arrived in York. Over the course of the nearly twenty-four-hour trip from London, Catherine, to her surprise, had taken a liking to their traveling companion. The ale (laced with brandy) that he sipped periodically had kept him calm and relatively quiet. Catherine herself had tried some at the stopover in Doncaster.

It took Catherine nearly two full weeks to arrange for transportation from York to Edinburgh. This leg of the trip would take another twenty-four hours, spread out over two nights.

On the morning of October 4, they finally reached Edinburgh, and Peter was poised to begin his university education.

As the eighteenth century drew to a close, both Edinburgh and its university were on the rise. In 1753, the city had consisted of only twelve streets and some twenty-two wynds (the local term for through lanes), leaving the city planners poised to undertake massive building projects. By the 1790s, the construction of New Town, the strip north of the main thoroughfare of Princes Street, which would become a wealthy enclave, was well under way. Likewise, the university, under the canny stewardship of William Robertson, had also initiated a major redevelopment project on its campus near Old Town, located a few blocks south of Princes Street. The architectural redevelopment of this medieval city, which also reinvigorated its cultural and intellectual life, elicited comparisons with the heyday of the classical world. This was the "Augustan Age" of Edinburgh, which, as one memoirist put it, had "gusto, grace, and gravity."

But just as the Rogets alighted in town, Edinburgh, like most cities in Great Britain, faced a major impediment—the war with the new revolutionary government of France. With many men and re-sources suddenly diverted to the war effort, the building renaissance came to a screeching halt. The university itself soon started to look like a war zone: many new buildings remained unroofed, stones and beams strewn all over the place. Roget wasn't as affected as much as other students because the new accommodations for the depart-ments of anatomy, physic, and moral philosophy, where he would spend most of his time, particularly in his last two years, went up as planned in the northwest section of campus.

Roget wouldn't begin taking classes at the medical school for two years. That first fall, he boned up on the classics, studying Latin with Professor John Hill and Greek with Professor Andrew Dalzel. Ever ambitious, Roget requested to take a second class with each professor—Roman Antiquities with Hill and Greek Literature with Dalzel. Both agreed, but insisted that he not tell any fellow students about his special arrangement. In those days, students paid their professors directly for the lectures—typically about three guineas a class (a guinea was worth slightly more than a pound).

Though Roget managed to handle the academic challenges of his first year in Edinburgh, he felt overwhelmed by the considerable so-cial pressures. At the time, university life was particularly alienating for entering students. The campus lacked any dormitories, and the students often had to walk several miles to get to class. The centers of social intercourse were the clubs—say, the literary or medical society—which were open only to advanced students. Most students lived isolated lives buried in their books. To borrow the words of Benjamin Constant, the celebrated Swiss novelist who had studied in Edinburgh a decade before Roget, "Work was the fashion there." The unpleasant Edinburgh weather—cold, windy, and rainy—didn't help matters.

Even Peter's classes left him feeling anonymous. In his Greek language course, Andrew Dalzel lectured to about a hundred students who rarely interacted much, either with the professor or with one another. The only saving grace was Dalzel's wit. In response to student complaints about the inconvenient entrance to the university grounds from South College Street, he quipped, "It was retained professedly for the professors, but principally for the Principal." At least in Dalzel, Roget and his classmates had someone who could empathize with their lowly station.

Not surprisingly, Peter's adjustment was far from smooth. New obsessions and compulsions emerged. In a letter to his uncle written at the end of 1793, he remarked: "Tuesdays and Thursdays I am in the college from 8 til 9 in the morn. and then from 10 til 3. The other days only from 8 to 9; from 10 to 11, and from 12 to 2. Mr Dalzel's class is at the top of the College; and as we live up two pairs of stairs, I every day go up at least 320 steps." Now, like Samuel Johnson, to manage his anxiety Roget, too, would study carefully the ground upon which he trod.

He also kept battling a host of other minor mental and physical ailments. Catherine expended considerable energy attending to each one as it popped up. For example, in an attempt to help Peter break his habit of stooping, she arranged for a high writing desk to be built for him. Once, while sitting close to the fire to combat a cold, Peter accidentally scalded his foot. Waxing somewhat philosophical, Catherine wrote Samuel Romilly, "Good is seldom very distinct from evil, or rather they lovingly go hand in hand together like twin sisters. The three large blisters on Peter's foot so effectively cured the cold and fever, that he has had no cough with it, and has not the smallest vestige of a cold remaining." In the same letter, Catherine added that "Peter is subject to malaise, languor and a bad digestion." For his "disordered stomach," Catherine urged him to eat warm gingerbread nuts. Unfortunately, he had to stop this regi-men, as purging remedies tended to weaken him. But, as Catherine informed her brother, she remained anxious because Peter still "looks ill."

Yet as Peter did swimmingly in all his courses, which included chemistry, botany, and natural philosophy (literally, the objective study of nature, but at the time also a catch-all phrase for science in general), his intellectual precocity became evident. His uncle Samuel Romilly wrote Peter on his own thirty-eighth birthday, March 1, 1795: "There are many persons who have been eminently distinguished in different sciences who have not even begun their studies at the age which you have attained." But Peter still had diffi-culty making friends. Dumont repeatedly expressed his concern to Catherine about Peter's isolation. In a letter sent to Catherine that May, he offered the following advice for Peter: "Some exercise, com-pany, conversation, not always books. It is necessary to talk about what one has read to imprint it on the spirit and learn it." Knowing Peter well, Dumont figured that the only way to get him to talk to his peers was to make a case for the practical advantages. Peter would eventually heed Dumont's advice. Throughout his life, the glue that cemented most of his friendships was a shared interest in specific scholarly matters.

In Edinburgh, Catherine continued to shuttle the family around from temporary abode to temporary abode, though not quite as fre-quently as during Peter's early childhood. In the summer of 1795, a few months before Peter officially began his medical studies, Cather-ine made an ill-advised move from the suburb of Fountain Bridge to Rose Street. To her horror, a few months later she realized that the Rogets were now living in the center of Edinburgh's red-light district. In November she wrote her brother: "I am sorry to inform you that we are in a sad low life neighborhood . . . [where] we are surrounded with

women of bad character. I was not a little vexed when I heard this
Street is famous for them, but a stranger may be supposed I hope to
be ignorant of it." Rose Street—an alleyway situated between Princes
and George streets—was a den of moral squalor. Catherine acknowledged a year later, after the family had found a new place near the university, that "the uncommon dirtiness of our neighbours and,
Landlady, made me, as the summer advanced, live in fear of all manner of filth."

The Rose Street days were particularly grim for the Rogets, as the
entire city was then down in the dumps. A couple of bad harvests
caused by the coldest weather in forty years, combined with the halt
in building, created a major economic downturn. Both inflation and
unemployment began to skyrocket, leading to a crime wave. In 1795,
nearly one-fifth of Edinburgh's population depended on emergency
relief from either charities or the government. Though Catherine
couldn't help noticing the terrifying predicament of the downtrodden,
she was, she confessed to her brother, not particularly sympathetic:
"The poor people here are starving, they have not the resources of
parish houses to apply to. The Scotch are liberal and charitable and
give much away even to common beggars, which (entre nous) I
should suppose does more harm than good."

Catherine's failure to steer clear of Rose Street was not just a temporary lapse in judgment. Mother and son shared the tendency to
categorize—rather than carefully observe and experience—the people and places in their midst. Peter's own fuzzy sense of place comes
through in the journal that he kept of his weeklong trip into the
Scottish Highlands with his uncle and Etienne Dumont that September. The trio entered the Highlands from Perth and traveled primarily by post chaise, though they often got out to do some hiking.

Peter's descriptions of the Scottish landscape lacked clarity. He
divided what he observed into two broad categories—"beautiful," an

adjective that he used dozens of times over the course of this forty-page travelogue, and "not beautiful." For example, in the entry for September 1, the day they left Edinburgh, he remarked that "Inverkeithing is a large village in a beautiful situation." As they approached Perth on the 2nd, reported Peter, they were presented with "a beautiful view of the river Tay." Likewise, he wrote that "the banks of the river"—referring to one near the village of Dunkeld, which they reached that same day—"are remarkably beautifull [sic]." By contrast, regarding the Duke of Atholl's House, which they toured on September 3, he concluded, "The grounds have nothing beautiful to recommend them." And approaching Kenmore the next day, he wrote that "The wildness of the scenes were not destitute of some sort of beauty."

Remarkably, Roget rarely explained exactly why he considered this or that river or village "beautiful" or "not beautiful." These holes in Roget's own adolescent prose highlight precisely how the *Thesaurus* can come to the rescue. By providing authors with synonymous terms for a given idea—in this case, "Beauty," 845 in the 1852 first edition—it can help them figure out what they are trying to say. If his own book had been available to him as a teenager, Roget would have seen such synonyms for "beautiful" as "fine, pretty, lovely, elegant, well-formed, well-proportioned, symmetrical, blooming, shining, splendid, resplendent, and sublime." With access to all these options, Roget might have expressed himself much more clearly.

These 1795 journal entries illustrate the full extent to which Roget's obsessive personality could leave him at a loss for words. They also provide evidence of the "deficiencies," which, Roget confessed in the preface to the *Thesaurus*, led him, in 1805, to write the first draft. Ultimately, Roget came up with the reference book that was targeted for people just like him. As he also noted in the preface, he went back and finished the *Thesaurus* a half-century later because he believed "that a repertory, of which I had myself experienced the advantage, might, when amplified, prove useful to others." This hypothesis was, of course, correct. Though not everyone is as wedded to categorizing the world as Roget was, his lack of verbal dexterity is common. In the introduction to the 1852 edition, he explained:

> We seek in vain the words we need, and strive ineffectually to devise forms of expression which shall faithfully portray our thoughts and sentiments. The appropriate terms, notwithstanding our utmost efforts, cannot be conjured up at will. Like "spirits from the vasty deep," they come not when we call; and we are driven to the employment of a set of words and phrases either too general or too limited, too strong or too feeble, which suit not the occasion, which hit not the mark we aim at.

Roget was here speaking from his own personal experience—that of an adolescent scholar seeking to record his trip to Scotland.

To write his travelogue, Roget relied on a Latin list—"Gray's Maxims In Travelling"—which he appended to the back of his journal. Gray is Thomas Gray, the famous eighteenth-century poet best known for his "Elegy Written in a Country Courtyard," published in 1751. In Gray, Roget saw a kindred spirit—one who, upon reading the tenth edition of Linnaeus's *Systema Naturae* in 1759, himself got bit by the classification bug. Avidly gathering his own collection of plants and insects, Gray began traveling all over Britain to see if the flora and fauna there were any different from Sweden's. Thirty years before Roget took his tour, Gray himself had gone to the Highlands. Of the magnificent landscape, he wrote, "In short, since I have seen the Alps, I have seen nothing sublime till now." Gray's letters on his

Scottish tour, published to considerable fanfare in 1775, also established him as an influential travel writer. In English, Gray's six Latin maxims read as follows:

1. See whatever is to be seen.
2. You should see whatever I have not seen.
3. Write down and describe, as faithfully as possible, whatever you see.
4. To write is not to admire; since you are not a painter, paint everything with words.
5. Whenever you can, abandon the footpaths, the worn crossroads of travelers.
6. Correct whatever can be corrected.

Following his own precepts, Gray had written rich descriptions of the Highlands. Unlike Roget, who saw "nothing beautiful" in the Duke of Atholl's House, Gray found much worth reporting:

> With its offices and gardens [it] extends a mile beyond the town [of Dunkeld] and as his grounds were interrupted by the street and roads he has flung arches of communication across them, that add to the scenery of the place, which itself is built of good white stone, and handsomely slated, so that no one would take it for a Scotch Town till they come into it.

To his credit, Roget must have been quick to figure out that his own manuscript fell far short of the standards set by his idol. A decade later—with his copious word lists by his side—Roget would be capable of much more finely wrought prose.

Peter's travel journal also contains his pen-and-ink drawing of the view of Glasgow from a road above the city, in which with a few quick strokes he captured the various buildings, such as the cathedral with its thirteenth-century tower, which then dominated the city's skyline. This was a rare artistic foray, as Roget would later show little interest in either creating or viewing art.

A comparison of Peter Roget's travelogue with one produced at the same age by his son, John—the second of his two children, born in 1828, three years after his daughter, Kate—is striking. John Roget's journal, replete with drawings, was based on a trip to the Continent he took with the rest of the family in 1844. In the narrative of this journey through Germany and Switzerland, John, though no mature literary stylist like Thomas Gray, still provided many more telling details than did his father. For example, John's description of the Cologne Cathedral gave a nuanced account of its beauty:

> [It] is an elaborate and magnificent structure, but its unfinished state gives it the appearance of some ruin of ancient splendour. . . . I cannot, however, admire the taste in pursuance of which the roof is gilded and painted with the brightest frescoes. This style does not suit the purposes of the building.

Likewise, John's drawings were much more true to life. For example, he accurately captured the German students he saw, whom he described as remarkable for their "short red beards, outlandish dress, swaggering gait and unstudious appearance."

If the son had the better eye for detail, the father had the better ear for language. Roget's emerging interest in the subject was already much in evidence in his account of his trip to the Highlands. In the entry for September 5, he related his conversation with a guide, "a hi-land boy who spoke English with difficulty." Asking the boy about his schooling, Roget learned he had received English instruction gratis from a small group of scholars who lived nearby. Roget came back to this surprising finding that many Highlanders can barely speak English in one of the handful of "End Notes" that he appended to the journal. In note 5, he observed, "The people in the Highlands do not speak English with a Scotch brogue, which prevails in the neighbor-hood of Edinburgh. . . . They speak it as if it was a foreign language." In the body of his travelogue, Roget also recorded his delight that some Scotsmen are educated in several languages. He mentioned running into one guide who reported having learned Gaelic, English, Latin, Greek, and French in school. He chalked this up to the "love the Scotch entertain for erudition."

Letting his obsession with counting get the better of him, Roget concluded his account by mentioning that his Scottish tour encom-passed a total of precisely 289 miles. Roget didn't say how he arrived at this figure, or whether he did his calculating during or after the trip. Whatever his method, he presumably relished the challenge of tallying up this total, as keeping track of relatively insignificant figures—like the number of steps he took every day—could help him maintain his equanimity.

The trip to the Highlands lasted just over a week, but it had a highly salubrious effect. Roget was delighted to be in the company of his two surrogate fathers. Peter also may have relished the breather away from his mother. Indeed, Catherine later reported to her brother on his improved state of mind:

Above all, I thank you for having taken him with you to the high-lands, the journey has certainly been of service to him, his complexion is better, and his spirits higher, for though he did not complain before you came, he was serious, had lost his relish for books and was growing yellow and stupid. He now appears himself again and is studying with fresh glee.

Roget really did need to rededicate himself to his studies because that winter he took his first round of medical school classes in anatomy, chemistry, and physiology. A month into the semester, his mother wrote to her brother, "His classes take up so much of his time at present . . . he has no leisure hours just now." Peter's health was good, but Catherine's anxiety increased severalfold as Peter began to see patients in the hospital. To reduce his risk of infection (and to get his mother off his back), Peter promised not to touch any of the very sick patients—not even to take their pulse.

The day was Monday, June 6, 1796. Peter had been living in Edinburgh for nearly three years; he had just finished his first semester of medical training. The summer term was beginning, and in addition to lectures on clinical medicine and his duties at the infirmary, he was slated to take Dugald Stewart's course on moral philosophy.

That morning, Peter had gotten up at six as usual. The hour before breakfast was often his only chance to keep up with his Latin. At seven, he ate breakfast with his mother and sister. However, he kept staring at the Latin grammar book propped up on the table. Immersion in the nuances of Latin prose composition, he found, could sometimes spare him from the barrage of questions his mother was prone to send his way—about his health and his sundry activities be-

tween classes. After saying a quick goodbye to his mother, Peter began the seven-minute walk from the second-floor apartment at Hope
Park End, where the family had just moved in May from Rose Street,
to the university. Their new home, which stood at the eastern end of
a strip of five houses, looked out over a lush meadow that contained
clusters of sycamore trees. Peter walked south along the edge of the
meadow and then dashed the one block west to reach George
Square. He then headed to the Department of Moral Philosophy,
which was located across the street from the university's hospital.

Peter was looking forward to Stewart's first lecture, set to begin at
nine o'clock.

Over the past three years, Peter had been a frequent guest in the
Canongate Street home that Stewart shared with his second wife,
Helen D'Arcy, an accomplished poet in her own right. In their many
extended tête-à-têtes, mentor and protégé would discuss the latest
developments in both the French Revolution and Western philosophy. Stewart would also frequently lend Peter books from his personal library. In fact, Stewart had invited Roget for a dinner the
following week to meet Lord Ashburton, a new student from London who was then boarding in what Roget's mother described as
Stewart's "not cheerful, but large and convenient" home.

But today was to be the first time Peter would see the famous professor in his natural element—the lecture hall. As Peter knew well,
Stewart was a living legend, widely considered the world's most influential philosophy professor outside of Germany. By way of response
to Königsberg's paragon of ratiocination, Immanuel Kant, the British
Empire had fired back with Stewart, who hailed from "the Athens of
the North"—to use the phrase that Stewart himself had coined to describe his hometown of Edinburgh. Frequently compared to Socrates,
Stewart had a reputation for mesmerizing his students.

Awarded the chair of moral philosophy at the University of Edinburgh in 1785—when he was just thirty-two—Stewart had an encyclopedic mind that ventured into numerous disciplines, including
mathematics, political economy, law, natural philosophy, history,
chemistry, and psychology. An adept organizer and synthesizer of
ideas, he gave a voice to what became known as Scottish liberalism.

A primary architect of Scottish "common-sense philosophy," Stewart had been heavily influenced by the work of Adam Smith, capital-
ism's first theoretician, and Thomas Reid, the moral philosopher who
had mentored him at the University of Glasgow. Stewart's *Biographical Memoir of Adam Smith*, published in 1793, just three years after
the economist's death, had rescued Smith's work from the dustbin of
history. As Stewart argued, the scientific method could be counted
on to improve the lot of humankind. Eschewing the skepticism of his
fellow countryman, the philosopher David Hume, Stewart strove for
practical knowledge that could help people lead virtuous and successful lives.

The classroom was packed. Though Peter got there early, he had a
little trouble finding a seat. He eventually settled in a row at the
back of the lecture hall. Like many of his fellow students—Stewart
attracted young men from all across the Western world to study with
him—Peter was soon sitting on the edge of his seat.

Peter looked up at the podium and stared at the professor. With
his piercing gray eyes staring out from his massive head, Stewart
was an intimidating presence. He was of medium height, yet his
lips were large and expressive. His gentle voice could convey a
wide range of emotion, and he often laced his mellifluous words
with humor. In short, Stewart was "quite the orator," as Roget's
mother once put it. Catherine had firsthand knowledge of just how
much the esteemed professor prided himself on his ability to captivate an audience, as it was to her that Stewart sometimes com-

plained when a bad cough impaired the smooth functioning of his precious pipes.

After clearing his throat, Stewart began by arguing that the central task of philosophy is to uncover the order in the universe. As Stewart asserted, the philosopher "can trace an established order where a mere observer of facts would perceive nothing but irregularity."

The topic of the day was the philosophy of mind and what Stewart termed "the intellectual powers of man." These powers, according to the professor, consisted of faculties such as attention, memory, and abstraction. Stewart then zeroed in on classification, which he defined as "attending to some of the qualities, or circumstances of objects and events, and of withdrawing the attention from the rest." Suggesting that abstraction and classification were synonymous, Stewart went on to call abstraction "the faculty by which the mind separates the combinations which are presented to it, in order to simplify the objects of its consideration."

Roget was already familiar with Stewart's ideas about classification from their one-on-one discussions, and his mind began to wander. But he could not help but prick up his ears when Stewart suddenly shifted his focus to language and issued the following lament: "As it is by language alone that we are rendered capable of general reasoning, one of the most valuable branches of logic is that which relates to the use of words. Too little attention has been bestowed on this subject." Toward the end of his lecture, Stewart came back to language and began listing the eight causes "of the slow progress of human knowledge." The first cause: "The imperfections of language, both as an instrument of thought and a medium of communication."

As Roget drifted out of the lecture hall, he couldn't stop thinking about the imperfections of language. He couldn't believe that no philosopher had ever made a systematic attempt to tidy it up. Such work was critical because, as Roget realized, without clear communication tools, all attempts to bring order to the world through knowledge would be doomed to failure. Rushing off to his next class, his mind kept coming back to the disturbing thought that chaos would forever rule the lives of men.

That June morning, Dugald Stewart had planted in Roget's brain a scholarly mission that would occupy him for the rest of his life. What Roget learned in Stewart's course that summer would work its way directly into the introduction to the *Thesaurus*, where fifty-odd years later Roget would write:

> In every process of reasoning, language enters as an essential ele-
> ment. Words are the instruments by which we form all our abstrac-
> tions, by which we fashion and embody our ideas, and by which we
> are enabled to glide along a series of premises and conclusions. . . .
> It is on this ground, also, that the present Work founds a claim to
> utility.

If his uncle was the person who instilled in Roget what it meant to be a man, Stewart taught him what it meant to be a scholar. In June 1798, Petrus Marcus Roget would dedicate his first scholarly text, his medical thesis (written entirely in Latin, as was required by the university until the mid-1830s), to "Samueli Romilly" and "Dugaldo Stewart."

Given the huge imprint this philosopher-king left on the adoles-cent mind of Peter Mark Roget, it's not surprising that a volume of the 1793 edition of Stewart's lectures, *Outlines of Moral Philosophy*, could be found on Roget's bookshelf on the day he died—nearly seventy-five years after he took Stewart's course. Just as Stewart's book had been designed "to exhibit such a view of the arrangement

In addition to Roget, Dugald Stewart's illustrious pupils included the novelist Sir Walter Scott and two future prime ministers, Lord Palmerston and Lord John Russell.

of my lectures, as may facilitate the studies of those to whom they addressed," Roget's masterpiece was "classified and arranged so as to facilitate the expression of ideas and assist in literary composition."

Now that he was a medical student, Peter had longer and more stressful days, but he also had the benefit of more contact with his fellow students. In the spring of 1796, in addition to his science courses and clinical work, Peter began attending the weekly meetings at the Royal Medical Society of Edinburgh, an activity that, Catherine reported to her brother, gave him "great pleasure." Not surprisingly, Catherine, who tended to treat Peter more as her spouse than her son, felt abandoned by his forays into the work world. But what most annoyed Catherine was what most excited Peter: the opportunity for lively late-night discussions with his classmates. At one meeting in 1797, Roget introduced his young friend Francis Horner, then studying politics with Stewart, to the group; a few years later, Horner would found *The Edinburgh Review*. Through his membership in the Royal Medical Society of Edinburgh, Roget also became acquainted with John Yelloly, Alexander Marcet, and John Bostock. A decade later, Roget, along with these three colleagues from his Edinburgh days, would play a critical role in establishing the Medical and Chirurgical Society of London (now the Royal Society of Medicine).

For the first time in his life, Roget began to mingle freely with peers whose company he could enjoy and with whom he could share an occasional laugh. One of these new friends was Lovell Edgeworth, son of the Irish inventor Richard Lovell Edgeworth. This new acquaintance, who had spent much of 1796 traveling around England demonstrating his father's model telegraph (dubbed the "pretty, delicate little telly") would remain Roget's closest friend for the next several years.

Despite his cordial and easygoing public persona, in private Peter could be very disapproving of others, even his friends. Having internalized his mother's critical nature, he was developing into a judgmental young man. While a few of Peter's comments appeared apt, many were unduly harsh. Peter described as "very pompous" Thomas Charles Hope, appointed a professor of chemistry in 1795. Likewise, Peter did not much care for Lord Ashburton, the teenage protégé of his uncle's who was staying with the Stewarts on Canongate Street;

Peter complained to his mother of his "talking so much and at random." Peter may well have been jealous of Lord Ashburton, who came from a wealthy London family, as he himself longed for even more personal attention from the two men he most looked up to. Of his classmate Arthur Aikin, who would later help found the Geological Society of London and edit the *Dictionary of Chemistry and Mineralogy*, Peter provided the following assessments: "rather heavy and not polite," and "rough in his manners."

In May 1797, a year before he was slated to graduate from medical school, Peter was sidelined with a serious bout of typhoid fever. Catherine felt as if her worst prophecy had come true—that Peter had indeed caught some incurable disease from his patients. Having lost her husband to tuberculosis, she began having flashbacks to Jean Roget's final days. Despite the lack of any corroborating evidence, she was convinced that Peter's lungs were irreparably damaged and that he was "at death's door." In early June, Catherine wrote her brother: "During all this time he has never had the least pain in his breast or even uneasiness there, nor does he breathe with difficulty, yet am I persuaded the seat of his present disorder is on his lungs. . . . My fears were so great that hourly I expected he would have a great spitting of blood."

Peter had the best doctor in town, James Gregory, who headed the medical school. Elevated to the university's chair of medicine in 1790, Gregory was also a formidable Latin scholar with a literary bent, who had taken a keen interest in the work of his late friend Robert Burns, Scotland's national poet. For Peter, who that fall would attend Gregory's lectures on clinical medicine, the learned physician could do little more than prescribe lots of bed rest and a little julep. With his patient often dozing, the musket-toting Gregory—like many of the city's residents, he had joined the Royal

Edinburgh Volunteers to protect his homeland from the French—
spent most of his time at the Rogets' listening to Catherine recite
her long list of fears.

Day after day, for weeks on end, Catherine sat at Peter's bedside.
Eventually, she moved his bed into the family's dining room, which,
as she emphasized, was larger and more airy than his bedroom.
Though she maintained that she took this drastic measure for Peter's
sake, her own convenience probably played a greater role. As with
her efforts to stake her own claim to pages in Peter's childhood notebook, Catherine once again showed little inclination to respect her
son's right to a modicum of privacy.

By the middle of June, Peter was at last feeling better. His fever
was gone and his coughing had abated. For the first time in weeks,
he was getting up out of bed and putting on his clothes. He was finally able to eat some solid food—occasional helpings of rice pud-
ding along with a little beef. He was also making plans to see Dugald
Stewart, who had visited him in his sickbed, for dinner. Though by
1797 Stewart was rarely inviting Catherine over to his Canongate
Street house anymore—she complained to her brother that she had
not even seen the Stewarts since the previous November—the famous professor continued to make himself available to Peter.

At the end of June, Catherine decided to take the family to Queens
Ferry, a small town just west of Edinburgh, for a three-week vacation.
Peter enjoyed being near the countryside. He would rise at seven to
take a long walk by the sea before breakfast. By August, Peter's recovery was in full swing. He was starting to regain all the weight that he
had lost. Catherine's descriptions of the various changes in her son's
body during his convalescence border on the comic. "When he first got
out of bed," she wrote, "we thought him grown tall, owing no doubt to
his being such a skeleton, for we now think him growing short." His
legs, Catherine added, were no longer "two sticks." Peter's mood was

also much more upbeat. What cheered him up the most was his ability to get back to his studies, for "without his books," Catherine observed, "he grows dull and weary."

Soon after Peter was beginning to feel like his old self again, Dr. Gregory informed him that in addition to the typhoid fever, he had briefly had a spot on his lungs. Upon hearing this unsettling news, Peter was deeply shaken for a few days. Despite having asserted a couple of months earlier that the thing she most liked in Gregory was "his frankness," Catherine now accused the doctor of being "imprudent" in telling Peter "that he had a narrow escape of his life."

Though Peter was the one coping with the aftereffects of a life-threatening illness, both his mother and uncle were so preoccupied with their own anxieties that they failed to offer him much room to process *his*. In fact, their hypervigilance only added to his distress. Catherine made it her business to "moderate his joy, lest any slight return should cast him down again." This bit of solicitousness, however, did not necessarily benefit Peter, as it was in fact his mother's way of coping with *her* abject terror of a relapse. Likewise, in a letter dated September 12, 1797, in which he promised to "entertain a regular correspondence," Romilly accused Peter of not being sensitive enough to the wishes of those who cared about him, namely, his mother. "I am afraid of your prosecuting your studies with more ardour and perseverance than your strength will allow of. I need not certainly impress upon your mind the value of life and health not on your account but for the sake of those who are most dear to you." It was a Roget family given that Peter was supposed to be living his life not for himself but for others.

Rather than protesting these subtle and not so subtle recriminations from his uncle, Peter quickly acquiesced. One reason may have been that Peter was thrilled, as he wrote in his response, by the prospect of "the correspondence in which you are so good as to indulge me." Living in Edinburgh, he sorely missed his uncle, and ever since the death of his father, he had suffered from a constant deficit of paternal attention. In that letter to Romilly, Peter also tried to offer reassurance by taking a peculiar tack—arguing that he was, in fact, being lazy:

> Far from being the studious person you imagine, I should—were the truth known—be often liable to the accusation of neglecting to execute what I might have done without fatigue. My application far from exceeding my strength, is, I am confident, not in the least degree prejudicial to my health; nor does it ever encroach upon those hours when exercise is necessary.

These statements didn't have even the slightest ring of truth, and Peter remained as wedded as ever to his books—his favorite escape hatch from stress. Eventually, to attend to his studies without opening himself up to the charge that he was failing to exercise, Peter learned how to pace back and forth across the room while reading. But as he entered what was to be his most demanding year of medical school, Peter hardly got a break from this suffocating attention from his mother and uncle.

That December, Samuel Romilly, then age forty, finally married. His wife was Anne Garbett, the daughter of affluent parents, who had grown up just a mile east of the border with Wales. With her dark curls and exquisite figure, Anne Romilly was ravishing. Fun-loving by nature, she was also a talented musician and painter.

Right after their first meeting, in October 1796, at Bowood, the estate of Lord Lansdowne, Romilly had described Anne as "the most beautiful and accomplished creature that ever blessed the sight . . .

of man." She possessed, he recorded in his journal, "a most intelligent mind, an uncommonly correct judgment . . . and an elevation and heroism of character." The courtship was swift—Romilly proposed marriage after just ten days—but his passion would never waver. Two decades later, Romilly still referred to her as "the most splendid beauty that human eyes ever beheld."

Though Catherine was eager to get to know her brother's new bride, she was worried about the possibility of rejection. Catherine was also disappointed that she was unable to see the newlyweds in London. For the time being, her only communication would have to be through letters. Given the difficulty and expense of travel, the Rogets never once returned to London during their five-year sojourn in Scotland. Catherine's various anxieties took the form of an odd speculation, which she shared with her brother: "Some people pretend to the knowledge of character and temper by the handwriting, but I hope my dear sister does not hold that doctrine good, as my dimunitive [sic] scroll will immediately give her a bad opinion of me. To judge from it, I must be mean and pitiful." Catherine's harsh diagnosis of her handwriting no doubt had more to do with her own shaky self-image than with her grasp of the then current state of graphology.

That winter, Peter felt overtaxed. Under the best of circumstances, the final year of medical school in Edinburgh was highly stressful. Graduation was by no means assured, as students often failed their exams and flunked out at the last minute. In fact, of the hundreds of students in each class, only about five percent graduated. Still not at full strength, Peter was unable to study late into the night like his classmates. But he also needed to catch up. "But unfortunately, his illness and long recovery have so prevented his studies," reported his mother to her brother, in her inimitable prose, "that he finds himself backward . . . [and] fears at present that he has lost more valuable time than he can repair." Right until the spring of 1798, Peter was thinking that he would need to spend at least another semester in Edinburgh.

That final spring semester, Roget took a second class in natural philosophy—this time with John Robison, another towering figure of the Scottish Enlightenment who was a close friend of James Watt, the inventor of the steam engine. Though once described by Watt as "a man of the clearest head and the most science of anybody I have known," in the classroom John Robison was no Dugald Stewart. Suffering from a mysterious nervous disorder that caused such severe concentration lapses that he had to stop teaching between 1791 and 1796, Robison was dry and plodding. His unpopularity among students, who were turned off equally by the complex subject matter, caused Robison some personal hardship, as a professor's income was then dependent on his ability to fill the classroom.

But Roget was drawn to Robison's intricate mathematical formulations. Greatly inspired by Robison, Roget would become a passionate student of natural philosophy. As befitted the era, Robison managed to inject classification into his examination of electricity and magnetism, which constituted the heart of his course. For example, in discussing electricity, Robison argued that "electrical bodies" are best arranged in two classes—"metals" and "those containing watery juices." Roget would dig out his notes from Robison's class (which still survive) when he wrote treatises on the two subjects some thirty years later.

Roget's fierce dedication to his studies combined with his innate smarts enabled him to complete medical school on time. On April 5, he passed his exams and on June 25, 1798, he was awarded his diploma along with about twenty other students, among them John Bostock, who would remain his lifelong friend.

Completed just before his graduation, Roget's medical disserta-
tion, "De chemicae affinitatis legibus" ("On the Laws of Chemical Affinity"), appears at first glance to be unrelated to anything else he
ever wrote. After all, the mature Roget never showed much interest in
chemistry. And chemical affinity referred simply to the way in which
certain atoms or molecules tend to bond. Ever since the Middle Ages,
this principle had been trotted out by any number of scientists—from
the medieval theologian Albertus Magnus to Isaac Newton—to explain the chemical reactions that lead to heat or fire. In 1775, the
Swedish chemist Torbern Olof Bergman had published the definitive
work *Disquisitio de attractionibus electivis (Concerning Elective Affinities)*,
which Roget cited respectfully in his opening pages.

But on a closer inspection, Roget's fifty-page Latin thesis would
prove to be tied to his lifelong obsessions. Chemistry—at least as it
was then taught in Edinburgh—was primarily concerned with abstract principles. Back in his first year of medical school, Roget had
taken the course offered by Joseph Black, the eminent chemist and
physician responsible for the discovery of carbon dioxide. (Among
his celebrity patients were David Hume and King George III himself.) As Black had defined the discipline, "Chemistry must be understood to have the same relation to many other branches of knowledge
that geometry has. It supplies principles by which many otherwise
dark and intricate points in these other sciences are clearly explained;
and thus throws much light on many of the great operations of nature." Roget saw in the principle of chemical affinity something that
had widespread reverberations. (So, too, did Goethe, whose novel
Elective Affinities, published a decade later, applied these new chemical discoveries to the realms of love and marriage.) "Among the many
qualities common to all matter," Roget wrote at the beginning of his
essay, "none is of greater influence or more worthy of being noted
than *mutual Attraction*." Both the massive planets in the heavens as

well as the smallest molecules, added Roget, adhere to this principle
of bonding.

Though Roget's thesis is nominally about chemistry, its real subject
matter is classification. That's why Dugald Stewart, who knew only a
smattering of chemistry, but whose overarching concern was the organization of knowledge, was the right advisor. And that's why Roget felt
free to sprinkle his Latin text with English quotations from *The Botanic
Garden*, a lengthy didactic poem written by the reigning British champion of classification, Erasmus Darwin. In the late 1780s, Darwin had
published translations of the two chief works by Linnaeus, *A System of
Vegetables* and *The Families of Plants*. A few years later, in an effort to
spread Linnaeus's ideas to a wider audience, Darwin translated these
works once again—this time into verse. *The Botanic Garden* turned out
to be a best-seller.

Just like his idols Linnaeus and Darwin, Roget, too, focused on
the order in the universe. To frame the body of his thesis, Roget
cited the following lines from a canto of Darwin's poem devoted to
the element of fire:

> *On the pain'd ear-drum bursts the sudden crash,*
> *Starts the red flame, and Death pursues the flash.*
> *Fear's feeble hand directs the fiery darts,*
> *And Strength and Courage yield to chemic arts;*
> *Guilt with pale brow the mimic thunder owns,*
> *And Tyrants tremble on their blood-stained thrones.*

Roget argued that chemical phenomena were the source of both
technological innovations such as gunpowder and the steam engine
as well as natural forces—namely, electricity and magnetism. Thus
his investigation into the laws that govern chemical affinity was no
trifling matter.

Shortly after submitting his thesis, Roget was to come back to classification in a fifty-page manuscript—also never published—titled "Classification or Arrangement of Knowledge." Roget divided knowledge into three classes: (1) *the material world*—namely, his beloved natural history; (2) *the intellectual world*; and (3) *signs*—that is, words. Roget's road map came directly from his professor Dugald Stewart, who once wrote that words are the glue that allow for scientific advances in the other two classes. Sharing Stewart's belief that "the progressive improvement of the species" depended upon the dissemination of knowledge, Roget would dedicate his life to filling in chunks of this outline with encyclopedic books and treatises.

In organizing the *Thesaurus* itself, Roget would also mine this outline from his youth. For example, the third of the six classes in his famous classification system, as he explained in its 1852 introduction, "includes all ideas that relate to the Material World." The fourth class, he noted, "embraces all ideas or phenomena related to the Intellect and its operations."

Roget was not Stewart's only student to become obsessed with the quest for the ideal classification scheme for knowledge. So, too, did Roget's friend Francis Horner, who later served with Samuel Romilly in Parliament. At about the same time as Roget wrote his fifty-page "Classification" text, Horner dreamt of writing a book called "A View of the Limits of Human Knowledge and a System of the Principles of Philosophical Inquiry." "A knowledge of the beings that compose the universe," Horner noted in his journal, "seems to consist in a proper classification of them." But what distinguished Roget from colleagues such as Horner was that his obsession with classification also seeped into the very fabric of his personality. Roget sought order in everything he did—both as a scientist and a man.

Though he had managed to summon up the enormous energy required to finish medical school, Peter felt exhausted and confused upon graduation. Not yet twenty, Roget had, as Dumont informed Catherine, "four or five years to fill up" before he could begin practicing medicine. To treat patients, he needed to look more mature. Dumont recommended that Roget plug up some of the gaps in his medical education by taking more classes in anatomy, a subject that most medical schools failed to emphasize. His uncle offered similar advice, writing to Catherine that "the only thing P has to do for some years is to pursue his studies and grow older." For Roget, who, paradoxically, tended to feel less anxious when he was weighed down by pressing responsibilities, the next few years would prove unsettling. Lacking clearly defined goals, the newly minted Dr. Roget would often find himself battling his own tendency toward melancholy.

3.

The
Idle and
Depressed
Young
Man

(841) WEARINESS, tedium, ennui, lassitude, fatigue, dejection.

Disgust, nausea, loathing, sickness, disgust of life, taedium vitae.

Wearisomeness, irksomeness, tiresomeness, monotony.

In the summer of 1798, Roget finally stood up to his mother. Despite her repeated assertions that she could not bear to be separated from him, he declared his emotional independence. Eager to get back to London to see her brother and the rest of the family, Catherine immediately returned to the capital. But Roget put off his return to his hometown for a few months. For the first time in his life, he would live apart from his mother and his sister.

Though still shy and socially awkward, Roget wanted to take the initiative and choreograph his own career. While his mother reported to Romilly that Peter was "not ambitious," this was far from the truth. He was highly motivated, and as he well understood, success in medicine at the end of the eighteenth century depended not so much on intelligence, expert training, or clinical acumen as on connections. Whether a young physician could attain a prestigious post at a hospital was largely a matter of who he knew. Roget thus chose to put his energy into networking—both with distinguished men of science and with the well-heeled.

To gain introductions to some eminent scientists, Roget leaned on his medical school colleague, Lovell Edgeworth. Through his father, the inventor Richard Lovell Edgeworth, the young Edgeworth had already formed close ties with several of the distinguished scientists belonging to the Lunar Society of Birmingham. (First assembled in 1765, this group held nighttime meetings once a month—typically when the moon was full, to facilitate travel—where they discussed new developments in natural philosophy and technology.) That September, Roget, accompanied by Edgeworth, went on a month-long trip to Derby, Birmingham, and Clifton, a small hill town above Bristol, to visit a few of these so-called "lunaticks," among them the eminent physicians Erasmus Darwin and Thomas Beddoes.

Derby was then home to Erasmus Darwin, and Roget was excited about the chance to talk with the man whose artful poetic renditions of Linnaeus he had cited in his medical thesis. Once described by the writer Samuel Taylor Coleridge as possessing "a greater range of knowledge than any other man in Europe," Darwin had a penetrating intellect. But this meeting turned out to be a disappointment, as were the majority of Roget's interactions with famous scholars over the next few years.

As Roget soon found out, he didn't have much in common with the renowned scientists who shared his obsessions with chemistry and classification. Like many avant-garde thinkers, Darwin espoused radical politics, which in those days translated into unequivocal support for the French Revolution. By contrast, Roget, though sympathetic to its ideals, was at heart a conservative. The thought of criticizing the British government during the war with France never occurred to him. Roget also felt uncomfortable around those who, like Darwin, thumbed their nose at convention. "A fool," Darwin had once observed, "is a man who never tried an experiment." Despite his brilliance, Darwin often fell for crackpot ideas. For example, he used electric shock to try to cure jaundice and advocated blood transfusions to treat consumption.

To borrow Richard Lovell Edgeworth's pithy description, Charles Darwin's grandfather was "large, fat and clumsy." Appearance meant a lot to Roget, and he could hardly stand being around someone so unkempt. Then nearing the end of his life—he would die in 1802 at the age of seventy-one—Darwin was so huge that a semicircle had to be cut out of his dining room table to accommodate him.

Though Roget would end up working much more closely with Thomas Beddoes than with Darwin, his stay in Clifton would also bring him little satisfaction. Beddoes was as physically unappealing as Darwin. Though still in his thirties, Beddoes, a former Oxford don in chemistry, was so obese that he could hardly walk. Richard Edgeworth had also come up with an apposite three-word portrait of Beddoes, calling him a "fat little democrat." By "democrat," Edgeworth was alluding to Beddoes's pro-French pamphlets, which had gotten him in trouble with the British government for allegedly "sowing sedition." Perhaps most unsettling to Roget was that Beddoes could be ill-mannered.

While in Clifton, Roget stayed in Beddoes's capacious home on 3 Rodney Place. Located on a hill, the town offered a scenic view of the western section of the port city of Bristol. Though Beddoes's house was surrounded by many charming villas, Roget could not help but notice that part of Clifton looked like a ghost town. As in Edinburgh, the resumption of the war with France in 1793—and the ensuing financial panic—had forced local businessmen to abandon their ambitious construction plans, leaving many buildings unfinished.

From his perch at 3 Rodney Place, Beddoes was turning his attention to what he envisioned as a radical new approach to medical care. At the time, despite advances in diagnosis, doctors often felt powerless when it came to treatment. For most patients, a comforting presence was the best they could offer. In 1793, Beddoes observed: "There are many diseases in which neither patients nor practitioners have much reason to be satisfied with the state of medicine; and multitudes will no doubt concur with me in endeavouring to put it on a better footing. Many circumstances indeed seem to indicate that a great revolution in this art is at hand." A product of the Enlightenment, Beddoes had an abiding faith in human progress. He soon became enthusiastic about the prospects for the emerging field of "pneumatic medicine," which concerned the effects of gases on the human body.

As Roget came to understand while working on his medical thesis, new discoveries in chemistry were then turning the scientific world inside out. With the appearance of the 1789 textbook *Elementary Treatise on Chemistry* by the Frenchman Antoine Lavoisier—considered the "father of modern chemistry"—the discipline had officially arrived; its associations with alchemy were now history. Chemistry was where the action was: between 1750 and 1800, about one-eighth of all scientists described themselves as chemists, making it the hottest specialty. On the heels of Lavoisier's discovery of the specific chemical composition of water, Joseph Priestley—another "lunatick"—had begun experiments to study the impact of inhaling various types of "factitious airs," or gases, such as oxygen, carbon dioxide, and nitrous oxide (laughing gas).

Beddoes was particularly interested in applying these new findings to the most pressing public health problem affecting England at the dawn of the Industrial Revolution—consumption. Beddoes was quick to concede that the prevailing "cures" were of little use. Since the end of the seventeenth century, tubercular patients had, for example, flocked to Bristol's Hotwells springs. Twice a day—at dawn and at five p.m.—they would drink the warm, milky water which trickled out of a rock from the river Avon. This potion, which contained lime, sulfur, and iron, rarely did any good, and Beddoes had nothing but contempt for such bogus medical practices. As a man of science, he sought to offer a sound alternative that could be empirically tested. But coming up with one wasn't easy. For a while, Beddoes personally conveyed cows into invalids' bedrooms in the hope that their health might be improved by inhaling the breath of the animals. Despite his penchant for unorthodox treatments, the scientific establishment embraced Beddoes. Erasmus Darwin, for example, encouraged him, writing, "Go on, dear Sir, save the young and fair of the rising generation from premature death."

By the time Roget and Edgeworth got to Bristol in the fall of 1798, Beddoes was putting the finishing touches on his Pneumatic Institution. A man ahead of his time, Beddoes was the first to envision the modern medical research institute—combining research, training, and patient care. He was also writing a book on the causes of consumption, and drafted the young Dr. Roget to do a little field-work for him. Tuberculosis was the disease that had taken his father, so Roget didn't hesitate to help. His task: to examine the prevalence of consumption among fishwives—the women who sold fish for a living—in Scotland. In his report, contained in Beddoes's 1799 book *Essay on the Causes, Early Signs, and Prevention of Pulmonary Consumption for the Use of Parents and Preceptors*, Roget concluded:

From what I have at length been able to collect, I have reason to believe that this class of women is less subject to the disease than the generality of poor people in this part of the country. I have made enquiries among the fishwives themselves, and was in particular informed by one of them, who, I am told, is one of the oldest in the place, and who by her own account was married in the year 1746, that the occupation they follow is, on the whole, a healthy one. . . . This account corresponded with that of several other fishwives with whom I conversed. They live much among themselves; they are a shrewd and intelligent set of people; and from the little intercourse they have with their neighbors, unless in the way of trade, their manners are in many respects peculiar.

Though Roget would be proud to see his name in print for the first time, he was not cut out for anthropological observation. Lacking much appreciation for the uniqueness of human beings, he tended to label individuals as either "ordinary" or "peculiar"—adjectives that he later subsumed under the neighboring ideas "Conformity" 82 and "Unconformity" 83, in the first edition of the *Thesaurus*.

Before Roget left Clifton that fall, Beddoes asked him to come back the following spring when the Pneumatic Institute was officially to open its doors. Beddoes had hoped to attract German researchers, sensing that the Germans were at the forefront of chemistry, but after his search proved fruitless, he readily turned to Englishmen. Beddoes had just hired a superintendent to direct the research. His selection: the nineteen-year-old self-educated Humphry Davy, who had been working as an apprentice to an apothecary-surgeon in his native Cornwall. Roget, who was just one month younger than his future boss, promptly accepted the job as Davy's assistant. Lovell Edgeworth would also return to Clifton and pitch in.

Described by the Bristol-born poet Robert Southey as "possessing extraordinary talents," Davy stayed in Bristol for only a couple of years before heading off to serve as a professor of chemistry at the Royal Institution, where Roget would meet up with him again shortly after his own move to London in 1808. Over the course of his legendary scientific career, Davy (later, Sir Humphry) would count among his many achievements the invention of the coal miners' lamp. Of all the scientists Roget encountered in the years between the end of his university studies and the beginning of his medical career, Davy was the one with whom he forged the strongest tie. Following Davy's scientific pursuits closely, Roget had nothing but the deepest admiration. "The name of Davy," Roget would later write, "will descend to distant ages, as associated with so many important discoveries in science." Davy, who died suddenly in 1829, was to make it onto Roget's hallowed list, "Dates of Deaths."

It was Thursday, April 25, 1799. It was the day a famous Londoner had chosen to retire. Though he was just thirty-six, Matthew Baillie, a physician at St. George's Hospital, whose anatomy course Roget was then attending, was calling it quits.

Baillie was not resigning from the hospital—though he would do so the following year—but giving up his post as a lecturer in Soho's Great Windmill School (also known as the Hunterian Medical School). He preferred to concentrate on his clinical practice—a decision he would not regret. Within a couple of years, Baillie would have the largest practice in London.

Roget had come to London in October for some extra training in anatomy because in this branch of medicine Edinburgh still lagged behind the capital. Due to the strict quotas imposed by the Crown limiting the use of cadavers by medical guilds, medical students had relatively few opportunities for dissection. Edinburgh's star anatomy professor, Alexander Munro, had to make do with just two cadavers for every one hundred of his lectures. Choosing not to play by the rules, the proprietors of London's private anatomy schools, however, availed themselves of the endless supply of dead bodies in the country's largest city—negotiating, for example, special deals with prison wardens to obtain executed prisoners. By the end of the eighteenth century, the Great Windmill School had evolved into a thriving business, thanks to its promise to deliver each student a fresh dead body to study.

Roget wouldn't have missed Baillie's final lecture for anything. Though Baillie wasn't as dazzling as Dugald Stewart, Roget found him equally inspiring. Baillie could make even the most abstract medical concepts comprehensible, both to his students and to patients. In the words of one student, Baillie "was singularly clear in his demonstrations, yet concise and condensed; he was never at a loss for an appropriate word or phrase."

Roget also identified with Baillie's personal style, which was simple and straightforward. Baillie had a plain countenance, and, disliking affectation, he dressed simply. A slender man of short stature, Baillie was both hardworking and sincere. The Scotsman came from a distinguished pedigree. His mother, Dorothea, was the sister of the two world-famous surgeons, William and John Hunter. After John Hunter's death in 1793, Baillie became one of the executors of the Hunterian Museum, which then housed some 15,000 anatomical specimens.

That same year, Baillie published his famous *Morbid Anatomy of Some of the Most Important Parts of the Human Body*. Baillie's one and only book, which, over the next generation, would go through ten British and three American editions (and be translated into all major European languages), constituted the first attempt to establish pathology as an independent discipline. Roget's course with Baillie that winter closely adhered to the professor's textbook.

On this final day, Baillie was discussing the diseased brain. While Roget looked at the specimen sitting on his desk, Baillie remarked, in his thick Scottish accent, "It is extremely common, when a brain is examined in a person who has been dead for several days to find its substance so soft that it can hardly be cut so as to leave a smooth surface and the smallest pressure of the fingers breaks it down into a pultaceous mass."

After Baillie uttered his final words, the students all stood up and applauded. As a token of their gratitude, they presented Baillie with a copper plate. Roget, like everyone else in the room that day, was profoundly moved. Of Baillie's last day in the Great Windmill Street auditorium one student would later recall that it was "one of the most affecting incidents I have ever witnessed."

Roget would incorporate much of what he learned from Baillie into his own lectures on comparative anatomy, which he later gave at many distinguished venues, including the Great Windmill School itself.

When Roget returned to Bristol in May 1799, he stayed in the center of town. Though he would have preferred to find a place in the airy hills of Clifton, the cost was prohibitive. Beddoes had offered him free lodgings on the top floor of 6 Dowry Square, the building that also housed the laboratories of the Pneumatic Institute. He was to live alongside his supervisor, Humphry Davy.

Bristol was not Roget's kind of town. In its natural situation, Bristol was a marvel, as it stood on seven hills—just like Rome, to which it was often compared. But at the dawn of the Industrial Revolution, the smoke issuing from its manufacturing plants—the brass and iron foundries, glass-houses, and distilleries—blanketed much of the city in an impenetrable dark cloud. With its population swelling to nearly 80,000 inhabitants, Bristol was densely populated and dirty—far from ideal, especially given Roget's aversion to crowds and chaos.

But the birth of Beddoes's Pneumatic Institute was greeted with considerable fanfare. On Tuesday, March 12, the day before its official opening, Robert Southey wrote to the scholar William Taylor (who, a decade and a half later, published one of the first English synonym books) of its potential benefit to medical students: "Studies here . . . would probably be of more importance than all the university lectures in Europe. I hope much from pneumatic medicine." Likewise, under the headline "New Medical Institution," an announcement published the following week in the *Bristol Gazette and Public Adviser* emphasized its potential to improve patient care: "The application of persons in confirmed consumption is principally wished at present; and though the disease has heretofore been deemed hopeless, it is confidently expected that a considerable portion of such cases will be permanently cured." This notice also mentioned that Beddoes had received the support of numerous subscribers, including "a large portion of the physicians of England." Among the key financial backers were Erasmus Darwin and Thomas Wedgwood, the inventor who later became known as the "godfather of photography." The Royal Medical Society of Edinburgh would also give Beddoes its seal of approval. Perhaps because the clinic's medical services were offered free of charge, patients began signing up in droves. By mid-April, Davy reported, "We have upwards of eighty outpatients, and we are going on wonderfully well."

At the same time as he was preparing for the influx of patients, Davy began setting up the research program. One of his first decisions was to experiment with nitrous oxide. On April 11, he discovered that pure nitrous oxide could, in fact, be inhaled. About a week later, with Beddoes looking on, Davy tried the gas for the first time. Over the next couple of months, Davy would repeatedly experiment on himself—sometimes inhaling as much as nine quarts of gas four times a day. Davy typically found the experience exhilarating—"I have felt a more high degree of pleasure from breathing Nitrous oxide than I ever experienced from any cause whatever." Once, while under its influence, he had a fit of grandiosity, in which he wrote his name next to Sir Isaac Newton's in big block letters.

To study the specific properties of nitrous oxide in a systematic fashion, Davy decided to recruit healthy volunteers. Over the next year, some forty people—including Beddoes, his wife, Anna, and his son, Lovell, not to mention such local avant-garde intellectuals as the poets Wordsworth, Coleridge, and Southey—would all take a turn as Davy's subjects. And among the first was Davy's trusted assistant, Peter Mark Roget.

On Friday, May 17, 1799, Roget got up early. Skipping breakfast, he walked down two flights of stairs from his bedroom on the top floor of 6 Dowry Square and entered the ground-floor laboratory. There he met Davy, who was already busy making preparations for the experiment.

To conduct the nitrous oxide trials, Davy relied on an apparatus personally designed by the famous inventor James Watt and manufactured by the industrial powerhouse Boulton and Watt, of nearby Birmingham. The gas was transported from a fire-tube to an airholder, and the patient would inhale it from an oiled silk bag. These bags, which could hold up to thirty quarts of gas, sometimes developed a foul odor, so Davy cleaned them with charcoal dust between uses.

With the gas now heated, Davy walked over to the row of silk bags hanging from the ceiling and plucked one down. Putting it next to the fire-tube of Watt's apparatus, he filled it with nitrous oxide through the small spigot at the back. Davy then handed the bag to Roget.

Roget felt queasy. Though he wanted to help Davy and Beddoes find a cure for consumption, he felt terrified by the thought of inhaling something that might make him lose control of his rational faculties. But despite his intense discomfort, he did not hesitate to proceed with the experiment. Closing his eyes, Roget put his lips on the wooden mouthpiece. He then took a deep breath, inhaling several quarts of gas.

Dropping the silk bag to the floor, Roget immediately became dizzy; he felt as if the room were spinning in circles. He also experienced a tingling sensation in his hands and his feet. He then got hit by a wave of drowsiness. Roget soon found that he had to force himself to inhale and exhale.

No longer able to speak, Roget briefly lost his sense of time and place. Suddenly, this torpor was replaced by agitation, and he heard a ringing in his ears. His whole body began throbbing, and thoughts of all sorts raced through his mind. But this state of violent unrest lasted for only a few minutes.

Fifteen minutes after first breathing the gas, Roget started to feel like himself again. He then began monitoring his own breathing. As he continued to take deep breaths, he excused himself, telling Davy that he needed to be alone for a few minutes to regain his composure.

The gas unnerved Roget, because for him pleasure was connected to the search for order, not to the senses, which he saw as a source of danger. In the 1852 edition of his *Thesaurus*, Roget distinguished between two types of pleasure—"Physical Pleasure" 377 and "Moral Pleasure" 827. For him, physical pleasure held little appeal, while moral pleasure was what life was all about; this state of "well-being" or "satisfaction"—to use two of the synonyms he listed under 827—typically required painstaking work.

Roget walked outside into the garden, shrouded by apple trees, at the back of the house. For the next half an hour he paced back and forth through the rows of strawberries. Roget then went back upstairs to jot down his reactions to the experiment in his notebook. Two months later, Roget reworked these notes into a letter to Davy, which Davy published in his book *Researches Chemical and Philosophical; Chiefly Concerning Nitrous Oxide, or Dephlogisticated Nitrous Air, and Its Respiration*. Of his only trial with nitrous oxide, Roget wrote: "I cannot remember that I experienced the least pleasure from any of these sensations. I can however, easily conceive that by frequent repetition I might reconcile myself to them, and possibly even receive pleasure from the same sensations which were then unpleasant." Overly formal and stiff, Roget lacked a sense of humor—a character trait that would have come in handy for this experiment.

By contrast, most of Roget's peers, including Davy, loved the gas, as it gave them an experience bordering on ecstasy. Coleridge, for example, who was perpetually intrigued by psychoactive substances—to cope with facial pain, he had begun using opium a couple of years earlier—was an eager participant when he returned from a trip to Germany in July 1799. Coleridge tried the gas a total of four times, breathing between five and seven quarts each time:

> The first time, I felt a highly pleasurable sensation of warmth over my whole frame, resembling that which I remember once to have experienced after returning from a walk in the snow into a warm

room. . . . The fourth time . . . my sensations were highly pleasurable . . . of more unmingled pleasure than I had ever before experienced.

Lovell Edgeworth was also delighted to find that the gas lived up to its moniker: "I . . . felt a strong propensity to laugh . . . and capered about the room without having the power of restraining myself."

Nothing was more important to Roget than self-control, but even so, he was eager not to see himself as belonging to a minority. Perhaps in an attempt to "normalize" his negative reaction, which, in part, reflected his own fear of and disconnection from his own bodily sensations, Roget came up with a dubious theory about the effects of nitrous oxide. In January 1800, he provided this assessment in a letter to the philosopher Jeremy Bentham: "I experienced no pleasurable sensations of any kind, but rather those of an opposite description. Nor was I singular in this respect; for some other persons on whom I saw the experiment made, were affected unpleasantly. The pleasure expressed by the rest might have arisen possibly from the novelty of the sensation." But novelty probably had little to do with anything. That's what Thomas Beddoes, who tried the gas more than anyone except Davy, concluded, "In two or three instances only has inhalation failed to be followed by pleasurable feeling; it has never been followed by the contrary." In Roget's case, the failure to experience pleasure revealed much more about the man than about the substance.

Made anxious both by the gas and the avant-garde intellectuals in his midst, Roget lasted just a month in 6 Dowry Square. Roget's sudden disappearance surprised his colleagues. Southey, in fact, wrote Davy in August to say that "I have seen nothing of Dr. Roget and can hear nothing of him." However, Roget would come back to town for another brief stay in September—this time staying in Clifton, with his mother and sister. But by then he no longer had any doubt that the Pneumatic Institute was not where his future lay.

The Institute's days, too, would be numbered. A year after conducting the experiment with Roget, Davy shut down the nitrous oxide trials. A conscientious scientist, Davy was forced to follow the data. Though the gas had some transitory effects upon the healthy volunteers, it did little for the tubercular patients. In his book, Davy concluded that "Pneumatic chemistry in its application to medicine is an art in infancy, weak, almost useless. . . . To be rendered strong and mature, she must be nourished by facts, strengthened by exercise and cautiously directed in the application of her powers by rational skepticism." Not long after Davy left in 1801 to begin his appointment at the Royal Institution, Beddoes closed the Institute. Beddoes died several years later, at the age of forty-eight. Though Beddoes left no direct intellectual descendants, in the mid-nineteenth century, anesthesiologists would discover the value of nitrous oxide for numbing pain during surgical procedures.

In the immediate aftermath of his Bristol sojourn, Roget was deeply discouraged. He felt as if he had wasted his time. For a man so obsessed with work and the pursuit of scientific progress, nothing could have been more frustrating. Shortly after his departure, he complained to his friend Alexander Marcet that Bristol had "afforded no prospect whatever of doing any thing in the way of my profession." Picking up on Roget's distress, Samuel Romilly sought to prevent him from blaming himself for what was essentially Beddoes's failure. That fall, Romilly wrote to Catherine:

Peter has no reason, I think, to regret that Dr. B's Institution has not been successful to him. It could not . . . be profitable, and as to any Reputation to be acquired by it, it could not, I think, have answered. . . . I am only sorry that P. is out of spirits about it, though I am not very much surprised. The first disappointment which a man meets on his onset in life is generally felt more sensibly than it ought to be.

Though Peter would never change his mind about his time in Bristol, he eventually softened his stance on Beddoes himself. More than twenty years later, Roget highlighted Beddoes's accomplishments when writing up his biography for the *Encyclopaedia Britannica*. In hindsight, Roget realized how much he identified with this profoundly erudite scholar. As Roget reported, after teaching himself French in just two months, Beddoes went on to learn German and Italian. Besides his interest in useful knowledge, Beddoes also had shown little patience for idle play. Summing up the arc of Beddoes's career, Roget wrote: "The strength of his intellectual powers was apparent at a very early period of his life: and he was remarkable from his infancy for his insatiable thirst for books, and for his indifference to the common objects of amusement, which usually captivate the attention of children." Roget here could also have been describing himself; as a child, he, too, had much preferred compiling his word lists to interacting with the other kids on Sloane Street. In researching Beddoes's life, Roget was surprised to have found a kindred spirit.

Another reason Peter may have found life in Bristol so unpleasant was that in between his stints there in the spring and fall, he stayed in a place that he soon fell in love with—Ilfracombe, the resort town off the north coast of Devon. Ilfracombe was everything Bristol was not: it was clean and sparsely populated. Known for its mild weather, it also had, as one nineteenth-century visitor put it, "the climate of paradise." Its name deriving from "Alfreincoma" (an Anglo-Saxon term meaning "valley of the sons of Alfred"), Ilfracombe was then a small fishing village with fewer than 500 homes and 2,000 residents. Described by the 1791 *Universal British Directory* as "a pleasant and convenient place for bathing and much resorted to by gentry for that purpose," Ilfracombe would by the early nineteenth century establish itself as a popular summer resort.

Roget's first visit with his mother and sister in June 1799 got off to a rocky start. Surprised to find the town so deserted, Catherine was initially convinced that they were all going to die of hunger. But they stuck it out—they had no choice, as Peter had developed a fever. In a letter to Catherine about this incident, Dumont suggested that Peter's illness may have had some psychological roots, remarking that "Peter has become a doctor for himself, and he studies carefully his temperament and learns how to manage it." By the end of their summer stay, though, they all had developed fond feelings for Ilfracombe.

Over the next seventy-five years, this North Devon town was to become closely entwined with the fates of three generations of Rogets. In 1803, Annette and Catherine would live there for about a year. Nearly twenty years later, they both moved back permanently. Throughout his life, Peter was a frequent visitor. Recording all the years he visited Ilfracombe between 1799 and 1857, Roget came up with a final tally—twenty-six—that exceeded by far the total for any other locale mentioned in the list "Visits To," contained on the first page of his "List of Principal Events." Beginning in the mid-1830s, Roget took his family there for about a month nearly every summer to visit his sister. For his children, Catherine and John, Ilfracombe would become a second home.

In the fall of 1799, as Roget was getting over his frustrating stint at Dr. Beddoes's Pneumatic Institution, his uncle was working to hook him up with another established scientific genius, the inventor and social philosopher Jeremy Bentham. On October 26, Romilly wrote Catherine:

> I have seen Bentham, and he told me what he hinted at once before: that he had a project respecting Peter. What it is I don't know, but I conjecture from some things which he said that it is some discovery in Chemistry which he has made—or thinks he has made—which he considers as very important and which he wishes to communicate to some person in whom he can have entire confidence, and who may, by experiments, ascertain the merit of it. He speaks of it as a thing which may be of great use to P. . . . B. is a man of so original a genius that it is possible the discovery . . . may be very important.

From Dr. B., Roget would eventually move on to Mr. B., though that collaboration would prove equally disappointing.

Romilly had first met Bentham in 1781. They were connected both by their shared interest in legal reform—Bentham was wont to supply Romilly with material for his speeches before Parliament—and their love of cats. "Romilly was," Bentham would write after his tragic death, "something between a brother and a son." By 1799,

Romilly had long been talking up the smarts of his favorite nephew to Bentham, and his word was enough to cause Bentham to place considerable confidence in Roget.

But it would take about a year before Bentham clarified to Roget himself the project that he had in mind. Since 1794, Bentham had been sketching out his ideas for a "frigidarium," an underground ice-house that could preserve foods such as fruit, vegetables, meats, and fish for long periods. The impetus for his proposed invention was the war with France, which had repeatedly caused food shortages throughout Europe. Bentham hypothesized that his device might enable the government to stabilize the price and supply of food by purchasing surpluses during boom times and distributing them to the needy during economic downturns.

With his mind prone to go off in so many different directions at the same time, Bentham thought Roget could help him both stay focused and bring his idea to fruition. Sending Roget, then in the country, all his notes, Bentham wrote on September 4, 1800: "I feel much the want of a confidential friend, whose sympathetic zeal might animate my languour and to whose information and intelligence I might look for a supply of my own deficiencies." Understanding just what Bentham needed—a few years later, Roget would turn to his private lists of synonyms to organize his own thinking—he provided a sympathetic ear and expressed his readiness to help.

The shy Roget was honored that such an esteemed thinker would seek his aid. Then in his early fifties, Bentham was considered a prophet in some circles—though typically not in his native land. "His reputation," as the noted essayist William Hazlitt would put it, "lies at the circumference; and the lights of his understanding are reflected, with increasing luster, on the other side of the globe." On account of Bentham's groundbreaking work in political theory, the

French, for example, had made him an honorary citizen in 1792. Writing back right away, Roget stated, "I feel extremely flattered at your having selected me as not unworthy of your confidence."

Roget was already planning to go back to London in the fall. When Bentham offered him the use of a couple of rooms in his house in Queen Square Place (now 50 Queen Anne's Gate, the site occupied by the British Home Office), he could hardly refuse. Eager to get started on the frigidarium, Roget downplayed his excitement. "It was already my intention to have been in town toward the end of October," he noted. "It will not materially derange my plans to hasten my journey a week or two earlier."

It was Saturday afternoon, October 11, 1800. Roget's long journey from Sidmouth, the Devon town where he had spent the summer with his mother and sister, was almost over. His carriage loaded down with his two valises, one of books and one of clothes, passed Westminster Abbey and then headed north toward St. James's Park. Its destination: the Hermitage, Jeremy Bentham's small but stately home.

As Roget got within a few blocks of what was to be his residence that fall, he was feeling apprehensive. In his recent letters to Roget, Bentham acknowledged that his house was often messy. The philosopher also kept contradicting himself. In his September 4 letter, Bentham had requested that Roget arrive in early October, citing a need to begin the work on the frigidarium before the weather became too cold. But in his last letter, dated October 4, Bentham was no longer so sure about the timing: "I can not look upon myself as warranted to summon you to my disorderly home." The reason for Bentham's change of heart was that his maid still needed to do some cleaning up—"without which," he wrote, "the obligation to attend to the frigidarium would be productive of some embarrassment." But Bentham urged Roget to come soon anyway, adding, "Yet time passes urgently." Roget was worried that he might be arriving too early.

The closer his carriage got to Queen Square Place, the narrower the streets became. For a moment, Roget feared its wheels might not have enough room. But passing through a gateway, he breathed a sigh of relief. At the end of the alley in front of him, he saw the neat courtyard that surrounded Bentham's house. Blanketed by shrubs and flower beds, the Hermitage looked like an oasis.

Roget got out of the carriage and walked over to the main entrance. Unable to find a knock, Roget banged away at the door for a few minutes with his fists. Bentham's secretary then emerged and ushered him in.

Walking down the hallway with his customary stoop, Bentham greeted his visitor. Of medium height and a bit stocky, Bentham had a double chin. The collar of his white shirt was open, and he wore a single-breasted coat. Every few minutes, his left hand would throw his long, stringy white hair back over his head.

Bentham began to give Roget the tour of his house. Each of the main rooms—the parlor, library, and dining room—was outfitted with a piano. Bentham then showed Roget the bedroom where he would be staying, which was located across from the library. Roget grimaced, as he noticed that this room—like all the other rooms in the house—did not have a lock on the door. Observing Roget's pained expression, Bentham asked him if anything was the matter. Keeping his thoughts to himself, Roget smiled wanly. But on the inside, he was unnerved.

"How can I live," Roget thought to himself, "anywhere where there is no privacy?" In a letter to his mother, Roget later complained that the only locks "in this house are those on my suit-case and a small drawer. All my papers are exposed."

Bentham was eager to show Roget the garden. As the two men stepped outside, they were suddenly in the dark, as huge cotton trees blocked the sun's rays. Hidden behind two of the trees was a neighbor's house, covered with mold. Pointing to the back of that house, Bentham said, "That's where John Milton once lived." As they went back inside, Bentham fished out a carved baluster that had come from the staircase of the poet's house. Handing it to Roget, Bentham asked, "What does it feel like to touch this relic—which the hand of the great bard of *Paradise Lost* himself once grasped?"

Like Roget, Bentham had spent a lonely childhood immersed in books. As a boy, Bentham had been on an even faster track than Roget, beginning Latin at the age of three and his studies at Oxford at twelve. Though Bentham's works spanned history, ethics, religion, and politics, he focused primarily on codification—the systematic arrangement of laws—which consumed him in the same way that classification consumed Roget. As Bentham once wrote, "Chess I could not play at without a [partner]. . . . Codification was a little game I could play at alone." Like Roget, Bentham also dedicated himself to the careful use of language, once noting, "Upon [logic] depends the choice of words: of those words by which, according to the interpretation put upon them, man is destroyed or saved."

With their shared academic passions, Roget and Bentham seemed destined to hit it off, and their work together started off promisingly. A few days after their first meeting, on a page of a letter marked "Roget's arrival," Bentham wrote to his brother, Samuel, a naval architect (known as "the General"): "Dr. Roget has been here since Saturday. . . . He is ready at calculations, mathematical included, which makes him already of use with regard to the Frigidarium."

But the honeymoon would be short-lived.

Within a month, Roget was already sick of his host. He was even less kindly disposed to the General and his wife, Mary, whom he found domineering. Even more troubling, Roget couldn't avoid this couple. To get to his room, Roget had to pass through the library, where Samuel and Mary would often be sitting. Right after seeing the Benthams, Roget would immediately wash his hands, muttering to himself, "I don't even know them."

Roget was also angry because the learned philosopher soon got caught up in other research and ignored both him and their joint endeavor. The two men hardly spoke. And, as Roget soon figured out, Bentham didn't even know enough about the underlying science of refrigeration to be of any use. On November 7 he wrote his mother that "the success of the experiment . . . is already doubtful. I assume that I will have all the responsibility. Mr. Bentham will contribute very little. . . . I am resolved to lose no time in it." Roget was also disgusted because Bentham's scientific equipment was filthy: "There are many instruments of iron and wood in the out-house in the garden, but all of it is in such great disorder and covered with such a pile of dust that I will only be able to use it very little. I have already lost a lot of time making the most simple preparations for my experiments." Mr. B., like Dr. B. before him, Roget was forced to conclude, wasn't all that he was cracked up to be.

Frustrated by the setup in Bentham's house, Roget started to focus on other activities in London. Borrowing the General's pass, he attended scientific lectures at the Royal Institution, which had just opened that spring. Two evenings a week, he took a course on anatomy from one of London's master surgeons, John Abernethy, of St. Bartholomew's Hospital, who attracted considerable acclaim for the clarity of his lectures. Abernethy, the surgeon Thomas Pettigrew later recalled, "so nicely disentangled the perplexities of many abstruse subjects: he made that so easy which was so difficult before." Though Abernethy's flamboyant style startled Roget—the surgeon was known to talk while sitting in a chair and swinging one leg over

the side—he also made a lasting impression on the soon-to-be lecturer. In January, Roget would take a follow-up course with Abernethy that met for an hour and a half every afternoon.

While staying with Bentham, Roget ate elsewhere—typically at
the Pratt Place home in Camden Town where Thomas Romilly, the
older brother of Samuel and Catherine, lived with his wife, Jane, a
first cousin, and their nine children. But to visit his uncle Thomas,
Roget had to walk more than three miles. "I hope I never again," Roget complained to his mother, "have to walk as much. . . . I lose half
a day on the road."

By the end of November, Roget had had enough of Bentham, his
scientific project, and his disordered home. He moved to 3 Great
Titchfield Street—just a half-hour walk from his uncle Thomas and a
five-minute walk from his uncle Samuel, then recently married and
living at 27 Gower Street.

On the surface, Bentham and Roget remained friendly. When Roget moved back to London for good in 1808, Bentham was one of
the first people he met for dinner. But deep down, Roget couldn't let
go of his anger and frustration about their failed collaboration.

Bentham would continue to conduct research, every now and
again, on the frigidarium until 1809, at which time he would officially abandon the project. Ten years later, Roget issued his final
assessment on Bentham's idea in a letter to a friend, the lawyer
Thomas Smith. "The term, Frigidarium . . . refers to a project he had
of a large conservatory of ice for preserving provisions through the
year and thus equalizing their price. It evaporated in smoke." Un-
derneath Roget's witty four-word epitaph for the frigidarium lay
deep bitterness. For Peter Mark Roget, "smoke" was a highly loaded
term that had scatological connotations. In the 1852 *Thesaurus*, he
stuck it in the same paragraph with "dirt, filth, soil, slop, dust, cob-
web, soot, smudge, smut, raff, and sordes," words that all fell under

one of the longest entries in the entire book, "Uncleanness," 653. The disorder that characterized both Jeremy Bentham's mind and his home had not sat well with Roget.

The date was December 31, 1800; the setting was Pratt Place in Camden Town, a couple of blocks east of Marylebone Park (now Regent's Park) in northwest London. In the annals of British history, the next morning, on which the nineteenth century would officially begin, would become known as the one in which Ireland finally became a full-fledged member of the United Kingdom by virtue of the Act of Union. But in the annals of the Roget family, January 1, 1801, would be remembered as the day Peter set the family record for the number of consecutive hours spent on the dance floor.

On the last day of the eighteenth century, Roget attended what he later called "a famous ball" at a palatial estate on Pratt Place. The invitation was for five in the afternoon, which, Roget later observed, was "a ridiculously early hour for a dance that was supposed to while away the century!" He had worked out a plan with his three teenage cousins, Caroline, Sam, and Margaret, and their parents, Thomas and Jane, to meet there at six.

On New Year's Eve, Roget left his apartment at Great Titchfield Street at five o'clock on the dot. Having made the walk to Pratt Place many times before, he knew that it didn't take an hour, but on this night, Roget wouldn't be going straight there. Though it was already dark and a light snow was blowing in a fierce wind, Roget wanted to stay outside in order to gather his thoughts. He was feeling nervous. The prospect of dancing rattled him. He had long wanted to dance but didn't know how. While in Edinburgh, he carefully avoided any parties that involved dancing, even those hosted by Dugald Stewart and his wife at their home on Canongate Street.

Walking briskly a few blocks north, Roget came upon Arlington Street, located at the eastern end of the park, which King George III was then leasing to tenant farmers. Glancing over at the snowy grass on his left, Roget paced up and down Arlington Street. He began counting his steps, first from Southampton Street, at the south end of Arlington, to Nelson Street, the first cross street, and then from Southampton Street all the way up to Warren—four blocks north. Eventually, Roget turned right on Warren Street and made his way over to Pratt Place.

Once he got to the party, Roget greeted all the Romillys. He then spotted a friend by the name of Robert Mudie, who had also taken classics courses with Professors Hill and Dalzel at Edinburgh. Roget and Mudie—later an editor at the *Sunday Times* and a celebrated author—instantly began reminiscing about old times.

At seven, the dancing began. This was the age of English country dancing in which several couples would dance together. The waltz and the quadrille wouldn't make their way over to England for another decade.

Roget felt relieved when his cousin Caroline, just a couple of years younger, looked over at him, whispered to him that he should relax and she would tell him what he needed to do. They then lined up next to three other couples and began to dance.

Roget smiled. Once he began dancing, he could hardly stop.

Roget remained on the dance floor until eleven, when he took a half-hour break to drink a bowl of soup. But then he was back at it. He danced away the rest of the century and continued until four-thirty in the morning.

A few weeks later, Roget recapped that night proudly to his mother, then living in the country. "Here is a feat which by far surpasses what Annette did at her ball! I danced all the dances except for one: admire, if you please, how I was able to dance for nine hours and could keep standing afterwards."

That night in Pratt Place, Roget had discovered a new side to himself. It was his coming-out party. Just shy of twenty-two, he had officially launched his career as one of London's most eligible bachelors, a career that would last almost a quarter of a century.

Peter spent the winter and spring of 1801 in a small apartment at 46 Great Russell Street in Bloomsbury, near the British Museum and a short walk from his uncle Samuel's home on Gower Street. Roget had frequent dinners with his two uncles as well as with his mentor, David Chauvet, who was once again living in Kensington. He would stay in touch with his mother by mail, informing her of his studies and health in lengthy biweekly missives, which typically ran a thousand words or more. At Catherine's request they would correspond in French. Though his mother kept badgering him to leave London and return to live in the countryside with her, he refused, claiming that he needed to be in the city "to make my career." This explanation was only half true. Roget also wanted to be in London to remain free of his mother's influence.

But Peter soon became miserable. He was often lonely, and chronically short of money. In the middle of January, he was worried about whether he could survive the winter on the twenty pounds he had recently received from his uncle. He wrote his mother, "My wardrobe is a bit worn . . . my ties have holes in a lot of places; they will need to be replaced, I fear, pretty soon." Despite his own distress, Peter still felt the need to parent her, stressing his eagerness to see her "well placed, at ease and enjoying society."

What appeared to bother Roget most was that he had too much

time on his hands. Without pressing commitments to help him organize his daily existence, he grew despondent. In a letter to his mother,
in February, he complained that "sadly enough everywhere that I find
myself, I find nothing but boredom and disgust. I have passed few
agreeable moments here. I detest London as cordially as you do. Not
having had a fixed plan, not having seen anything stable or certain for
the future, I have not been able to enjoy anything." Roget never could
conceive of pleasure without structure, which typically consisted of
mountains of work. In contrast to those nineteenth-century intellectuals such as Oscar Wilde who sought to create "art for art's sake," Roget
sought to engage in "work for work's sake." Work did not so much provide joy and satisfaction in its own right as stave off negative states,
such as boredom and despair.

Roget immediately regretted being so frank with his mother
about his feelings. This momentary lapse, in which he had forgotten
just how little Catherine could tolerate hearing about anyone else's
distress, set off a chain of recriminations. Though his mother's response does not survive, Roget's self-effacing next letter suggests
that Catherine became very distraught. He apologized profusely for
letting "my imagination have empire over me," reassuring his mother
that his unhappiness would soon abate. In signing off, he implored
her to write back at once to confirm that she had gotten over her
sadness.

Samuel Romilly, like his sister, Catherine, also shamed Roget for
his normal feelings of sadness. A few months later, his uncle exhorted
him to "be a little more cheerful," observing, "I know by experience
that melancholy may be very much increased by being indulged." According to Romilly, the only way to stave off depression, which he
once called "the great defect of our family," was to numb out painful
emotions.

The harsh rebukes Roget received from his family for his bout with depression in his early twenties had profound effects. From then on, he would rarely open up to either his mother or his uncle— or to anyone at all, for that matter—about his moments of anguish. He had learned to become a true Romilly. He, too, would begin to criticize others who failed to keep a stiff upper lip.

4.

Napoleon's
Captive

(754) PRISONER, captive, détenu, in custody, in charge.

By early 1802, shortly after his twenty-third birthday, Roget was feeling more energized. The debilitating depression that had plagued him the previous year had lifted. What boosted Roget's spirits was the resumption of gainful activity. As long as his daily life had a purpose, he could keep feelings of anxiety at bay.

Roget's upbeat mood could be traced back to the actions of one man: the First Consul of France, Napoleon Bonaparte. Between the fall of 1801 and the fall of 1803, Napoleon—to whom Roget would never be personally introduced, but of whom he was to catch a few glimpses in Paris—was to have more influence on the course of his life, both for good and for ill, than anyone else.

Napoleon's political calculations proved instrumental in helping Roget land his first real job. On October 1, 1801, the French leader agreed to a preliminary peace treaty with England, halting the war that had hindered travel between the two countries for a decade. Shortly after the announcement of what became known as the Peace of Amiens, Roget's uncle, Samuel Romilly, planted an idea in the mind of John Philips, then the owner of the largest cotton plant in

Manchester: to hire Roget to lead his two teenage sons, Burton and Nathaniel, on a Grand Tour of Europe.

Prior to the commencement of the war with France, the Grand Tour was a well-established rite de passage for the sons of England's upper crust. This tradition dated back to the late seventeenth century, when the priest Richard Lassels wrote of his trips to Italy for the purpose of educating "young lords" about art and architecture, as well as the political realities of the world. The Continental sojourn, which could last anywhere from one to five years, often took the place of a college education. Many distinguished scholars would do a stint as a bear-leader (or traveling tutor) early in their career. Besides broad learning, the other key qualification for the position was a knowledge of French—two requisites Roget had no trouble demonstrating.

On December 1, 1801, John Philips wrote Roget, inviting him to his home in Manchester. Having gotten some background information about Roget from both Arthur Aikin, the young scientist with whom Roget had studied in Edinburgh, and from Richard Sharp, a business partner of his brother, George, Philips was eager to seal the deal:

> I received a letter from my friend Sharp yesterday informing me of the interview which had taken place between himself and you on the subject of sending my two sons into France. . . . From the very handsome terms in which both Mr. Aikin and Mr. Sharp have spoken of you to me, I consider myself singularly fortunate in the prospect of placing my sons under your care.

As John Philips clearly understood, Roget was also an attractive candidate because he would be able to avail himself of Romilly's many connections among Europe's intellectual and political elite, including Talleyrand, Napoleon's foreign minister.

But John Philips's wife, Margaret, was reluctant to send the boys away, and she needed to meet the prospective tutor. A master at reducing the anxiety of nervous mothers, Roget easily won her over. He also convinced her husband to allow them to travel not only to Paris, but also to Geneva. Roget's charge was to help the boys learn French while tutoring them in science and math, for which he was to receive the considerable sum of 400 pounds a year (about $40,000 today) plus expenses. Roget was particularly excited about what would be his first trip back to his ancestral homeland of Switzerland since the death of his father.

Roget found himself among a swarm of thousands of English visitors who traveled to Paris soon after Napoleon reopened its gates. Britain's professional elite—its doctors, lawyers, and military men—were all curious to see what Napoleon had wrought with his country. And with the round-trip fare costing just ten guineas, middle-class tradesmen were for the first time crossing the Channel as well.

Meeting the Philips boys in London—Burton was then sixteen and Nathaniel fifteen—Roget took them to Dover, where they set sail for Calais on February 18, 1802. The trip in the sailing packet—a ship that ran a regular route between two ports—took about fifteen hours. From Calais, Roget and the boys traveled by post chaise at the rate of about sixty miles a day. Of this leg of the trip, Nathaniel Philips wrote:

> The mode of traveling is curious. The horses go three abreast when there are three persons in a chaise. The positilion has something

very ridiculous about him. He wears immense jack-boots, one of which you could hardly lift up with your hand, and carries a long-lashed whip with which he announces his entrance to a town, so that horses may be prepared without delay. Every five or ten miles (English), which are here called "posts," the horses are changed.

After passing through Montreuil, Amiens, and Chantilly, on February 23, they finally reached Paris, where they checked in at the sumptuous Hotel de l'Europe on the Rue de la Loi.

Roget's first impressions of Paris were mostly negative. He felt that the French capital was not of sufficient grandeur even to warrant comparisons to London. Paris covered much less space—a deficiency, which, he noted in his journal, the French made a feeble attempt to compensate for by erecting tall buildings, some with as many as seven stories. Throughout the nineteenth century, many foreign observers would echo this sentiment. For example, some fifty years later, the composer Richard Wagner, while working as a guest conductor in London, observed that in contrast to this "large city, Paris is simply a village."

Roget's chief complaint was that Paris was too full of chaos. For a man obsessed with order, the city's disorganized and dirty streets were an abomination. In his journal he commented:

The total want of foot pavement renders it really dangerous to walk in the streets, till you are trained to feats of agility. You are required every instant to hop from stone to stone and to dart from one side of the street to the other. . . . The pavement consists of large round stones, very far from being level and very irregular. They are either covered with mud, or, which is generally the case, greasy and very slippery.

Roget was also shocked to find filth, which young Burton Philips referred to as "the particular foible of France," nearly everywhere, even inside hallowed buildings. Of the Théâtre Français, he remarked that it "has a gloomy appearance; the walls of the pit are very dirty and black." With his mind so focused on assessing the thoroughness of the clean-up crew, Roget failed to offer any comments on any of the plays or actors he saw in this landmark theater.

The French way of doing things also annoyed Roget to no end. He was irked that shops did not have signs identifying what they sold, but rather painted pictures of the items (say, wine or shoes) on the outside walls. Likewise, the appearance of the French rubbed him the wrong way. Roget could not stomach the French penchant for fashion. In his eyes, self-expression through one's clothing was an affront to civilized society. Of Parisian women he observed that they "walk about in caps, without hats, in jackets. . . . In the markets, they sit under red oilcloth parasols fastened to posts. The men in general wear cocked hats, and are very dirty in their persons."

Yet Roget acknowledged, albeit grudgingly, that Paris had a few advantages over London. He was impressed by the carefully constructed hackney coaches, which were pulled along by well-trained horses. But the narrow streets, he was compelled to add, often prevented smooth travel on these vehicles. He also admired "some handsome buildings," such as the Faydeau and Odéon theaters, and "nothing," he remarked, "can exceed the magnificence of the Tuileries and the Louvre."

In the first couple of weeks, Roget and the boys made the rounds among his family's many high-placed friends, all of whom were exceedingly kind. They saw Dumont and his pupil, Henry Petty, later known as the third Marquis of Lansdowne. Through Romilly, they also received an invitation to the house of Etienne Delessert, a wealthy banker. There they met Delessert's daughter, Madame Gautier, to whom a generation earlier the French philosopher Jean-Jacques Rousseau had dedicated his *Letters on Botany*.

Roget took on the task of steeping the boys in French culture. To teach the boys French pronunciation and grammar, he hired a tutor by the name of Bousset, an Englishman who had lived in Paris for some forty years, to come to their rooms every other day. Despite his impressive academic résumé, Roget lacked the whimsy required to serve as an able guide to Paris—though he managed to whisk the boys off to many of the major sites, he couldn't help them bask in the city's magic. The best way to appreciate the "City of Light" is by making use of all five senses, not by making lists of its contents. But patterning themselves after their instructor, Burton and Nathaniel did precisely that. In their letters home, the boys wrote largely of trivial facts and figures. Of the Louvre, Nathaniel observed, "The large room contains 209 statues and busts. . . . Above this is a gallery of pictures, and at present there are 980 of them." Like the eight-year-old Peter scribbling away into his notebook, Burton and Nathaniel were taking an inventory of Paris rather than experiencing it. No matter what the venue or the occasion, the boys always seemed to be most concerned about getting the count right. Referring to a ball, Burton wrote, "The company numbered 150. Only about 16 danced." And upon visiting the Cathedral of Notre Dame, Burton noted that the tower had 360 steps and the organ had 3,800 pipes.

Rather than finding their obsessive behavior odd, Roget was of course delighted. From his vantage point, the boys were being intellectually rigorous. To their father, he wrote, "I must say that they deserve praise for their attention and assiduity, and their behaviour towards me calls for my loudest commendation. I believe they are as attached to me as I to them, for more they cannot be." Roget was thrilled to have two young charges who mirrored his peculiar take on the world.

After a couple of months in Paris, Roget started to feel more comfortable. Rather than dampening his spirits, the move from the plush and centrally located Hôtel de l'Europe, which was necessary because of its lack of dining facilities, to Madame Polier's boarding-house on the Rue Cadet cheered him up. Roget much preferred the new lodgings up in the hills of Montmartre, where, he observed, "the air was better." He was pleased with the clean rooms, which looked out over a garden. Much to his satisfaction, this living arrangement also put the boys in closer contact with others with whom they could practice their French.

Roget was also exhilarated because he could now begin teaching the boys about the proper arrangement of the plant and animal universe. In mid-April, he wrote to John Philips:

> Now that we are settled we are able to apply to business without interruption. We go daily to the Botanical Gardens, of which the Museum of Natural History forms part. Here is the most superior collection in Europe. It is a most complete inventory of Nature, and arranged in a way that greatly facilitates the study of that branch of science.

Beyond providing an ideal classroom in which to instruct the Philips boys, the museum also would inspire Roget's later work. His *Bridge-water Treatise*, which mapped out all the flora and fauna, was, like the museum, "a most complete inventory of nature." And just as the contents of the Museum of Natural History were "arranged in a way that greatly facilities the study of that branch of science," so, too, were the entries of his *Thesaurus* "classified and arranged so as to facilitate the expression of ideas." Ultimately, Roget would do for words what naturalists such as Linnaeus and Georges Cuvier—then in charge of the Paris museum—did for plants and animals. Roget acknowledged as much in a footnote lodged at the end of his introduction to the *Thesaurus*: "The process of verbal classification is similar in principle to that which is employed in the various departments of Natural History."

Roget was well aware that the French—even more than the Germans or English—had been major contributors to the field of natural history. He assigned the boys readings from the massive *Histoire naturelle* by Georges-Louis Leclerc so that they could compare the actual object with the description by this towering scholar. At the time, Leclerc, better known as the Comte de Buffon, was regarded as a philosopher of the same stature as Rousseau and Voltaire.

Roget was so taken by Buffon that he insisted that Burton and Nathaniel buy all sixty-five volumes of his encyclopedic work, which began with the following warning to readers: "Natural History . . . is an immense history because it encompasses all the objects that the Universe presents us with." Inspired by Linnaeus, Buffon was interested not only in classifying the natural world but also in describing it as accurately as possible. Buffon's magnum opus was not a book of lists, but a series of finely wrought essays:

> Of the great number of authors who have written on Natural History, only a few have written good descriptions. To represent simply and clearly the things—without changing them, nor diminishing

them nor adding anything of one's imagination is a skill. . . . In description, one must enter the form, the size, the weight, the colors, the situations of rest and of movements.

To become a scholar of his beloved Natural History, Roget would have to work especially hard to overcome the deficiency that had manifested itself in his Scottish travelogue: his own inability to write clear, descriptive prose. As they made their way through Buffon's massive text, Roget asked the boys to keep a notebook where they could jot down their own observations. Carefully following Buffon's precepts, Roget also worked on honing his own powers of description.

Despite the dry academic path laid out by Dr. Roget, both Nathaniel and Burton rarely expressed any dissatisfaction. On the contrary, they seemed thrilled by his pedagogical assignments. In a letter to his parents, Nathaniel suggested that the hefty price they paid for their edition of Buffon—eight pounds (or about $800 today)—was a bargain. "We are engaged chiefly," Burton wrote home, "with French and the study of natural history. Now that there are all these collections in Paris, natural history is very interesting."

Though the boys' curriculum in Paris was top-heavy with plant and animal physiology, Roget also took them to see plays by France's great playwrights, such artists as Moliere, Racine, and Voltaire. To make sure that they could follow along, Roget insisted that they both read the play beforehand and take a copy of the book to the show. This measure insured that the boys focused exclusively on the text—almost to the exclusion of the action on stage. Roget tended to view these classic plays not so much as human dramas replete with emotional significance but as concatenations of words.

. . .

The date was April 18, 1802. On this Easter Sunday, religion was coming back to France after a decade-long hiatus. To mark the occasion, Napoleon was staging a celebration at the Cathedral of Notre Dame, in the heart of Paris. Sunday, Napoleon decreed, was once again a holy day. Nearly a year earlier, under a concordat reached with Pope Pius VII, Napoleon had recognized Roman Catholicism as the religion of the vast majority of French citizens. The First Consul of France did not, however, make it the official state religion. Roget interpreted this gesture as a sign that Napoleon was eager to atone for the sins of the French kings who had persecuted his Huguenot ancestors. But this was not the case. Napoleon's openness to other religions—including Judaism—was simply a way to humiliate the Church of Rome, by forcing it to yield its supremacy. The pope was now Napoleon's vassal. As Napoleon is reported to have declared, "If there had not been a pope, I would have made one for the occasion."

This carefully choreographed Easter Sunday would proceed exactly as Napoleon had planned it. The festivities began at the crack of dawn, when sixty shots from a cannon heralded the announcement of the new laws concerning public worship. At eight that morning, French police distributed pamphlets containing this information throughout the streets of Paris. At ten o'clock, Napoleon took up his position next to the Battalion of Egalité in the Jardin des Tuileries. First, the Corps Législatif marched to Notre Dame, followed by the pope's French prelates. An hour later, the First Consul himself began his walk, saluted by some sixty guns.

Roget and his charges had hoped to be present at the church service, but couldn't procure tickets, as the ceremony was limited almost exclusively to French soldiers. Two days earlier, the tutor Bousset had helped Roget and the boys gain access to a parlor normally reserved for French governors, where they had seen Napoleon ride by them twice in his monthly military parade at the Tuileries. Of his excitement, Burton wrote, "It is the only way to see him well, and the Review is a most entertaining spectacle. There were this time 6,000 soldiers." They all felt they couldn't pass up the chance to get another peek at the First Consul.

And so, late on Easter morning, Roget and his pupils eagerly joined the huge throng that watched Napoleon's procession as it wound its way toward the Ile de la Cité. Standing at a window next to the Philips boys and his mentor, David Chauvet—in Paris for a few days en route to Geneva from London—the young doctor cheered along with tens of thousands of other spectators. In response, Napoleon, whom Burton Philips had described in a letter to his father as "thin and of low stature" but with an "animated countenance," waved back to the crowd.

Roget could not help but admire the orderly precision of the 10,000 soldiers marching in unison behind Napoleon's carriage, which was drawn by eight highly ornamented horses. Following immediately after, came six Arabian horses, led by Mamelukes—an elite group of Egyptian soldiers.

When Napoleon reached his destination, the cathedral's great bell was sounded. Napoleon was seated at a throne near the altar while an orchestra of some four hundred musicians—not including those needed to handle the six rows of keys of Notre Dame's massive pipe organ—performed the *Te Deum* by the composer Giovanni Paisiello, recently recruited from Naples.

Leading the ceremony was Jean de Dieu-Raymond de Cucé de Boisgelin, the archbishop of Aix, who had presided over the coronation of the last French monarch, King Louis XVI, in Rheims. Then seventy and in failing health, Boisgelin spoke in hushed tones. Few could hear his sycophantic speech in praise of the First Consul.

That evening, as Paris was fully illuminated, Napoleon expressed his delight with the day's events. As he proudly remarked to his generals, "Well, then, wasn't everything like old times?" Reluctant to contradict France's leader, General Jean-Baptiste Bernadotte, who would later stand up against him, glumly responded, "Yes, except for the two million men who died for liberty and are no longer here."

Though Roget fell hard for Napoleon's pageantry and public relations gimmicks, more astute political observers already had an inkling of what his real intentions were. Madame de Staël, the famous novelist whom Roget would meet a few months later in Lausanne, called the *Te Deum* event an "odious spectacle," and noted in her journal that Napoleon "meant the Concordat to serve him as the pretext for presenting the people with the dress rehearsal for his coronation." Sure enough, that August, Napoleon declared himself First Consul for life. Two years later, he would crown himself emperor in a similar ceremony at Notre Dame.

Romilly, whom Roget saw a few times in Paris that month, also was not seduced by Napoleon's apparent charms. Offered a chance to be presented to the future emperor, he refused:

> What strikes a foreigner as most extraordinary is that the despotism which prevails, and the vexations and trifling regulations of the police are all carried on in the name of liberty and equality. . . . His character is of a kind which inspires fear much more than it conciliates affection. . . . That he meditates gaining fresh laurels in war can hardly be doubted.

But Roget, who was often naïve about the motivations of others, could be a poor judge of character. As Romilly predicted, France would soon be back at war with England, and Roget—then still on the Continent—would be caught in the crossfire.

. . .

O n May 22, 1802, in the company of his trusted friend Lovell
Edgeworth, who had shared with him adventures both in Edinburgh and Bristol, Roget and the Philips boys traveled the 350
miles from Paris through the French countryside to Geneva. Roget
and the teenagers traveled in a special post chaise that they purchased in France for fifty pounds. Larger than a typical British
one—for example, the one used by Edgeworth and his squire—it
contained a box in front that afforded them a place to put their huge
trunk filled with hundreds of books.

Choosing to avoid the irregular pavement of the city's boulevards,
the travelers first drove southeast, to Charenton, where they crossed
the Seine. Once he was outside the city, Roget instantly felt energized. He recorded in his journal:

> To emerge at once from the busy scenes of a large and gay metrop-
> olis, to enter from these of a sudden upon extensive plains, deserted
> and forlorn, appears to be the effect of magic. . . . Undisturbed by
> the rumbling of wheels, you glide along lengthened avenues of
> trees, perfectly straight and uniform, and where the sight of an in-
> habitant or even the traces of a human footstep are rarely met
> with. . . . The sounds that formerly annoyed us are banished far
> away. Once more we inhale the country breeze; the eye again re-
> poses on verdure, and the mind is left at liberty to pursue unmo-
> lested the train of her reflections.

After a day, the two carriages had made the forty-five-mile journey
to the forest town of Fontainebleau, the so-called capital of French

history, which had once been home to dozens of French kings. Roget was impressed by the town's landscape, but showed surprisingly little interest in its famous castle. He was horrified that mob violence had ransacked the famous gallery of Francis I with its numerous frescoes where the Italian Renaissance had been introduced to France. "The château of Fontainebleau," he complained, "presents but a shabby outside, and the inside offers but little that is worth seeing." But he did carefully examine the queen's boudoir, the only room untouched by the revolutionaries. Its large mirrors, he found, produced intriguing optical illusions.

Even the paintings by Leonardo da Vinci failed to pique Roget's curiosity because, he noted, they were "faded." The only kind of history he really cared about was natural history—the makeup and organization of plants and animals. By contrast, human history and the lives of those who came before him mattered much less.

From Fontainebleau, Roget and the boys, rising at three a.m. every morning to beat the oppressive heat, headed for Lyons, stopping in Cosne along the way. From there, they traveled through La Charité in the Loire Valley. This stretch of the trip, Roget remarked, offered "a great variety of gay and pleasing landscapes," but they were disappointed with Moulins, a large town where they spent the night. Once again, the boys' observations reflected the sensibility of their tutor. Burton wrote:

The inns are shocking; the beds dirty—two or three in a room; where you have to dine. The apartments are badly fitted, the walls whitewashed, and the tapestry so old and ragged as to be a fit nest for spiders and moths. For a table there is only a board laid on cross-bars. The oak chairs have rush bottoms. Their perpendicular backs defy all attempts at rest. Doors give music as well as

entrance. . . . Mops, brushes and brooms are not in the catalogue
of the belongings of a French inn.

Though Roget and his pupils couldn't stand their accommodations,
they were delighted by the frogs, ducks, grasshoppers, and crows
that serenaded them with mellifluous tones during an after-dinner
stroll around the city's ramparts.

To get to Lyons required going through the mountains of the
Massif Central. They all took an immediate liking to this region,
which featured well-cultivated plains and woody meadows. Taking in
a valley near Mont Tarare, Roget wrote, "A scene like this would at
all times have highly gratified us, but after three months' confine-
ment in the atmosphere of Paris it was capable of inspiring us with
transport." The farther Roget got from Paris, the more he realized
how imprisoned he had felt there.

Roget was shocked by what he saw in Lyons. As a result of the
fierce fighting during the French Revolution and Counter-Revolution,
the city lay in ruins. However, the destructiveness of war was not what
most disturbed him. Understanding industriousness to be the hall-
mark of virtue, Roget felt a sense of moral outrage that the citizens of
Lyons had made hardly any efforts to rebuild the city. "With a population estimated at 150,000," he observed, "none has the courage to
step forward. The spirit of enterprise seems totally extinguished, and
all is at a stand."

To be fair, a belief in progress was an article of faith among most
nineteenth-century British intellectuals, but Roget's impatience with
feelings of hopelessness was extreme even by the standards of the
day. Having been chastised by his mother and uncle for wallowing in
his own melancholy, Roget could sometimes show little empathy for
those in need—even helpless victims of wartime atrocities.

Once Roget and the Philips boys reached Geneva on June 5, they were taken under the wing of his former instructor, David Chauvet, who had returned to his native city following his retirement. For the next few days they stayed with Chauvet at his country home in Pacquis, just outside town. His house was too small for an extended visit, so Chauvet arranged for them to stay somewhere nearby for the rest of the summer.

Having been annexed by France in 1798, Geneva, then an independent republic and not part of Switzerland, was a city under siege. Surrounded by some 3,000 French soldiers, its gates were shut at ten p.m., and anyone found out past that hour without a lantern could be sent to jail. On account of the occupation by Napoleon, the Genevans detested the French. Chauvet's 1798 pamphlet "The Conduct of the Government of France Toward the Republic of Geneva," which he posted to a U.S. congressman in an attempt to rally support for his beleaguered countrymen, captured these feelings of betrayal and humiliation:

> After the taking of the city, the Genevans consented to a kind of capitulation or agreement, in order to save, if possible, a few planks from the wreck. . . . This city, once so happy and so prosperous, will soon lose her character, her manners, her religion, her commerce, her literary establishments; she will soon be only a garrison-place, where we shall look for Geneva, but where, alas! we shall no more find her.

By the time Roget arrived in 1802, the fear that the city might lose its identity was even more pronounced.

Looking also to England as a potential savior, Genevans tended to give a warm reception to British citizens; Roget and the Philips boys were no exception. "We were surrounded by friends," Roget observed, "warmly attached to our interests and devoted to our cause, to whom we could open our minds without reserve, and from whom we could never expect to perceive any symptoms of our being in an enemy's country." Roget was delighted to be back in the city of his forebears. Though his grandparents were long dead, many relatives still lived there—including his uncle, his late father's older brother, Jean Samuel Roget, who was an engraver.

In fact, despite all the political tension, Roget felt as if he were in paradise. The climate suited him perfectly. In June 1802, he wrote to John Philips, "I find myself better than I was in Paris . . . the air being so much drier." In addition, he loved the landscape: "Geneva has surpassed my expectations. The beauty of the situation, the appearance of comfort that surrounds us, and the excellent society give us every prospect of passing our happiest days in this enchanting spot."

Once in Geneva, Roget began instructing the boys in what he called "more serious studies," such as mathematics. Buffon, too, was still a key item on the agenda. In addition, Roget tried to instill in Burton and Nathaniel a love of Latin by having them translate the Roman historian Sallust, the staunch defender of morality best known for such works as *The Conspiracy of Catiline*, which exposed the degeneracy of the Roman aristocracy. Summing up Roget's pedagogical approach, Nathaniel wrote to his father, "It has been Dr. Roget's aim to conduct our studies so that we can derive pleasure from them." But Nathaniel didn't fully understand that Roget held an idiosyncratic definition of pleasure. For Roget, pleasure had little to do with enjoyment, but everything to do with the intellectual challenge of learning about order.

During the summer, the trio made numerous hikes in the Alps.

Their tour guide was the famous climber Jacques Balmat, who had been the first to scale Mont Blanc, in 1786. Burton couldn't help but use these forays as a chance to get his hands on some comforting facts and figures. Upon eyeing Mont Blanc from the town of Chamonix that August, he reported to his mother that it was 15,662 feet high, part of a chain of mountains that extended more than a hundred leagues in length. Burton substituted these digits for a physical description of these magnificent sites. As the summer wound down, the Philips boys began attending the chemistry lectures of Marc-Auguste Pictet, an international authority on astronomy and chronometry (the study of the temporal sequencing of information), at the local university.

That fall, Roget and the boys moved into Chauvet's Geneva townhouse in the Rue Beauregard. Roget felt as if he were back with the Chauvets in Kensington—the only home he ever really had. Despite the worrisome political currents that swirled around them—Napoleon's increasingly bellicose rhetoric began to make the peace feel tenuous—the mood at the Chauvets' was upbeat and playful. Madame Chauvet enjoyed cooking for Roget and the boys. One night at dinner she asked Burton, in her heavy French accent, "Well, Pheleps, how do you find the pâté?" After Burton said he liked it and took two more helpings, with a sly smile, she announced its source: frogs. Burton was startled, to everyone's amusement.

But this pleasant domesticity would prove to be only temporary. On February 9, five months after Roget and the boys had first moved in with Chauvet, Roget's mentor suddenly died. Though Chauvet had been ill for a while, no one had understood how serious his condition was. In fact, just a few days before his death, Burton had written his father that Chauvet was "out of danger." In the middle of February, Roget discussed Chauvet's death in a letter to John Philips. After mentioning that three hundred people showed up to the funeral, Ro-

get homed in on the practical ramifications—his need to find new accommodations:

> No man could be more universally regretted by all who knew him.
> The despair in which his niece and widow are plunged may be
> imagined. To us the loss is particularly sensible. Never shall we find
> a house where we can enjoy so many advantages and comforts as
> in this one, which we are now obliged to leave.

Like Chauvet's niece and widow, Roget had grounds for being af-
flicted with deep despair, as he had lost one of his surrogate fathers.
Though at the time Roget never talked too much about his grief, he
never forgot Chauvet. In his "List of Principal Events," written more
than fifty years later, he both highlighted the date of Chauvet's death
as a key event in 1802 and inserted his tutor's name onto that treas-
ured list, "Dates of Deaths."

A week later, Roget solved his housing problem by moving with
the boys to the home of Jacques Peschier, a local pastor, and his wife.

John Philips initially thought that Roget should stay in Geneva with
his sons until the fall of 1803. But as the tension between France
and England started to mount, it became increasingly difficult to stick
to that plan. In early 1803, the two countries began firing harsh words
back and forth. Roget felt uneasy, but he continued to assume they
would be safe. Explaining his thinking at the time, he later wrote, "All
my friends were unanimous in their opinion that no possible inconve-
nience, far less danger, could be incurred by delaying our return to
England, and that even in the event of a war, we should be allowed to

stay or go as we pleased." After spending nearly a year in territory where Napoleon was universally hated as an occupier, Roget, too, was now starting to feel nothing but disgust for the French ruler's domineering ways: "I felt all the while a reluctance to remain in an enemy's country. To accept protection from a foe, to eat of his bread, to be sheltered under his roof, was repugnant to every feeling of delicacy."

By March, the conflict between the two countries had reached the boiling point. The Peace of Amiens was officially ruptured; negotiations broke down once Napoleon rejected England's offer to evacuate Malta if he withdrew French troops from Holland. On May 10, England recalled its ambassador, Lord Whitworth, from Paris. A few weeks later, the British navy captured a handful of French ships. Napoleon responded by ordering the imprisonment of all British nationals aged eighteen through sixty who happened to be traveling in France and any territory occupied by France. Though this edict didn't apply to the Philips boys as they were underage, it turned Roget into a *détenu*.

As soon as John Philips heard about Napoleon's decision to take action against British nationals, he wrote to Roget, urging him to bring the boys back to England. Philips was particularly concerned about keeping his wife's anxiety at a tolerable level. He tried to enlist Roget in the effort to make sure that the boys will "not fail to give every possible consolation to their mother, who only errs by being too fond and amiable a parent." Over the next few months, Roget would eagerly oblige, but right then he had more pressing concerns than the anxiety of Mrs. Philips. In fact, by the time he received this missive, in early June, he had already tried to leave Geneva—only to realize that there was no easy way out.

At eight o'clock on the morning of May 28, Burton rushed into Roget's bedroom, followed by Moré, the fellow who groomed his horses. Moré announced that the English in Lyons had been arrested. Grabbing nothing but a couple of shirts, Roget immediately decided to go with Edgeworth and the boys to Secheron, a small town a mile northeast of Geneva. The plan: to escape from Secheron into Switzerland proper. But on his way out the door, he ran into the commandant of Geneva, General Dupuch, then living on the ground floor of Monsieur Peschier's house, who said, "Did you suppose that you would have been more in safety in Switzerland than here? Quite the reverse; the order, if it had come, would have extended as well to Switzerland as to Geneva." He also assured Roget that if such orders had come, he would have given him advance warning. At the time, Roget felt that he could trust Dupuch. He wrote John Philips, "We are also fortunate in being acquainted with the Commandant de la Place, who is charged with the execution of these orders and will contribute all in his power to make us easy." That morning, still believing that it was in his best interest to stay, Roget changed course and sat down for a leisurely breakfast.

But before Roget had a chance to finish his meal, a neighbor, the philosophy professor Pierre Prevost, rushed in, and reported that he had just come from the prefect's office. Confirming that the order to arrest Englishmen had been issued, Prevost advised Roget to leave Geneva right away. Quickly shaking the hands of the Peschiers, Roget raced to Secheron in an attempt to put his previous plan back into action. But once he got there, he heard that Napoleon had ordered gendarmes to guard all the roads to Switzerland. Lovell Edgeworth refused to ride in his carriage (for fear of being arrested at the border), and Roget began to deliberate about what to do. At that very instant, Madame de Staël's teenage son, Albert, brought Roget a note from Madame Peschier. (Then living in her château in the nearby town of Coppet, Madame de Staël was a close friend of the Peschiers.) It was official: General Dupuch, the commandant of Geneva, had ordered all British nationals eighteen and older to surrender themselves to him within twenty-four hours. Given that the same regulation had also been put forth in Switzerland, Roget decided to stay in Geneva, where he would at least have a personal familiarity with the commandant. Once he got back to town, Roget spoke to the commandant himself, who confirmed that he would have to surrender by noon on the following day.

Roget studied the order and decided that the commandant had made a mistake. According to Roget's interpretation, it applied only to British military men, not all British nationals. Several other key city officials such as the secretary of the prefecture and the commissary of the police, Roget soon learned, shared this view. So, too, did Madame de Staël, who was more in the know than practically anyone else in Geneva, thanks to her close ties to many influential Parisians. Of that spring, she later wrote in her memoir, *Ten Years of Exile*, "I was at Geneva living . . . in the society of the English when the news of the declaration of war reached us. The rumour immediately spread that the English travellers would all be made prisoners, but as nothing had ever been heard of in the law of European nations, I gave no credit to it."

That night, Roget slept soundly, thinking he was still free. The next morning, he had no intention of turning himself in. But just before noon, both Monsieur and Madame Peschier told him that there was no time to waste, that the commandant had, in fact, received orders to detain all Englishmen over age eighteen, regardless of their status. Shortly thereafter, Roget bumped into the commandant, who confirmed the account of the Peschiers but said that he still had another twenty-four hours of freedom.

In the evening, Roget took a walk in the hills beyond Secheron and was struck by their beauty. Nature, like words, he acknowledged, could often provide him with some comfort:

I enjoyed for the last time the magnificent spectacle of the glaciers, which then appeared in all of their grandeur, and of the contrasting sweetness of the opposite shores of the lake, which that evening assumed a most peaceful stillness. The air was uncommonly clear and the setting sun tipped all the snowy summits of the Alps with fire, till at length Mont Blanc, standing aloof from the rest, was alone refulgent with its beams, and received alone the parting rays. The sun, which was again to enlighten them would find me in captivity.

Roget anthropomorphized these objects of nature; while the shores of Lake Geneva were "sweet," Mont Blanc "stood aloof." For a brief moment, Roget felt safe; in the spectacular Swiss landscape, he had found friendly companions. But as he well understood, on the following morning, he would be in imminent danger of being thrown into prison, if not killed.

Two days later, Roget gave his word to the commandant that he would not leave French territory. He also made various pleas to officials in Paris—including one to the French minister of war, Talleyrand, whom his uncle, Samuel Romilly, had gotten to know during the Reign of Terror—that an exception should be made in his case since he was not a soldier. But these entreaties came to naught. For the next two months, Roget's fate remained in the hands of the French government.

Roget came up with an emergency plan. As a last resort, he could declare himself a citizen of Geneva because of his father's roots there. With this stratagem, though, he ran the risk of being drafted into the French army.

. . .

On Saturday, July 16, 1803, Roget learned that the French weren't kidding. After several weeks of issuing threats, they had finally stepped up their aggression toward all foreign nationals.

The day began without incident. As Roget ambled through the Peschiers' living room early that afternoon, he saw a familiar face: it was the author Madame de Staël. Though she was not beautiful, Madame de Staël was a captivating personage. A little chubby, she was full-breasted and had an olive complexion, thick black hair, and large, dark eyes.

Then in her mid-thirties, she had been born Anne-Louise-Germaine Necker in Paris. Her estranged husband, the Swedish diplomat Erik Magnus de Staël-Holstein, had died the previous year. De Staël had recently been ordered out of Paris by Napoleon, who objected to the ideas about liberty expressed in her widely read novel *Delphine*, published the previous year. But in contrast to Roget, she was then safely ensconced on the estate of her ailing father, Jacques Necker—once the finance minister to King Louis XVI—on the banks of Lake Geneva.

Before Roget could get comfortable on the Peschiers' sofa, Madame de Staël turned to him and said, in English, "I have very bad news for you. You are going all to be sent to Verdun. I have it from an unquestionable source. No reclamations will be attended to. You will set out in about a week." As Roget well knew, on matters concerning Napoleon, de Staël was definitely to be trusted, as she maintained close contacts with the prefect's office in Geneva. De Staël also informed Roget of the apprehension in Baden of two British intellectuals whom she had befriended—John Campbell, then a young law student, and Dr. Robert Robertson. Campbell, she stated, had managed to escape across the border wearing women's clothes, while Robertson was still in custody.

Roget, as he later would confess, was "thunderstruck."

Madame de Staël then apologized to Madame Peschier for switching into English (a language that Roget's landlady did not understand), but said she could not resist the opportunity to practice this foreign tongue. De Staël then proceeded to go downstairs, and Roget followed her to ask if he could share the information with Lovell Edgeworth. Grudgingly, she consented.

Roget felt he had no choice but to take decisive action. In the burning July sun, he marched off to Secheron—a mile outside Geneva—to see Edgeworth. To Roget's surprise, his friend no longer believed that the English were in serious danger of being arrested. Edgeworth's stubbornness would eventually have dire consequences for his future.

Roget then began trying to track down the commandant. He raced all over town but couldn't locate him. Roget's anxiety was becoming nearly unbearable.

Two days later, when Roget finally met up with the commandant, they immediately exchanged bitter words with one another.

"All your requests for exemptions have been refused by Paris," General Dupuch barked at Roget. "I have orders to send you away."

Roget was well prepared for this moment. "If that is the case," he stated confidently, "I shall *réclame* myself. I am a French citizen and no longer consider myself your prisoner."

"Well, you don't have a moment to lose to get the necessary paperwork. Otherwise you may be arrested as soon as the day after tomorrow," the commandant replied.

But before Roget could think about his own fate, he first had to help the Philips boys prepare to leave. The next morning, Tuesday the 19th, he walked them to Secheron, where they set off for Neuchâtel, across the border in Prussia.

Roget was soon able to procure a certificate from the mayor's office testifying to his Swiss citizenship, but his struggle for freedom was far from over.

On Thursday morning, July 21, Roget got a note from the prefect's secretary requesting that he see the prefect at three that afternoon. The prefect informed him that unless he could come up with the necessary documentation—specifically, his father's birth certificate and a local identity card—to prove that he was who he said he was, by seven the next morning, the commandant would ship him off to Verdun, the town in Lorraine where Napoleon's agents were herding British prisoners like cattle.

His heart pounding, Roget began a terrifying race against the clock. He quickly tracked down a copy of his father's birth certificate. But getting himself a local identity card proved much more difficult. The justice of the peace, who typically handled such matters, lived ten miles away from the city. Though his assistant lived in town, that evening he was engaged in a game of "boules."

Bursting through the door of the notary's social club, Roget demanded to speak with him. But the notary refused to listen. Roget had no choice but to resort to bribery. At last, the notary said the document would be ready by six the next morning, at which time Roget would also have to present him with the names of eight witnesses who could sign it later that day.

Traveling through the night, Roget got to the notary's house at the crack of dawn. Rousing him while he was still in bed, Roget left with his identity card within half an hour. A couple of hours later, he began rushing around town to collect the necessary signatures.

Roget would be permitted to stay in Geneva, while all the other English, including Edgeworth, were sent to prison in Verdun just two days later.

It was Monday, July 25, 1803. At eight o'clock in the evening, Roget went to see Monsieur Maurice, the mayor of Geneva, who promised him that his French passport would be ready the following day. He hurried back to his room at the Peschiers', and immediately finished packing.

Though his eyes were red from a lack of sleep, Roget was not yet ready for bed. Late in the evening of what he knew was to be his last full day in Geneva, it suddenly occurred to him that there was someone he urgently needed to see. Hurrying toward the city's gates, he began briskly walking the mile to Coppet, the neighboring town that Madame de Staël now called home.

Since her recent exile from France by Napoleon, Madame de Staël had set up a salon in the family's Coppet estate that nearly rivaled her celebrated one in Paris. Like the learned storytellers of Boccaccio's *Decameron*, who sat out the Black Death in a villa outside Florence, Europe's most brilliant minds would come to Coppet to discuss music and art while the world around them crumbled. The salon's core members included Roget's surrogate father, Etienne Dumont, the well-known botanist Augustin-Pyramus de Candolle, the philosopher Pierre Prevost, and Marc-Auguste Pictet, the physics professor who was teaching the Philips boys chemistry. And at the center of de Staël's Coppet orbit was Benjamin Constant, the Swiss novelist and politician who had been her lover since 1796. After all, she was a seductress whose reputation spanned the entire Continent. Other prominent conquests included Charles-Maurice de Talleyrand, the bishop of Autun, and Count Adolphe-Louis Ribbing, the man who had helped to engineer the assassination of Gustavus III, the king of Sweden.

Roget was on edge. As he headed toward Coppet, his mind was racing. He kept worrying about whether he had organized all his books and other belongings in the most efficient manner. Would he be able to find what he needed when he needed it? He thought about Nathaniel and Burton, and wondered how they were getting along in Neuchâtel without him.

Roget was also overwhelmed by anger. He couldn't believe that Napoleon was forcing him out of the city where his father had been born. A Frenchman was kicking him out of Switzerland!

Images of Madame de Staël kept popping up in his mind. She was such a sensible woman! That was the phrase that he and the boys kept using to refer to her. At that instant, he tripped on a log along his path. Dusting himself off, Roget felt ashamed of his clumsiness. He was also feeling embarrassed that he hadn't caught on to Napoleon's treachery as quickly as the woman he was about to visit.

Up ahead, through the darkness, Roget caught sight of the red-tiled roofs of Coppet. Geneva was on the right side of the castle, which stretched along the hills separating the Jura Mountains from Lake Geneva. Nearby were the mountains of the Savoy, lined by huge trees that de Staël referred to as "her friends who watched over her destiny." Like Roget, she, too, was inclined to turn to nature for comfort. On the left side was the lake, whose blue waters pointed the way toward Lausanne.

Roget knocked at the main entrance to the castle, which consisted of three separate buildings and a courtyard. A servant let him in, and in the wide hall, with its white walls and stone floor, on which stood a statue of de Staël's father, Roget waited. A few minutes later, the woman he so much wanted to see during his final moments in Switzerland came bounding through the library's glass doors.

Madame de Staël's shoulders were bare and she wore no shawl, just a white muslin blouse. In her left hand, she carried a twig, which she kept twiddling.

De Staël's dark eyes fell on Roget with a mix of concern and affection. *"Pierre!"* she exclaimed. *"Comment vas-tu? Je m'inquiète pour toi."* ("How are you? I'm worried about you.") Putting her arms around Roget, she peppered him with questions about how he was managing to deal with the imminent threat of prison. Grabbing his left hand with her right, she escorted him past the library, which, Roget noticed, was lined with carved wooden bookcases and bronze statues, to the upstairs bedroom where she both entertained her guests and composed her famous books. Roget and his hostess sat down on the sofa, situated across from the bed, armchair, and writing desk—the only other pieces of furniture in the room.

What earthly pleasures were then enjoyed? Did de Staël then serve Roget a full meal consisting of her standard fare, stewed beef and fried potatoes, washed down by her excellent wines? Did this learned temptress initiate the handsome young doctor—roughly a dozen years her junior—in the art of love? Roget's diary presents little more than the following summary: "Called on Mme de Stael."

Whatever happened that night, it was, presumably, to Madame de Staël's liking. The next day, Roget would later note in his diary, he "received an invitation from Mme de Stael." But, sticking to his plan to leave the city of his ancestors as soon as possible, Roget declined her offer.

At noon on the next day, July 26, the mayor of Geneva issued Roget a Parisian passport. A few hours later, he was outside the city limits.

On the afternoon of the 27th, Roget rejoined the Philips boys in Neuchâtel. Roget could finally catch his breath. He no longer needed to spend every waking moment thinking about his survival. As he gradually began to feel less threatened, he was overcome by feelings of rage and indignation. He felt most angry not with Napoleon, but with his minions—in particular, General Dupuch and the Genevan government. What particularly infuriated Roget was Dupuch's duplicity, the way he had terrorized him, all the while pretending to be his friend. He felt, he wrote in his journal that summer, as if Dupuch

had toyed with him, the way a cat might sadistically taunt a helpless
mouse:

> He drags the victim, bound hand and foot, before him and with
> the greatest civility spits him in the face. The imperious tone of
> vanity when invested with authority, the sharp accents of waspish
> irritability, or the assumed politeness of an exalted foe: these are
> what he must expect to bear alternately, according to the humour
> of the moment. Of all these the last is the most cutting and bitter.

Roget would hold on to his hatred of the French for the rest of his
life.

But even in Neuchâtel, Roget and the boys were not entirely out
of harm's way. They still had to go from Prussia, then an independent state, into Germany. Safe transit was not a given. As Roget
later wrote, Neuchâtel was "full of English who had flocked from
Switzerland to avoid arrest by the French troops, of which the Swiss
government had given notice. Two or three were attempting an escape in disguise as peasants; the rest were waiting without knowing
what to do." Roget also opted for peasant garb. On July 30, shabbily
dressed, toting pipes in their mouths, and carrying long sticks, Roget
and his charges—along with a guide whom Roget had brought from
Geneva—started walking through the Swiss countryside en route to
Germany. To escape notice, they traveled very early in the morning
and refrained from speaking English.

They faced one last hurdle: crossing the Rhine, the dividing line
between Switzerland and Germany. On August 1, they arose at three
a.m. To get across the river, they had to go through either Baden,
where Madame de Staël's other English friends had been arrested, or

Brugg, a small town that had a French garrison. They chose Brugg, and to their great relief, as they passed through a corner of the town, the sentinel's back was turned, so he failed to stop their carriage. But he immediately halted the next one. Fortunately, riding in that carriage was an innkeeper favorably disposed toward Roget and the boys who made the sentry the following offer, "Let the carriage pass; I know the persons, and am answerable for them and their carriage. You come and drink a bottle at my house when you come off duty." This little bribe enabled the three travelers to catch a ferry boat before the commandant of Brugg had a chance to send after them.

After bathing in the Rhine and eating breakfast, Roget and the Philips boys made it to Stuttgart, the first town on the other side of the German border. Roget could hardly believe that he was finally out of enemy territory: "I repeat to myself frequently in the course of the day, 'I am free; the ground on which I tread is friendly; I am on my way towards England, towards all that is dear to me; I am once more a man.'" In Stuttgart, they changed gears and did some sightseeing. Eager to get back to some "business," Roget could not pass up the chance to show the boys the town's natural history museum. Burton felt compelled to compose a letter to his mother to keep her anxiety at bay. "It is with concern," he wrote, "we hear you have been so anxious on our account, but I hope all fears will, from the moment you receive this be dissipated."

From Stuttgart, Roget hoped to travel directly to Berlin. Though he had been terrorized by Napoleon's army, Roget had not lost his appetite for military precision. He was eager to get to Berlin so that he could witness "the great Review of the Prussian Army" that September.

But they were forced to postpone the trip to Berlin. Shortly after they got to the Hôtel d'Angleterre in Frankfurt, on August 12, Roget fell ill. He soon recovered, but Burton then developed what Roget would describe to John Philips as "a brain fever." He had memory lapses and other troubling mental symptoms such as feelings of lethargy and disorientation. Burton may well have been suffering from a psychosomatic disorder, as the stress of the escape from Switzerland no doubt had shaken him. And perhaps he also possessed the same anxious temperament as his mother.

John Philips was appreciative of Roget's attentive medical care. He was also thankful that Roget asked Dr. Samuel Thomas von Soemmerring, a renowned expert on anatomy who was based in Frankfurt, to examine Burton. Roget knew of Soemmerring because he had also taken Matthew Baillie's course in London (and was in fact then translating Baillie's *Morbid Anatomy* into German). Yet Philips remained very worried and suspected that the news would shatter his wife. In late September, he wrote Roget, "I dare not show Mrs. Philips your letter at present, but shall wait for your next, which God grant may be more favorable."

By early October, Burton was, as Roget put it, "sufficiently restored to bear the motion of a carriage." After being on the road for a few days, Burton abruptly declared himself fully recovered from his monthlong illness. One afternoon, he went up to Roget and shook his hand, making the startling assertion that he had not seen his tutor for a while. Never again did Burton complain of any symptoms.

Roget and the boys finally reached Potsdam on October 17. Though they did not reach Berlin in time to see the particular military review Roget had been so looking forward to, they still got to witness a parade of the Prussian military. Roget also accompanied the teenagers on a tour of the principality's architectural wonders— Frederick the Great's palace of Sans Souci, Frederick William II's Marble Palace, and the opera house.

Arriving in Denmark a week later, Roget was thrilled to catch his first glimpse of the North Sea. As he later recalled, he felt like Xenophon—the Greek general who, upon reaching the Black Sea after leading thousands of his soldiers in a retreat across Persian territory, had issued the famous cry *"Thalassa, thalassa"* ("The sea, the sea"). Unfortunately, in Roget's case, the sighting of the salt water provided no guarantee of safety.

Due to fierce storms, the trio would be stuck for nearly three weeks in the port city of Husum. They could hardly relax, as reports kept circulating that the French navy had gained control of the North Sea. Other unforeseen dangers also beckoned.

On November 16, Roget and the Philips boys boarded the packet *Diana* bound for Harwich, a coastal town in northeast England, seventy miles from London. For about a week, the small ship led by Captain Stewart was tossed about on the North Sea. Then the *Diana* came upon a frigate, which fired a gun, then lowered a small boarding boat. Roget and the boys were terrified.

Roget feared that Napoleon had somehow tracked him down. But the lieutenant who stepped onto the *Diana* spoke English, not French. What's more, he was friendly and issued a dinner invitation. Soon the passengers on the two ships were chatting amiably with one another.

Roget's extended nightmare—his five-month stint as Napoleon's captive, during which he often feared for his life—was finally over.

On November 22, 1803, Roget and the boys reached Harwich. After first stopping off in London to see his uncle, Samuel Romilly, then still living on Gower Street, he accompanied the boys back to Manchester. He enjoyed his stay at John Philips's home in December, but he longed to move on. "I find at length," he wrote his aunt Anne Romilly, "that there is no end to the dinners and invitations, and that I must sooner or later make my escape from this hospitable place and retreat to the more tranquil and sequestered vales of Devonshire." To recover from the terrors that he had experienced on the Continent, Roget urgently needed a dose of country living. Roget soon trekked off to Ilfracombe, where he spent the winter with his mother and sister.

Though Roget was able to pick up his life where he left off, not so his friend Lovell Edgeworth, who would remain a prisoner of the French until 1814. In Verdun, the French authorities had stuck Edgeworth in a small shack by the river, where he spent his days chasing flies. In a letter sent shortly after his capture—one of the few that he managed to send to Roget during his internment—he thanked him for a loan of 120 pounds, lamenting:

Nothing in heaven above, earth below, nor the waters under the earth can be more truly melancholy than this spot. . . . My health is getting worse and worse. My stomach has been very bad ever since I came here; so that in time I think that the best and cheapest plan will be for me to lay me down and die. . . . The only way is to have, if possible, no thought at all, and no care, for the morrow.

Even after his release, Edgeworth was still in a constant state of despair. When his wealthy father died, in 1817, Lovell made such a mess of the estate that he had to be relieved of his duties as a trustee. He lived until 1842 but remained a broken man, given to frequent bouts of dissipation and drunkenness. Roget's remarkable resourcefulness, and a little luck, had enabled him to escape his friend's tragic fate.

5.

Manchester: Both the *Thesaurus* and a Medical Career Begun

(653) UNCLEANNESS, immundicity, uncleanliness, soilure, soiliness, foulness, impurity, pollution, nastiness, offensiveness, beastliness, defilement, contamination, abomination, taint, tainture.

Slovenliness, slovenry, untidiness, sluttishness, coarseness, grossness.

Mud, mire, quagmire, slough, alluvium, silt, slime, spawn, offal, recrement, feces, excrement, ordure, dung, guano, manure, compost, dung-hill, midden, bog, laystall, sink, cess, cesspool, sump, sough, cloaca, sewer, shore; hogwash, bilge-water.

After spending a few months with his mother and sister in Ilfracombe, Roget, now twenty-five, began to look for work as a doctor in Manchester. By August, a job opened when a senior physician at the city's infirmary, Thomas Percival—still remembered today as the author of a treatise on medical ethics—died after a long illness. In October, with the help of his patron, John

Philips, who chaired the hospital's board of trustees, Roget replaced
Percival.

Roget was suddenly knee-deep in professional responsibilities.
Besides a hospital, the institution that later became known as the
Manchester Royal Infirmary included a dispensary for outpatients, a
ward for the treatment of fever patients, and a psychiatric facility—
then called a "lunatic asylum." Manchester's hospital was busier
than any in London: about 6,000 patients a year, split evenly between inpatients and outpatients, came through its doors. The entire
town housed but a handful of licensed physicians.

In the first decade of the 1800s, Manchester was a boomtown.
The Industrial Revolution was revamping all of Great Britain, but
nowhere else were its effects felt more keenly than in Manchester.

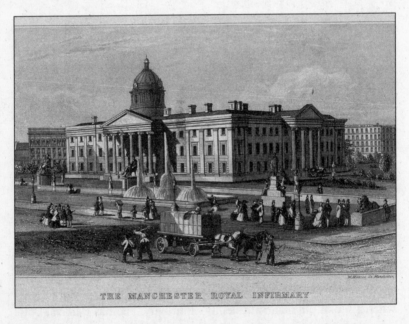

THE MANCHESTER ROYAL INFIRMARY

*Founded in 1752, the Manchester Royal Infirmary was in the center of town (near where
Piccadilly Gardens now stands) until 1910.*

Between 1780 and 1801, the population of England and Wales grew from 7.5 million to 9 million. Yet over the same period, the number of Manchester's inhabitants nearly quadrupled, reaching 90,000.

The reason for Manchester's meteoric rise can be summed up in one word: cotton. Two decades before he designed the apparatus that Roget used to inhale nitrous oxide, James Watt had invented the first rotary steam engine, which, as numerous manufacturing firms soon discovered, could help with the spinning of cotton. A few years later, in 1783, Manchester saw its first steam cotton mill open; by 1825, the city would be home to some 104 spinning factories. As England's cotton exports expanded nearly fortyfold between 1781 and 1811, Manchester emerged as that industry's focal point. More than a quarter of the population of "Cottonopolis" would toil in its newly built factories.

But rapid economic growth brought with it a nasty by-product: industrial waste. Manchester was rapidly becoming the filthiest place on earth. In early 1804, Dumont wrote Catherine that "Manchester has nothing agreeable about it. The smoke which rises from all the chimneys covers the city in a thick vapour." Even in the first decade of the nineteenth century, many could barely restrain their horror, such as the visitor from Rotterdam who declared, "The town is abominably filthy, the Steam Engine is pestiferous, the Dyehouses noisesome and offensive, and the water of the river as black as ink or the Stygian lake." The famous verdicts of a generation later—Alexis de Tocqueville and Friedrich Engels both arrived at the same conclusion, the former calling Cottonopolis "a new Hades" and the latter "Hell on Earth"—also applied to Manchester during Roget's stay. So, too, did Dickens's description of the fictional Coketown—delivered in his novel *Hard Times*: "It was a town of red brick or of brick that would have been red if the smoke and ashes had allowed it; but as matters stood it was a town of unnatural red and black like the painted face of a savage."

As Manchester would not build an adequate sewer system until 1844, its streets in the first few decades of the nineteenth century were often swimming with garbage. Roget was literally living in a dump. Dirt was an everyday evil. Perhaps that's why so many Mancunians (the Latin-derived term for Manchester denizens) gravitated toward the teachings of John Wesley, the founder of Methodism, who preached that "Cleanliness is, indeed, next to Godliness." Manchester was home to more Methodists than any city but London. A frequent visitor, Wesley himself had, shortly before his death in 1791, opened the Methodist Chapel, located just a few doors away from Roget's first apartment, which stood at 18 Oldham Street.

Though Manchester suddenly was asserting itself as a major player in international trade, it was stuck in a time warp. Still run like a medieval village, Manchester had no mayor, relying for leadership on a few town administrators; it would not have any representation in Parliament until 1832 and would not be officially incorporated as a city until 1847. Lacking a police force, early-nineteenth-century Mancunians remained dependent on the vigilante justice doled out by justices of the peace and the militia—consisting of part-time soldiers.

Roget was under no illusions. He knew all along that the combination of chaos and uncleanliness would be tough to take. He never harbored any intention of settling in Manchester. In January 1802, while staying with the Philipses just before beginning the Grand Tour, he noted, "I have been told that the area around Manchester is flat and ugly. . . . The town itself is horrible: dirty and black, paved only with small stones, the air always heavy by the smoke of the factories." What appealed to Roget was not the town but his new position. First jobs for physicians were hard to come by, and Roget figured this one would enable him to reach his ultimate goal of establishing himself in London as quickly as possible. In 1804, he wrote his uncle:

> Having obtained a situation in an Infirmary is of itself a degree of success, and will be considered so by the world: and the celebrity that is attained in a large town appears to admit more easily of transference to another town, than the described reputation, however great, of a country practitioner, which is obstinately attached to the spot where it sprung.

The initial plan called for Roget's mother and sister to live with him. Catherine and Annette arrived in town on October 21, 1804, just a week after Roget started at the Infirmary. But within a couple of weeks, Catherine had had enough and started planning their escape. Though she wasn't sure exactly where they would spend the winter, on November 17, she and Annette left town. Forced to choose between living in what she described as "such a smoky town," and living apart from her beloved son, Catherine opted to become a "country rambler" once again.

Hearing about this sudden turn of events from Roget, Dumont was critical of Catherine for acting so precipitously. While acknowledging Manchester's downside—"the fumes in the air" and its "unhealthfulness"—Dumont was convinced that Catherine should have tried living there for longer than a month. Offering words of consolation, Dumont assured the young doctor that he could understand his disappointment at the separation from his mother and sister. Little did Dumont know that deep inside Roget felt more relief than sadness about the family's new living arrangements.

Roget figured that he would no longer have to cater to his

mother's whims, but he was mistaken. Once settled in the surrounding countryside, Catherine, heedless of her son's hectic schedule, continued to pester him through the mail. "But can you employ your time better," went the rhetorical question she posed in one of her frequent letters, "than in endeavoring to make those happy, who most sincerely love you?"

Roget enjoyed living apart from his mother and sister that first winter, but he felt lonely in his Oldham Street rooms. Except for the Philips family, he knew very few people in Manchester. Both his mother and uncle were extremely worried about his isolation, but, as before, their concerns only increased his own feelings of distress. In early January 1805, Catherine, who had not received responses to two previous letters, was nearly frantic: "I really long to hear from you, no doubt you thought of us these holidays, spending them quite alone, having not a soul to talk to! . . . Send us all the news you can, and that immediately as you receive this, or I shall fear you are ill, and shall go to Manchester to inquire after you." Then residing in Parkgate, a seaside town thirty miles from Manchester, Catherine, as her son well knew, could have easily carried out her threat to show up on his doorstep. Writing her back as soon as he could, Roget succeeded in fending her off—at least for the time being.

Roget managed to disengage himself from his mother, but he still had to figure out how to cope with the problems Manchester posed for *him*. How could he tolerate the loneliness? How could he stand to live surrounded by so much filth and disorder? He often felt enraged and horrified; he felt as if his body would be forever encased in dirt.

But by the beginning of 1805, Roget had devised a survival strategy for enduring the pestilence that was Manchester. To keep his distress at bay, he went back to the reliable formula that had worked so well as a child: he would once again create a new world made entirely of words. Whenever he had a few free hours in the evening, he would beef up his word lists. That was the year Roget was to complete the first draft of his immortal book of lists.

M anchester's industrial toxins not only spurred Roget to get cracking on his word lists but also, increasingly, became the focus of his day job. The more Roget immersed himself in his duties at the Infirmary, the more he realized how uncleanliness could lead to serious illness, if not death. Both in his daytime medical pursuits and in his nighttime literary endeavors, Roget kept focusing on the same goal: how to save the world from disorder and disease. Swept up by this crusade, he had little time to feel anxious and depressed.

The omnipresent filth was causing havoc among the poor, most of whom lived in unsanitary conditions. A decade before Roget's arrival, an alarming infectious fever broke out at a cotton factory at Ashton-under-Lyne—right outside town—affecting some three hundred workers. This epidemic, in turn, led to the establishment of the city's Board of Health the following year, which was headed by Dr. John Ferriar, Roget's supervisor at the Infirmary. Ferriar, who personally examined the residences of the indigent, had begun to connect the dots:

In a house in Bottle Street, most of the inhabitants are paralytic, in consequence of their situation in a blind alley, which excludes them from light and air. Consumptions, distortion and idiocy are common in such recesses. In Blakely Street, under No. 4, is a range of cellars let out to lodgers, which threaten to become a nursery of diseases.

They consist of four rooms, communicating with each other, of which the two centre rooms are completely dark; the fourth is very ill lighted, and chiefly ventilated through the others. They contain from four to five beds in each, and are already extremely dirty.

Understanding the environmental roots of disease, Ferriar identified uncleanliness as the major threat to the city's public health.

These insights led Ferriar to devise a new approach to treating those fevers—specifically, typhus, malaria, and scarlet fever—that in the early nineteenth century constituted the most common ailments seen by physicians. He emphasized prevention over cure, and the means he advocated were more political than medical. With his assistant Roget by his side, Ferriar began using his pulpit at the Board of Health to argue for a variety of social reforms, including the licensing of rooming houses and improved ventilation systems in factories.

Cleanliness reigned supreme in the fever ward that Ferriar and Roget manned at the Infirmary. As soon as patients were admitted to the hospital, the staff provided them with new garments—a jacket and trousers for men and a wrapping gown and petticoat for women. Their old clothes were then taken into the yard to be washed, scoured, and ventilated. As the two men emphasized in an annual report written in 1806, on account of the various sanitary measures they had put in place, the ward's census began to drop steadily. In 1802, a total of 1,070 fever patients had stayed at the hospital; three years later, the number was down to 184. But Roget's first year would still prove grueling: the fever cases admitted in 1805 were of a particularly virulent kind, and nearly one in five of the patients died; the ratio that had typically prevailed since the establishment of the ward in 1796 was one in nine. Facing so much death did little to ease Roget's transition to Cottonopolis.

Roget and Ferriar, despite such setbacks, helped to put Manchester on the map as a center of the nascent field of public health. Of his work with Roget during this period, Ferriar stressed the successes:

The progress of infectious fever has been effectually arrested; and the destructive epidemic of scarlet fever, which was actually introduced into the town during 1805, from Liverpool, has been completely suppressed. In effecting these purposes, so important to society, so consoling to humanity, the physicians have regarded the public good more than their own immediate reputation; and have preferred the solid benefit of preventing the wide diffusion of contagion, to an ostentatious list of cures.

In addition to working for the passage of new laws and regulations to improve the city's public health, Ferriar and Roget also sought to persuade the poor to change their behavior. These exhortations took the form of a pamphlet titled "Advice to the Poor," which they co-wrote. What they were aiming at was similar to what Roget would attempt some fifty years later with his *Thesaurus*. Just as the *Thesaurus* offered the masses tips on how to clean up their prose, here Roget, who "accommodated the language to the persons for whose benefit it was designed," offered them tips on how to keep their bodies clean: "You are requested to read the following paper with attention, by persons who are endeavoring to relieve you from the misery and fatality of fevers, and other infectious diseases. . . . Much depends on your own conduct, for preventing the first occasions of sickness." The recommendations included obvious measures such as moving out of damp cellars and investing the time each week to clean clothes and bed linens. Distributed free to the city's residents,

the pamphlet was also laced with a rigid moralism: "It should be un-
necessary to remind you, that much sickness is occasioned among
you, by passing your evenings at alehouses, or in strolling about the
streets, or in the fields adjoining to the town." As a scientific expert
on the ill effects of uncleanliness, Roget was not averse to shaming
those who were lax about maintaining their own personal hygiene.
On this subject, he lacked empathy because he couldn't identify
with his readers.

During his four years in Manchester, Roget would greatly benefit
from his association with Ferriar. Visiting Roget shortly after his
arrival in town, Dumont described Ferriar to Catherine as "an interesting man of solid merit who takes a genuine interest in his young
colleague." Though largely forgotten today, Ferriar had wide-ranging
scholarly concerns that encompassed not only public health but also
pharmacology, psychiatry, and literary studies. The first person to
notice the effect of dried leaves from the plant known as *Digitalis
purpurea*, Ferriar discovered digitalis, the heart medication still in
use today, which increases the amount of blood pumped in each
heartbeat.

In Ferriar, Roget found a scholar he could learn from, but also a
man who shared some of his eccentricities. Like Roget, Ferriar was
plagued by literary obsessions and compulsions, which, in his case,
involved collecting not words, but books. As a physician steeped in
psychiatric diagnosis, Ferriar coined a new term to describe his
own disorder: "bibliomania." At the time, Roget was still only a
bibliomaniac-in-waiting, as he was too poor to indulge his whims as
often as he might like. But once he moved to London, in 1808, he
would give free rein to his own bibliomaniacal tendencies, eventually
amassing a library of some 4,100 volumes. Just as Roget was leaving
town, Ferriar finished up his highly regarded satiric poem "The Bibliomania," about his own inner struggle—

What wild desires, what restless torments seize
The hapless man, who feels the book disease. . . .

Like Poets, born, in vain Collectors strive
To cross their Fate, and learn the art to thrive . . .
The tyrant-passion drags them backward still:
Ev'n I, debarr'd of ease, and studious hours,
Confess, mid' anxious toil, its lurking pow'rs.

During Roget's four years in Manchester, his sister's life would begin to fall apart. In Ilfracombe, where Annette had stayed for over a year, she had enjoyed perhaps the happiest period of her life. In this seaside paradise, Annette, who turned twenty-one in 1804, had pursued a wide range of social activities, including horseback riding, card games, dances, and musical parties (in which she and her friends would perform musical numbers). She also had been courted by a suitor identified only as "Mr. Lock," who appeared to be on the verge of proposing marriage. In a letter to Roget dated May 20, 1804, she described Mr. Lock as her "constant [dance] partner." She also wrote of Mr. Lock's many kindnesses to her—he would lend her books as well as the use of his horse. "Mr. Lock," she stated, "is always contriving to procure me pleasure—in every shape."

As Annette prepared to leave Ilfracombe for Manchester at the end of that summer, she felt a deep sense of dread. She complained to Roget:

Cannot you form an idea of what I must feel when on the point of bidding adieu, perhaps for ever, to friends who evince for me the utmost kindness and whose pressing arguments for our stay seem

dictated by something more than common, everyday polite-
ness. . . . Where shall I dance with so much pleasure and spirit as
here?

Though Catherine had focused most of her maternal energy on her
son, she had also managed to suffocate Annette with her flurries of
attention, incapable as she was of treating anyone dear to her as a
separate human being. Lonely and isolated as a child, in her late
adolescence in Ilfracombe, Annette was starting to come out of her
shell and to experience some of the joys of connectedness, something that had been in short supply in the Roget family.

But Annette's worst fears were soon realized. Right after she left
Ilfracombe, she fell into a deep depression. The precise cause is un-
clear. The change of venue may well have been enough to trigger this
crisis, which bordered on a complete breakdown. In addition to her
acute emotional distress, Annette also developed a host of medical
ills, including both intestinal and vision problems. In a poem she
sent to her brother that December, shortly after the move from
Manchester to Parkgate, Annette observed:

> The bracing air invigorates my shatter'd frame
> And bids me call Parkgate by ev'ry tender name.
> But ah how oft when strolling on the lonely shore,
> My sighs the friendly gales have back to Devon bore;
> The sad comparison my heart oft draws
> And oft laments, with tears, Fate's cruel laws!
> My thoughts from this in vain I strive to keep
> And, ev'n at night, they haunt me in my sleep.

Annette's thoughts may well have kept returning to the Devon shore simply because she loved its landscape and missed her many friends there.

But in all probability Annette was enduring many a sleepless night because Mr. Lock had jilted her. That December, Annette sent Roget another poem that tells of the woe of a woman, named Louisa (Annette's middle name), who sought protection from the sun's "ardent rays" in a "shady bow'r." Assuming that Mr. Lock had turned his attention to someone else, Annette may well have needed to resort to another identity to write about her intense feelings:

> *But sighing deep and seized with sudden pain,*
> *"And this was I," she cried and sigh'd again.*
> *"Young, blooming, happy, pleasing all I pleas'd. . . .*
> *Till cruel love his hapless victim seized."*
> *Thus with her future peace a woman parts*
> *Deceived by looks, by words, and winning arts.*

Her older brother was perhaps the worst person imaginable to send such confessional poetry. Roget couldn't relate to Annette's creative impulse. For him, immersion in words had everything to do with tackling lexicographical challenges, but little to do with self-expression. The word lists he was then obsessing over in the late evenings enabled him to escape from—not to face—painful emotions.

By May 1805, Annette's mind, Catherine wrote to Peter, continued to be "very gloomy." Describing Annette as "the most nervous girl I ever saw," Catherine tried to force Annette to snap out of her depression. In her desperation, Catherine thought to punish her daughter for her sadness. She wrote Peter, "I told her she had certainly better not write to you, till her spirits were better." Expressing feelings of loss and despair in the Roget family was strictly verboten. But by silencing her daughter's emotional pain, Catherine, then living with Annette in Tenby, crushed her spirit. Annette soon cut back on her creative pursuits—her poetry, her drawing, her piano playing, and her needlework. Family history would eventually replay itself: just as Catherine never got over her husband's death, Annette would never recover from the loss of Mr. Lock.

Roget responded to Annette's obvious cries for help in much the same way as his mother. His letters to his sister during this period reveal a remarkable insensitivity and lack of empathy. In September 1808, he wrote her:

Look upon your present trouble as an opportunity which has been presented to you to exercise your patience, and use the offensive passages to fortify your constancy in undergoing the *real* evils in life. . . . Forget the past and begin again to take courage. One should not expect to enjoy the pleasures of life without a little self-preparation, without some salutary self-discipline.

Though Roget could get angry about injustice in the abstract—say, the perfidy of Napoleon's minions—he couldn't comprehend the rage resulting from abandonment by a flesh-and-blood lover. For Roget, deep interpersonal hurt rarely registered. Romilly also felt that such "evil" wasn't real. During Annette's long bout with what he called the "family defect," Romilly observed: "Her indisposition is imaginary. . . . Instead of trying to overcome the depression of spirits which she labours under, she indulges it to the utmost."

Peter, who had difficulty dealing with his own losses, was unable to help others mourn theirs. He had buried his grief about the early death of his father and thought Annette should do the same with her loss of the love of her life. Roget tried to impose on Annette the family's sole strategy for coping with setbacks—to deny feelings of sadness and anger and just plow straight ahead. Unfortunately, neither Roget's advice nor anything else, for that matter, proved helpful to Annette. She would give up both on men and on her own prospects for a fulfilling life.

E arly in 1805, Peter moved from Oldham Street to a cozier apartment at 7 King Street, in the heart of the city's financial district. Though Roget's immediate surroundings were posh, he was now living even closer to the most dilapidated part of Manchester— Old Town, where the workers camped out in their filthy huts. To help him cope with the chaos of his new living situation, Roget would work well into the night, building his word lists.

Roget called the manuscript that he would complete that year in his King Street apartment *Collection of English Synonyms Classified and Arranged*. Though the word "thesaurus" appears nowhere in the title, Roget's manuscript reflects his attempt to create a new kind of book, one that organizes all of language. In the preface to the 1852 edition of the *Thesaurus*, Roget would write:

> It is now nearly fifty years since I first projected a system of verbal classification similar to that on which the present Work is founded. . . . I had, in the year 1805, completed a classed catalog of words on a small scale, but on the same principle, and nearly in the same form, as the Thesaurus now published.

This first draft of his famous book contained some 15,000 words and came to ninety-nine pages, not including a two-page index listing all the key concepts, along with their page numbers, which Roget inserted at the beginning. Given Roget's love of symmetry, it's surprising that he resisted the chance to cap off his text at a clean one hundred pages.

Long considered lost, this unpublished manuscript surprisingly resurfaced in a London auction held by Philips (now Bonham) in 1992. No one—not even Roget's first biographer, Donald Emblen—has written anything about this document, which provides a fascinating window into the mind of a creative genius.

Roget was by no means the first writer—or even the first English writer—to put together a book of synonyms. That distinction belongs to a French monk, the Abbé Gabriel Girard, who in 1718 published *La justesse de la langue françoise* (called *Synonymes françois* in its subsequent editions). In his preface, Girard boasted, "I did not copy anyone; I don't even believe that there is anyone to copy on this material." Though no one would challenge Girard's claim to originality, his English successors would all judge him harshly for his overweening pride in his native tongue. Of all the European languages, Girard argued, French was "furthest along on the path to perfection." Sensing that Latin was on the decline, the abbé maintained that French should emerge as the next universal language. And to promote his cause, Girard felt compelled to draft some general guidelines for French word usage.

Girard was also motivated by two other practical concerns. First, he felt that speech was the central force that held society together. Second, he believed that clear thinking depended on the ability to express oneself clearly. Girard addressed himself not to scholars but to ordinary users of the language, whom he sought to help improve their conversational skills. Girard's method was to group together words that signify a common idea—say, *ordre* ("order") and *règle* ("rule")—and then write a few paragraphs on the appropriate usage of each synonym. The first edition consists of 295 such articles.

In 1766, an Englishman, John Trusler, widely considered a hack writer—he had received just a smattering of university training in medicine and theology—published a translation of Girard's book, *The Difference Between Words, Esteemed Synonymous, in the English Language; and the Proper Choice of Them Determined: Together with So Much of Abbé Girard's Treatise on This Subject, As Would Agree, with Our Mode of Expression.* Noting that Girard's book had become an instant classic, Trusler sought to reproduce its success in England: "It is hoped, the great esteem, the Abbé acquired by his piece, and, the many editions . . . are sufficient proofs of its excellence, and, will be some excuse, for this similar attempt." Trusler included a translation of Girard's preface, though he had the good sense to delete those passages in which Girard rhapsodized about the superiority of the French tongue.

Trusler's book contains 371 articles, all of which are either direct translations or adaptations from Girard's text. Far from comprehensive, Trusler's book is limited to those groups of words that have readily identifiable French cognates, such as "add" (*ajouter*) and "augment" (*augmenter*). Though Trusler's guide met a huge demand—in addition to numerous London editions, it also appeared in Paris—scholars were scathing. As a writer noted in *The Critical Review,* "We can by no means think this author equal to the task he undertakes, which requires the most critical discernment. . . . Few critics write nonsense with a better grace."

About thirty years later, Hester Lynch Piozzi followed with *British Synonymy or, An Attempt at Regulating the Choice of Words in Familiar Conversation, Inscribed, with Sentiments of Gratitude and Respect, to Such of Her Foreign Friends As Have Made English Literature*

Their Peculiar Study. Dismissing Trusler as a mere "imitation" of Girard, Piozzi—better known as Mrs. Thrale (after the name of her first husband)—aimed to create a truly British book of synonyms that would come closer to capturing the spirit of Girard. She had begun her foray into the genre while living with her second husband in Italy, where she often felt the need to explain the nuances of English to non-native speakers. Like Girard, Piozzi focused on the art of conversation, and as a woman, she felt she had much to contribute: "While men may teach to write with propriety, a woman may at worst be qualified through long practice—to direct the choice of phrases in familiar talk."

A close friend of Samuel Johnson, Piozzi looked to the famous lexicographer as an authority, mentioning him dozens of times in her 310 unnumbered articles. In his *Dictionary*, Johnson was determined to improve the "elegance of language," and Piozzi shared his vision. "Synonymy," wrote Piozzi, "has more to do with elegance than with truth." Her book proved to be as popular as both Girard's and Trusler's. In its 1804 edition, the editors tried to convince readers of its value by noting that "the successive editions it has passed through [are] the best proof of the estimation in which it is held."

However, Piozzi's impressionistic work lacked academic rigor. Her articles combined odd factoids, personal opinions, and celebrity reportage. Shying away from a systematic overview of language, Piozzi, like Girard, also cherry-picked her words, evincing a preference for those related to emotional and moral states. Not surprisingly, the critics also had a field day with *British Synonymy*. *The Critical Review* pointed out its "uncouth language," its "total want of plan," and its political "rancour" (Piozzi was prone to insult the French every chance she got). Another reviewer referred to her "utter incapability of defining a single term in the language."

Roget was also deeply dissatisfied with Piozzi's ode to elegance. A scientist, he didn't think truth could be dispensed with so easily. He was also troubled by its lack of comprehensiveness—a point Piozzi herself conceded: "My little book then—*levior cortice* [more fickle than a cork]—may . . . direct travelers on their way, til a more complicated and valuable piece of workmanship be found." Unlike Piozzi, Roget saw language as more than just the means with which to engage in idle chatter. Like Dugald Stewart, Roget looked to words as an essential tool in the fight to advance human knowledge.

Since the previous synonym books lacked any philosophical moorings whatsoever, Roget was forced to look for theoretical insights elsewhere. He found some in a widely read Platonic dialogue on grammar, *Epea pteroenta* (*Winged Words*), published in 1786 by the philologist and radical pamphleteer John Horne Tooke. Soon after the appearance of the eagerly awaited second volume in 1805, which earned Tooke the then staggering sum of 5,000 pounds, *The Annual Review* called Tooke's work "the most valuable contribution to the philosophy of language which our literature has produced."

A muscular five-foot-nine, Tooke was a man's man, and Roget's sensibility was much closer to his than to Piozzi's. Of Tooke, the essayist William Hazlitt would write, "His mind was the reverse of effeminate—hard, unbending, concrete, physical, half-savage . . . [he] saw language stripped of the clothing of habit or sentiment, or the disguises of doting pedantry, naked in its cradle, and in its primitive state." In contrast to Piozzi, Tooke looked at language through a scientific lens, applying the principles of natural history and anatomy.

Tooke's lengthy treatise centered on the argument that all the parts of speech except for nouns and verbs—for example, prepositions, adjectives, and conjunctions—were "winged words," or "abbreviations," and ultimately could be traced back to a noun or verb. Though Roget didn't agree with everything in Tooke's treatise—such as his convoluted theory of the evolution of language—Tooke clearly shaped his thinking. For example, accepting Tooke's central dictum, Roget typically included only nouns and verbs in his early word lists.

Despite its title, Roget's 1805 *Collection of English Synonyms Classified and Arranged*, was more than just another book of synonyms. Like Tooke, Roget also sought to make a theoretical statement about the nature of language itself. Decades later, when publishing the first edition of the *Thesaurus*, Roget would mine Tooke's work for his epigraph: "It is impossible we should ever thoroughly understand the nature of the *signs*, unless we first properly consider and arrange the *things signified*." Roget's 1805 manuscript was his first attempt to both classify "the things signified" (ideas) and explore the meanings of "signs" (words).

Tooke had inspired Roget to think big—and to think systematically. But then there was the matter of pulling it off. To organize his inventory of synonyms, Roget turned for assistance to the 1668 book *An Essay Towards a Real Character and a Philosophical Language*, by Bishop John Wilkins. Not a book of synonyms, but a topical dictionary, Wilkins's treatise provided an elaborate thematic arrangement of all the concepts that make up the world.

The man who had the biggest impact on Roget's *Thesaurus* had also been a scientist first and a wordsmith second. Educated at Oxford, Wilkins had wide-ranging interests that included theology, mathematics, and philosophy. Wilkins was also obsessed with mechanical devices and inventions: in fact, he entertained the then fantastical idea that man was destined to journey to the moon. But Wilkins lost his academic appointment at Cambridge in 1660, the year Charles II regained the crown. Moving to London with his wife, one of Oliver Cromwell's sisters, Wilkins worked doggedly on his magnum opus for six years. Shortly after the manuscript went to the printer, in September 1666, the Great Fire struck, destroying all copies. Wilkins dusted himself off and created a new version, based on his surviving notes. The 1668 edition, which so delighted King Charles II that he soon handed over the vacant bishopric of Chester to Wilkins, is the one that Roget consulted.

The ultimate objective of Wilkins's treatise was to put forth a new international language that could replace Latin. But unlike Abbé Girard a generation later, Wilkins turned not to another European language, but to a "philosophical" or artificial language—one that he invented. This new language, which was only to be written, relied on characters representing abstract ideas. By his term "Real Character" Wilkins was referring to "the expression of our Conceptions by Marks which should signifie things, and not words." Wilkins saw many advantages to this pure form of language that, by circumventing words, would "refer directly to what knowledge and thought are about." Given that the ambiguity inherent in most languages, including Latin, was a constant source of error, tying common notions to idiographic characters, he thought, could speed the growth of knowledge. And as a theologian, Wilkins was also convinced that this new international language could help spread the Gospel around the world—particularly to the denizens of the new American colonies.

But before he could get around to the guts of his book—the unveiling of his new universal language—Wilkins faced a daunting task. He first had to provide, as he put it, "a regular enumeration and description of all those things and notions to which marks or names are to be assigned." This was Wilkins's famous classification scheme, laid out across some two hundred pages at the front of his book, where he divided all ideas into some forty classes, plus numerous subclasses. As it turned out, by the time Roget was rifling through Wilkins's treatise, this preliminary material was the only part anyone ever consulted. Within a decade of its publication, most members of the

Royal Society—with the notable exception of Newton's archrival, the physicist Robert Hooke—had panned Wilkins's universal language as too complicated to be of much use.

Wilkins's systematic arrangement of ideas, though more widely read than the rest of his book, also promised more than it delivered. It, too, was confusing. The forty classes didn't parallel one another. Some were extremely broad, others very narrow. While the first three classes ("GENERAL," "RELATION MIXED," and "RELATION OF AC-TION") all covered what Wilkins called "things called TRANSCEN-DENTAL," classes ten through eighteen covered specific plants and animals (such as "TREE," "FISH," "BIRD," and "BEAST").

Despite its many inconsistencies, Wilkins's classification scheme would prove enthralling to many scholars prior to Roget, including the naturalist John Ray, whom Wilkins had enlisted to help him categorize plants and animals, and the young naval administrator Samuel Pepys—then also engaged in composing the entries in his famous diary—who would help Wilkins craft class 39, "NAVAL." Ray became so consumed with his physiological research for Wilkins that he ended up elaborating on his findings in several famous books of his own, such as *A New Method of Plants* and *A Methodical Synopsis of Birds and Fish*. Ray, who also translated Wilkins's treatise into Latin, laid the foundation upon which the famous eighteenth-century naturalists— among them Roget's heroes, Linnaeus and Buffon—would build.

To get started on his synonym book, Roget leaned heavily on Wilkins. Compare, for example, the first page of each manuscript. Under his first class, "GENERAL," Wilkins labeled "BEING" as idea number one. Next to "BEING" he listed a series of synonymous terms beginning with "entity, essence, existence." Eager to highlight the interrelationships between ideas, Wilkins often included what he calls "opposites" (the word "antonym" had not yet been coined). Un-derneath "BEING" he inserted "NOTHING," and then listed a series

Existence

1

Ens, entity, being, exist..
Essence, quintess.. quidess..
Nature thing substance
course world frame
position constitution
Reality, (v. truth) actual
exist.. — fact.
course of things, under.. sun
extant, present

Nonentity, nullity, nihility
nonexist.. noth.. nought
void zero, cypher blank
empty
unsubstantial
Unreal, ideal, imaginary
visionary, fabulous
fictitious, supposititious
absent, shadow. Dream
phantom, phantasm

Positive, affirmation absolute
intrinsic, substantive
inherent
Negation, virtual, extrinsic
potential. adjective

To be; exist, obtain, stand
pass, subsist, prevail, lie
— on foot, on ; tapis
to constitute, form, compose   to consist of
scope, habitude, temperament
State, Mode of exist.. condition, nature, constitut.. habit
Affection, predicament, situat.. point.. posture contingency
place
Circumstance, case, plight, train, tune, — point, degree
juncture, conjuncture, pass, emergency, exigency

— Mode, manner, style, cast, fashion, form shape
Strain, way, degree. — tenure, terms, tenor
footing, character, capacity
Relation, affinity, alliance, analogy, filiat.. (v. connect..)
ship
Reference about, respect.. regard.. concerning, touching
in point of, as to — pertaining to, belong.. applicable to
relatively, according to
Comparable, commensurate   incomp.., incoun.. -ble,
correspondent   -able   irreconcilable, dissident
accordant

The first page of Roget's 1805 manuscript.

of synonyms, beginning with "nought, null, none." The first line of Roget's 1805 text, "Ens, entity, being, existence," which appeared on a page with the idea "EXISTENCE" emblazoned across the top, was essentially a shorter version of Wilkins's (*ens* is the Latin equivalent of Wilkins's first word, "entity"). Similarly, in the right-hand column of this page, just like Wilkins, Roget came up with a list of "opposites" for his first idea: "Nonentity, nullity, nihility, non-existence, nothing, nought, void, zero, cipher, blank, empty." Roget, too, felt that a collection of synonyms could not be complete without antonyms. Though the 1805 manuscript didn't contain "opposites" for every idea, Roget would attend to this when he got around to preparing his *Thesaurus* for publication a half-century later.

Roget's method involved first coming up with a concept and then making a list of all the synonyms he could think of that related to it. Though Roget's 1805 manuscript did not include a formal classification scheme—his division of his ideas into six classes would not come for another half-century—it served his purposes. His immediate concern was not to prepare a book for publication, but to complete a private book for his own use. Having taken a concrete step toward putting language in order, Roget now felt that he could endure Manchester—no matter how much uncleanliness would come his way. With his word lists by his side, he experienced a surge of pride and confidence. He was now ready to begin his career as a scientific writer and lecturer.

It was six o'clock in the evening on January 29, 1806. After a busy day of seeing patients at the Infirmary, Roget walked back to his apartment at 7 King Street. He had about an hour before he had to rush out again, but he couldn't relax. He was gripped with terror. That night he would be giving the first of eighteen lectures on physiology to university students. Never having spoken in front of an audience before, Roget feared that he might clam up. He also kept worrying if his remarks would be clear and well organized. "And what would happen," he wondered, "if I am suddenly at a loss for words?"

For months, Roget had been dreading this day of reckoning. He had frequently written his relatives back in London about his mounting anxiety. The most supportive response came from his aunt Anne Romilly, who, in early January, had tried to reassure him. "I pity you for the nervous sensations you feel when you think on your debut," she wrote. "Yet as I have no doubt you will acquit yourself to universal satisfaction I do not feel at all anxious about it but I depend upon hearing from you as soon as you have commenced your part of the course."

Roget had done everything he could to prepare. In the fall, while he was polishing off the last few pages of his synonym book, he was also crafting a detailed syllabus for his lectures, which the Manchester firm of Nanfan and Company had published that November. In an apologetic introduction, Roget noted, "It may be sufficient to state, that the arrangement detailed in the following pages will be as much as possible adhered to in the Lectures, and, it is hoped, will facilitate to the reader the remembrance of the leading facts, as well as furnishing him with the general outlines of Anatomy and Physiology."

The course was to take place in the anatomy museum of the revered elder statesman of Manchester medicine, Charles White. Roget was to teach the physiology portion, and the surgeon Benjamin Gibson, who, like Roget, had trained with Baillie in London, would take on anatomy. A protégé of White, who called him "ingenious," Gibson had already been lecturing at the museum for years on both anatomy and the gravid uterus. Wanting to provide the students with an overview of the material—in the manner of his college adviser, Dugald Stewart—Roget had convinced Gibson to join him in cranking out the syllabus.

"At least I don't have too far to walk, and I don't have to go into a smoky part of town," Roget thought to himself as he made his way over to the museum, which Charles White maintained in his home, just a few doors away, at 19 King Street. (White's museum no longer exists. Today, a branch of Lloyds Bank stands on this site, which is commemorated by a blue plaque.)

Widely considered the "most eminent surgeon in the North of England," White was a living legend. Then in his late seventies, White still had a sharp mind. However, he had recently contracted ophthalmia and was slowly going blind. Back in 1752, seven years after Liverpool had established Britain's first hospital for the poor, White had founded the Manchester Infirmary. Long before even Ferriar had sniffed out the perils of dirt, White had begun addressing puerperal fever—then a prevalent killer of new mothers—by devising measures to sanitize maternity wards. Of his *Treatise on the Management of Pregnant and Lying-in Women*, published in 1773, a colleague once observed that "few medical books have been Productive of greater important reform in medical practice."

More recently, White had shifted his focus to natural history. In 1799, he published *An Account of the Regular Gradation in Man, and in Different Animals and Vegetables; and from the Former to the Latter*, a book based on lectures that he had given before the Literary and Philosophical Society of Manchester in 1795. (Roget had just become vice president of this learned society.) Though White was interested in classifying all of God's creatures in a systematic way, he realized that at his advanced age he wasn't up to so monumental a task.

White greeted Roget as he came into the hallway, then led him into the lecture hall, which contained hundreds of anatomical specimens. A total of eleven skeletons—lined up next to each other, from the tallest to the smallest—were dangling along the front wall. Nine were of Europeans; one was of a pigmy and one was of a monkey. A glass case along the same wall contained a variety of skulls, marked "Negro," "American Savage," "Asiatic," "European," "Roman Painter," and "Grecian Antique." Standing alone on the bottom shelf case was a jar labeled "African Penis: Multo Firmior et Durior" (much firmer and harder).

Stepping up to the podium, Roget noticed the famous grandfather clock at the back of the room—the one that would make an unforgettable impression on generations of Mancunians. Some years earlier, a grateful female patient had left White 25,000 pounds in her will, with the stipulation that he view her embalmed body once a year. To keep up his end of the bargain, White had stuffed the mummy inside an English clock-case, draping a white velvet veil over the face. Accompanied by a couple of witnesses, White would dutifully perform the annual ritual of peeking inside.

Roget quickly averted his eyes from the clock-case, preferring to look straight down at his papers on the podium. He continued staring at his syllabus while with his right hand he gently stroked his book of lists, which lay at the bottom of the pile.

Roget began with what he called some "prefatory observations." "The study of Nature," Roget stated with a sigh, "is highly interesting. So, too, is Anatomy, especially on account of its connection with Physiology. But scholars currently face a major difficulty," he added before pausing. "No, that's not quite it," he muttered to himself. He quickly riffled through his synonym book and turned to page sixty. Next to "difficulty," he saw "obstacle, embarrassment, rub, restraint, emergency, exigency, pinch, quandary, and lurch." And across the page, he spotted out of the corner of his eye, the correlative terms "facility, ease, smooth, light, easy, on velvet, and glib."

"What I am trying to say," he resumed with a sudden air of confidence in his voice, "is that until now scientists have faced a major *obstacle*. There has been no systematic arrangement of physiology. But that's what you will get in this course. I have discovered a natural order in which the field should be studied, dividing it into four classes: Mechanical Functions, Respiratory Functions, Nervous Functions, and Reproductive Functions. One could also make the case that 'peculiar functions' compose a fifth class, but I will discuss this point later.

"Tonight, I will be talking about Mechanical Functions—by which I refer to the mechanical conditions of the body such as *cellular substance*, which forms the basis of animal structure. Mechanical Functions can be divided into the following subclasses"—and he listed these five:

1. Mechanical properties of cellular texture
2. Chemical composition of cellular substance
3. Membraneous connections
4. Provisions for the defence of the body
5. Muscular action

Roget breezed through the rest of his lecture. That night, he felt he had hit his stride as a scholar.

Nearly sixty years later, when he wrote his official "autobiography"—an unpublished manuscript that was little more than an expanded version of his "List of Principal Events"—he still remembered the date: January 29, 1806. In the handful of lines devoted to his Manchester years, his remark "introductory lecture in a joint course with Mr. Gibson" figures prominently. The following year, on the same date, he began, as he also recorded, "a course of evening lectures on Animal Physiology at the rooms of the Philosophical Society." For this follow-up course, Roget, who would serve as the vice president of the Literary and Philosophical Society through the end of 1807, managed to attract a much larger audience, consisting not just of students but of fellow academics as well. Roget's teaching stint would help pave the way for the founding of the city's medical school a generation later.

I t was March 5, 1807, and Dr. Roget had a surprise announcement. "Dr. Ferriar," Roget said softly, "this is the last meeting for which I will be writing the minutes. I hereby submit my resignation as Secretary."

A hush suddenly came over the committee room of the newly built Portico Library, where twenty-one of Manchester's most literate men, drawn from the ranks of medicine, law, and business, sat in attendance. Just two months earlier, on the first anniversary of the library's governing committee, both John Ferriar, its chairman, and Roget, its secretary, had agreed to remain in their posts for another year.

Since the mid-eighteenth century, subscription libraries had been cropping up all over northern England—first in Liverpool, then in Birmingham, Warrington, and Leeds. Eager to jump on the bandwagon, in 1802, a group of four hundred Mancunians—each purchasing a subscription at a cost of thirteen guineas—hired Thomas Harrison, the architect who had built the Lyceum Newsroom and Library in Liverpool, to construct a domed neoclassical structure to house what was originally called the Manchester Library.

The major impetus for the rise of subscription libraries such as the Portico was the birth of the daily newspaper. Particularly for the residents of northern towns like Manchester, access to this new technology posed a vexing problem. The newsstand price of the new four-page broadsheets such as the *Manchester Gazette* (the *Guardian* was not founded until 1821) was typically a hefty sixpence—roughly $20 today. But Mancunians also craved the latest news from the capital, and by the early 1800s, London put out not just *The Times*, established in 1785, but also more than fifty other daily papers. The additional shipping cost could also be astronomical, given that stagecoach travel from London to Manchester often took as long as forty hours. Subscription libraries provided a solution, as the city's professionals could now share the considerable expense of staying informed.

One of Roget's first official duties as secretary was to order sixteen London newspapers, as well as numerous periodicals, including *Cobbett's Political Register* and *Votes of the House of Commons*. He then faced the unenviable task of trying to order the London newspapers on more affordable terms. His charge: to keep the cost at under one shilling for delivery by the evening after publication. For the better part of 1806, Roget tried to negotiate with the papers and the coach lines. Finally he threw up his hands in defeat. On January 5, 1807, Roget reported to his fellow committee members:

> Repeated endeavors have been made to procure by the Coaches the London morning papers on the evening after their publication. But the scheme was found to be impracticable on account of the great *irregularity* in the time of their delivery: and the charges made for carriage were such as far exceeded the limits within which the Committee thought it their duty to confine themselves. [Emphasis mine.]

In his synonym book, Roget had placed "irregularity" next to its opposite, "order"; it was something for which he had little patience.

Roget also had another reason to feel irked: the state of the library. As secretary, Roget had initially been in charge of ordering books. And over the first few months of 1806 he had not been shy about requesting those volumes that most inspired him, books such as John Horne Tooke's *Diversions of Purley*, Dugald Stewart's *Biographical Works*, and such reference works as *Dictionnaire raisonné de bibliogie* and *Dictionnaire d'histoire naturelle*. But on May 15, 1806, the Portico hired a librarian named James Watson, at an annual salary of forty-two pounds. A well-known local bibliophile, Watson went by the honorific "the Doctor," in acknowledgement of his wide reading.

Roget was not troubled that he had to cede control over the ordering of books to "the Doctor." But he questioned the Doctor's fitness for producing a library catalogue. As Roget well understood, this challenge, which Watson was given just a couple of months after his appointment, involved organizing the library's books. And to come up with a classification system from scratch—there was as yet no universally recognized tool such as the Dewey decimal system—required a bona fide scientific background. That February, Roget got a glimpse of the catalogue as it was about to be printed and he was aghast at its lack of a sound organizing principle. Watson, Roget was convinced, had never bothered to read Wilkins and didn't know the first thing about classification.

With the eyes of his fellow committee members turned toward him, Roget explained that "Unfortunately, my other avocations do not leave me sufficient leisure to attend to the duties of Secretary." In an effort to make a diplomatic exit, Roget offered this white lie. In truth, Roget was so consumed by his career that he devoted little time to any pleasurable diversions; the word "avocation" is not to be found either in his 1805 draft or in the 1852 first edition of his *Thesaurus*. He even approached one of his favorite pastimes, chess, as if

it were an academic discipline (decades later, he published the celebrated theoretical paper "Description of Moving the Knight over
Every Square of a Chess-Board Without Going Twice over Any One"
in a philosophical journal). On that late winter day, Roget felt that if
he had to stand back and put up with Watson's assault on classification, he would be better off directing his energy elsewhere.

After making his announcement, Roget was concerned that his
colleagues would be disappointed, perhaps even angry. But after a
moment's silence, Lieutenant Colonel John Leigh Philips, a cousin
of Roget's patron, John Philips, rose and said, "I move the thanks of
the Committee be given to Dr. Roget for the very essential services
he has uniformerly [sic] rendered to this Institution, and that a copy
of this resolution signed by the Chairman be transmitted to the
Doctor." Roget looked over at the lieutenant colonel, and the two
men smiled at one another.

Since his arrival in Manchester, Roget and the former military
man (in 1777, at the age of sixteen, Philips had been commissioned
in Manchester's famous 72nd Corps of Volunteers) had formed a
strong bond. Owner of a silk and cotton manufacturing firm, Philips
was also an amateur scientist. He was a founding member of the Literary and Philosophical Society, and had presented academic papers
on such arcane subjects as the "The Uses of Insects." Philips also
achieved renown as one of the city's most symptomatic bibliomani-
acs. After his death, a decade later, his heirs needed a full nineteen
days to dispose of all the volumes in his library; the sale would rake
in proceeds of nearly 6,000 pounds. The elder Philips and Roget
spent long hours talking about classification. As dictated by his will,
John Leigh Philips's extensive collection of plants and animals would
form the basis of the city's first Natural History Museum.

After Roget resigned as secretary, he still remained on the Portico's committee until he moved out of town a year and a half later. A month after Roget's announcement, James Watson also assumed the position of secretary, for which he was paid an extra ten pounds a year. But beset by chronic alcoholism, "the Doctor" failed to carry out his various duties conscientiously; he would resign in disgrace from the Portico three years later. By then, Roget was busily engaged in classifying and arranging the vast library of the Medical and Chirurgical Society of London.

While Roget was languishing in Manchester, Samuel Romilly's legal and political career was taking flight. His annual income was growing exponentially—it would eventually reach some 17,000 pounds—as he was taking on many high-profile clients, such as Maria Anne Fitzherbert, a lover of the Prince of Wales (who continued to live with her after King George III annulled their 1785 marriage). In 1805, as Romilly made the move from Gower Street, then populated almost exclusively by barristers, to more commodious quarters on Russell Square, the prince himself offered Romilly a seat in Parliament. Seeking to preserve his independence, Romilly turned down the future monarch (the prince would become King George IV in 1820). However, in 1806, when the Whigs came to power under Lord Grenville, Romilly was appointed solicitor general and entered the House of Commons as an MP from Queensborough. That same year, he was also knighted.

Romilly was also busy raising a family—the last of his seven children, Frederick would be born in 1810—and so he had precious little time to write to Roget. But he kept trying to rescue his favorite nephew from the filthy byways of Manchester. In February 1808, his wife, Anne, wrote Roget:

> Your uncle and I have very frequently been conversing about you lately and lamenting that your time and talent should be so thrown away . . . in Manchester. . . . Your uncle has always wished you to settle in London and upon the 18th of last month [Roget's twenty-ninth birthday] when we drank to your health he could not forbear how time had slipped and thought at your age the trial was to be made.

That fall, Romilly took the matter one step further. He would use his considerable resources to help Roget set himself up in London. He lent Roget 1,500 pounds to buy a house and also provided him with some temporary employment—hiring him as a private tutor to his oldest son, William, then nine.

On October 30, 1808, Roget, though he had not yet obtained a new medical post, bid adieu to Manchester. During his four years in the city's Infirmary, he had succeeded in turning his personal obsession for order into his professional obsession. Having found a way to meet his existential needs for comfort and security through his intellectual labor, Roget was ready to move to the big stage—London. Now that he had organized the world, he could finally conquer it.

PART TWO

Bloomsbury Doctor, Inventor, and Scientist

(1809–1848)

(492) SCHOLAR, savant, pundit, schoolman, graduate, doctor, gownsman, philosopher, philomath, clerk.

Linguist, literati, dilettanti, illuminati.

Pedant, pedagogue, bookworm, bibliomaniac, blue-stocking, bas-bleu, bigwig.

6.

The Best-Looking and Most Gentlemanly Bachelor in England

(904) UNLAWFUL MARRIAGE: a left-handed marriage; misalliance.

    CELIBACY, singleness, misogamy, single blessedness.

    An unmarried man, bachelor, agamist, misogamist.

On January 12, 1809—on the eve of his thirtieth birthday—Roget moved out of his temporary London apartment into his new Bloomsbury townhouse at 39 Bernard Street. The plan that Romilly had orchestrated, which he referred to as "the Experiment," also involved Catherine and Annette—he asked them to try residing in London for three years. Overcoming their aversion to city life, Roget's mother and sister agreed to move back to London. For the first time since Edinburgh, the Rogets were living together as a family. As it turned out, Catherine and Annette lasted about a decade in the nation's capital. Roget himself would remain a Bloomsbury fixture until his death some sixty years later—though he would relocate his home and office to the slightly more upscale 18 Upper Bedford Place, now Bedford Way, in 1843. Perhaps to compensate for a childhood marked by frequent moves, as an adult Roget stayed put.

Like many London residences of the era, 39 Bernard Street contained four stories, each with a front and back room, and one floor below ground, consisting of the kitchen. With plenty of space to house servants, Roget immediately hired a cook and maid. Centrally located, Roget's perch was within walking distance of the cornerstones of English cultural and intellectual life: the British Museum, where he would spend many a day toiling away in its illustrious Reading Room, the Medical and Chirurgical Society, and the University of London, founded two decades after Roget's move to town.

In its outward appearance, London hadn't changed much since Roget was an adolescent boarder in Chauvet's Kensington rooming house. The war with Napoleon had put a freeze on all new construction, except for the Bank of England, erected on Threadneedle Street. With few office buildings to speak of, the coffeehouse—for example, the Stock Exchange Coffee House, adjacent to the new central bank— remained the primary locus of business. London was still bounded by Marylebone Road to the north, Hyde Park to the west, the Thames to the south, and City Road to the east. However, its population continued to expand rapidly. During the first decade of the 1800s, it added more than 100,000 new residents, becoming the first city in the world to reach the million mark in 1811.

But once Napoleon was exiled to Elba in 1815, London would undergo a face-lift, largely engineered by the architect John Nash. He was the Prince Regent's favorite architect and had designed Regent's Park, St. James's Park, Trafalgar Square, and Buckingham Palace. A close friend of Romilly's, Nash often invited Sir Samuel and his wife to stay at his country home on the Isle of Wight. The building boom also extended to churches, which began sprouting up in the wake of the Church Building Act of 1818. Among the nearly fifty new churches, which the government got for the million pounds it allocated under this law, was the Church of St. Pancras on the corner connecting Euston Road and Upper Woburn Place—designed by architect William Inwood and his son in 1822 at the cost of 82,000 pounds. Built during the phase of English architecture known as the Greek Revival—its west galleries were propped up by columns copied from the Elgin Marbles—the new St. Pancras was consecrated by William Howley, the bishop of London, in May 1822. Roget would regularly attend services at what one critic has called "the parish church, par excellence of Regency England" for the rest of his life.

While Roget saw nothing unfamiliar in the face of London, since his childhood the city had been busy refashioning itself into the world's most imposing and dynamic city. As Roget was settling into his Bernard Street townhouse, Georgian London had already given way to Regency London, though the oldest son of King George III wouldn't be officially installed as the prince regent until February 1811. "Prinnie," as the head of state was affectionately known, was a colorful character, a gourmand who enjoyed both dancing late into the night and engaging in amorous adventures. In 1809, he was married to Princess Caroline, still involved with Maria Anne Fitzherbert, and seeing at least one other woman—the courtesan Frances Villiers—on the side. In contrast to most of the other members of the House of Hanover, the Prince Regent—with his bright blue eyes and "shapely legs"—also had charm and style. His official residence was Carlton House in Pall Mall, which he arranged to have redesigned at considerable expense to taxpayers.

Regency London was to mirror the personality of its leader. Gluttony and gambling were in; so, too, were bed-hopping and decadence. The Prince Regent's sidekick, the dandy George Bryan ("Beau") Brummel, likewise embodied the era's flamboyance. Brummel, a fashion trendsetter, rejected the extravagance of the typical eighteenth-century outfit in favor of an elegant simplicity—though he himself could require as long as five hours to dress. He preferred trousers to buckskin breeches and cloth overcoats to long-tailed ones. (The present-day uniform of the Western male professional—the coat and necktie—traces its provenance to Brummel.) While his sartorial manner was understated, his taste was more than a little bit outrageous. Brummel polished his riding boots with champagne. When once asked for the name of his barber, Brummel could not supply a direct response as he had three—one for his temples, one for the front of his head, and one for the back.

The Regency also produced a flurry of new artistic activity—the flowering of English Romanticism. In the visual arts, the painters J. M. W. Turner and John Constable, not to mention the visionary artist William Blake, Roget's former Soho neighbor, were all toiling on their best works. In literature, poets such as Lord Byron and John Keats were coming into their own. In 1817, Keats would give up his medical career—he had been training to be a surgeon at Guy's Hospital, where he attended lectures given by Roget's best friend, Dr. Alexander Marcet—to focus full-time on his poetry. That was the same year that Jane Austen, one of the Prince Regent's favorite authors, died. Austen had dedicated *Emma*, her last novel published before her death, to His Royal Highness. Yet the creations of these immortal artists—by 1819, *Emma* had sold only about five hundred copies—didn't necessarily have as much of an impact on Roget's contemporaries as on posterity.

Roget's response to the lively cultural milieu of the Regency was the same one he took toward whatever environment he found himself in—say, the deprivation of his childhood world, or the smokiness of Manchester—he sealed himself off from it. He continued to ignore the developments in his immediate surroundings, preferring to live as much as possible inside his own mind. A product of the Enlightenment, he would forever be immersed in his quest to amass and organize scientific knowledge. In the early nineteenth century, academic disciplines were much less specialized than today, and Roget kept up with the latest scientific findings in everything from anatomy to zoology. Though Roget had little interest in the latest in literature, art, or fashion, he was an avid theatergoer. The high cost of tickets—six shillings (the modern equivalent would be about $100) for seats in the boxes—didn't prevent the frugal Roget from seeing occasional performances by the legendary actors John Kemble and Edmund Kean at Drury Lane and Covent Garden. However, he tended to prefer outings to the less expensive French theater.

Despite his seriousness, Roget was no prig. He enjoyed going to parties and dances. A lively conversationalist, he could also be entertaining and amusing. In 1822, a young Scottish surgeon, James Colquhoun, who was then trying to woo the Bloomsbury denizen Jane Griffin, was simply bowled over by Roget. As Griffin, whose own romance with Roget had by then fizzled out, wrote in her diary of the impression her former love interest made on Colquhoun:

> Dr. Roget . . . held the highest place in his opinion, and he even affirmed him to be by far the handsomest man in the room and the most gentlemanly-looking. . . . He thinks him and Lord Aberdeen

whom he saw at the Royal Society the best-looking men he has
seen in England. Dr. R . . . is so gentlemanly and has such a fine
head.

During Roget's extended bachelorhood, which would last until 1824,
he would also create quite a stir among the ladies—particularly Jane
Griffin, who spent a few years trying to win him. Though he shied

*Of this lithographed engraving, Roget, pictured at age sixty, wrote,
"Most of my friends think it a good likeness."*

away from casual sex, which was more common during the fun-loving
Regency than during the subsequent Victorian period, Roget would
have a long string of romantic entanglements.

One factor behind Roget's decision to delay marriage until age
forty-five was the typically precarious economic situation of neophyte
doctors. In contrast to other professionals, doctors almost never married before their early thirties because of the considerable time it took
to establish a client base. For example, upon informing Jane Griffin—
then already north of thirty—of his affection in 1822, Colquhoun
thought nothing of asking her to wait another five or ten years for a
marriage proposal, by which time he expected to have acquired the
requisite wealth. Though Roget was thirty when he moved to Bernard
Street, he was essentially starting over from scratch. To supplement
his meager income, Roget would still require subsidies from Romilly
for nearly a decade.

In the spring of 1809, Roget began to lay down the foundation for
his medical career. In March, he had received his license from the
Royal College of Physicians, the governing body first established by
the crown in the sixteenth century. Roget whizzed through the licensing exam, which at the time was still entirely in Latin. On May 1,
he began a series of twelve lectures on animal physiology at the Russell Institution, a newly formed subscription library. Roget didn't
have to prepare much, as he could recycle the talks that he had given
in Manchester. Lecturing was then often a major source of revenue
for doctors. Roget's Monday-afternoon lecture series—as mentioned
in the advertisement that ran in *The Times* of London on April 24,
1809—was open to the general public at a cost of one guinea.

With Roget unable to find a medical appointment in London,
Romilly created one especially for him. In the middle of 1809, Romilly

helped to found the Northern Dispensary, a free clinic that served the indigent in several sections of London, including St. Pancras and Camden. The clinic opened its doors on February 13, 1810. Romilly headed the committee that ran it, which also included a couple other MPs. The project was funded by some 120 backers, all of whom paid a guinea for an annual subscription. Roget worked there as a senior physician along with Dr. Charles Wittell and a surgeon, Mr. John Want. Though Roget received no salary, this position allowed him to make many important contacts in the medical community.

Roget's first scientific paper, published in 1811, concerned his treatment of a young woman suffering from arsenic poisoning, whom he had first seen at this clinic. Heartbroken by the end of a love affair, the nineteen-year-old woman had eaten a piece of bread sprinkled with arsenic. As Roget reported in his detached clinical prose, he carefully monitored her for a few weeks as she struggled with troubling symptoms, such as convulsions, burning sensations, insomnia, and headaches. His scholarly contribution involved his development of a new laboratory test to detect the presence of arsenic in the bloodstream. He would continue to see indigent patients at the clinic until 1825. Upon his resignation, the governors of the Northern Dispensary presented him with a silver plate—valued at 110 pounds, as he made sure to note in his autobiography—for "his able, humane and gratuitous services as a Physician."

In the spring of 1810, Roget repeated his course of lectures at the Russell Institution. That fall, he also began teaching at the Great Windmill School of Surgery. Two years later, he picked up a class at the Royal Institution, joining his former boss in Bristol, Humphry Davy, who had already been teaching chemistry there for more than a decade. On June 1, 1812, Roget obtained his own appointment at the Royal Institution as a professor of comparative anatomy. These affiliations further increased Roget's visibility, so that by 1813, as he noted in his autobiography, his "practice [was] beginning to be more considerable."

Upon his move to London, Roget also became active in the Medical and Chirurgical Society of London. Cofounded in 1805 by Marcet, this democratically run group—originally composed of "26 secessionists" from the Medical Society of London who were angry with its leader, Dr. James Sims, for his autocratic rule—was formed for "the purpose of conversation on professional subjects, for the reception of communications and for the formation of a library." Annoyed by Sims's twenty-year reign, the members of this splinter group, which excluded apothecaries, decided to limit its president to a two-year term. In 1810, the Medical and Chirurgical Society established its headquarters at 3 Lincoln's Inn Fields, and Roget began marshaling the effort to catalogue the books in its new library. A year later, Roget became the Society's secretary, a position he would hold for sixteen years. He also began serving as an editor of its journal (where his paper on arsenic poisoning was published). Through his active participation, which eventually included a stint as president from 1829 to 1831, Roget came into frequent contact with many prominent London doctors, including his mentors, the surgeons Matthew Baillie and John Abernethy, who served as trustees.

But Roget's transition into the London medical scene was far from smooth. He faced constant anxiety about the arc of his career. He frequently suffered from fevers—a brutal one in March 1811 sidelined him for nearly six weeks. On July 28, 1811, feeling besieged by both another fever and debilitating neck pain—a condition that kept recurring—he wrote Marcet of his woes:

> I presume the world is turning around just as usual; yet to me, who
> have been out of it for some time, it appears to be standing still,

and that I have myself been moving backwards. . . . You will always find me at home and your conversation will be a great pleasure.

Throughout his first several years in London, to ensure that he could get a good night's sleep, Roget, like many of his contemporaries, would resort to taking opium.

D r. Roget, I'm so glad to see you," gushed the petite poetess. "I am delighted to be here," responded Roget, beaming.

It was Thursday, March 12, 1812, and Roget had made his way over to the house of the architect William Porden at 58 Berners Street in the St. Marylebone Parish of London. The Porden residence was just a few blocks north of Roget's first home in Soho and a few blocks south of the apartment on Great Titchfield Street where he had lived after finishing medical school. Roget was attending a meeting of the Attic Chest Society, a literary club whose members discussed the issues of the day as well as their own poetic creations. This was a rare evening meeting, as the group usually gathered on Sunday afternoons after church.

The poetess with the dainty figure who greeted Roget at the door was the architect's daughter, Eleanor. With her dimpled arms and bright eyes, combined with an infectious optimism and joie-de-vivre, she made quite an impression. Though Eleanor was just seventeen, she already possessed a degree of erudition and wisdom few could match, not even the many distinguished artists and scholars who had already fallen in love with her. In addition to making her own clothes and canning preserves, she also had a reputation for dancing quadrilles in a style then termed *con amore*. There seemed to be hardly anything that Eleanor Anne Porden couldn't do.

She also ran the lively meetings of the Attic Chest Society. Ever since she had begun caring for her invalid mother in 1809, Eleanor had been firmly established as the mistress of the house. Her father, William, harbored literary aspirations, though architecture was where he had made his mark. A few years earlier, Porden had designed the riding house at the Royal Pavilion in Brighton—one of the few new constructions to emerge in England during the Napoleonic War. Greatly influenced by the French, he looked down upon English architecture. "It's always ding dong in my ears in Paris, we have a serious want of porticos and columns," he would often say.

Well connected in the artistic community, William Porden had reached out to his impressive array of colleagues to help launch his daughter's literary society. Among the guests in his drawing room that evening were the sculptor John Flaxman, recently appointed the first professor of sculpture at the Royal Academy, who lived just a few blocks away in Buckingham Street. Flaxman brought his sister, Maria, also a sculptor. Thomas Phillips, a fellow of the Royal Academy of Arts, was there along with his wife, already nestled in a ladies' easy chair. It was to Phillips, then London's foremost portrait painter, to whom the city's most prominent intellectuals and political leaders—Blake, Byron, the Duke of Wellington, and the Prince Regent himself—would invariably turn. Likewise, the writer and lawyer Henry Crabb Robinson—just back from Spain, where he had done a stint as the world's first war correspondent for *The Times*—was ensconced in a horsehair armchair in a corner.

William Porden had devoted considerable time to educating Eleanor, and he was proud of his daughter's many accomplishments, including her solid grounding in Greek and Latin, her growing poetic oeuvre, and her broad learning in science. But her father alone wasn't responsible for all of her erudition. Ever since the age of nine,

Eleanor had attended lectures at the Royal Institution, where she had feasted on the offerings of Britain's most illustrious scientific minds, among them Humphry Davy and Roget, who had begun lecturing on natural history a few months earlier. Eleanor would later write that she considered herself "a pupil of the Royal Institution."

All eyes were on her as she began to speak.

Just then, one more visitor—a bald and toothless octogenarian—limped into the room. Though William Franklin was frail and battling a chronic heart condition as well as gout (an illness that had also plagued his father, Benjamin Franklin), he was still a commanding presence.

He wasn't really a military man, but everyone still called him "the General" (he had attained the rank of brigadier general for his service to the crown). Conceived out of wedlock, the only son of Benjamin Franklin had served as the last Royal Governor of New Jersey back in the 1760s. He ended up siding with the Loyalist cause, a decision that estranged him from his legendary father. In London, however, he was still seen as a man of honor.

Introductions were made all around. Roget, who had never met Franklin, walked up to him and said, "Your father made quite an impression on my uncle, Sir Samuel Romilly, when they met in Paris in 1783. And my natural philosophy professor in Edinburgh kept emphasizing how much we owe to Dr. Franklin for his many contributions to the field of electricity. That's one of my major interests. I would like to write a book about it one day."

"And of course, you know," Franklin responded, "I was my father's only companion on the day he performed the famous experiment with his kite. I was then twenty-one."

Roget's jaw dropped.

"And I'm sure you don't know," added Franklin, "that I was much more involved in 'bringing lightning from the heavens' than most people—probably even your professor—ever realized. I also helped my father with the preparations and then conducted numerous mathematical calculations to support our theories. In truth, I was his scientific collaborator."

Eleanor Porden then retook the floor, and all returned to their seats. "After Dr. Roget's lecture last week, I invited him to join us because I am writing a poem which is based on some of the material in his course. Just as Erasmus Darwin in *The Botanic Garden* put Linnaeus's *Systema Naturae* into verse, I want to do the same for the work of some of today's leading scientists. Inspired by Alexander Pope's *The Rape of the Lock*, my poem is entitled *The Veils; or the Triumph of Constancy*."

She continued: "One day not long ago while I was gathering shells on the coast of Norfolk, a gust of wind blew the veil off my head. That incident inspired me to write the story of three beautiful ladies who have lost their veils. The search brings these ladies to the far reaches of the universe—to the center of the earth, to the bottom of the sea, and to the boiling streams of the volcano on the Aeolian Island of Stromboli. I'm now working on the fourth section, called 'The Sea.' At his lecture last week, here's how Dr. Roget described how fish survive on the contents of the seawater:

> Many of the larger tribes of fishes feed on the smaller kinds and are exceedingly voracious, but most fishes appear to derive their subsistence from the element which surrounds them. . . . Did the majority of fishes require any other food than what is afforded by the water which surrounds them, where would the immense multitudes which inhabit the ocean find provision?

"And the corresponding lines in my poem are as follows:

> Like swallows marshall'd for their annual flight,
> The smaller tribes in countless shoals unite,
> Still as they roam, inhale the briny flood,
> At once their liquid atmosphere and food."

Roget smiled at Eleanor, who, he felt, had captured exactly what he was trying to say. "Now that my efforts to classify the animal world are wrapped up in your immortal verse," he told her, "perhaps I, too, shall not be soon forgotten."

Most contemporary literary critics agreed with Roget's assessment of both Eleanor's extraordinary grasp of science and her poetic gifts. "Miss Porden," declared *Gentleman's Magazine* in a glowing review of *The Veils*, published in 1816, "with half the scientific knowledge which pervades the whole of her Poem, would still be entitled to our most unfeigned admiration." Her book won a special prize from the Institute of France, a rare distinction for a work of British literature.

The man was arrogant, and he rarely admitted his errors. That's why his scientific colleagues called him "the Pope." His name was William Hyde Wollaston, and on the evening of November 17, 1814, he would help usher Roget into the inner sanctum of British science. The bald Wollaston—just a few strands of curly white hair encircled each of his ears—was then nearing the end of what would be a dozen-year tenure as the secretary of the Royal Society. It fell to him to read before that hallowed body Roget's mathematical paper on the slide rule.

Wollaston was then a close colleague of both Roget and Marcet, as he, too, was affiliated with the Medical and Chirurgical Society. It was to Wollaston that Marcet would later dedicate his own magnum opus—his book on urinary calculi.

Roget could see much of himself in his scientific elder. Trained in medicine at Cambridge, Wollaston had shut down his clinical practice in 1800. One reason may have been that he never managed to get a hoped-for appointment at St. George's Hospital. In addition, treating patients tended to make him anxious because he overidentified with their distress: their suffering became his suffering. Conducting research out of his private laboratory at 14 Buckingham Street, Wollaston had made a series of pioneering discoveries in chemistry, optics, and physiology that earned him the Royal Society's prestigious Copley Medal in 1802. By 1814, Wollaston had also become wealthy by discovering a malleable form of platinum, which he sold to gun manufacturers.

Wollaston had more than a passing interest in Roget's efforts to fine-tune the slide rule. A year earlier, Wollaston had devised a chemical slide-rule, which enabled scientists to compute complex equations involving chemical proportions. Wollaston figured that Roget's discoveries might help him refine his own invention, which was about to make its mark. A decade later, Britain's premier chemist, Michael Faraday, who in 1814 was still working as Humphry Davy's assistant at the Royal Institution, would refer to Wollaston's chemical slide-rule as a common tool.

Though his vision was starting to go, Wollaston could still make out Roget's words—carefully crafted with the help of his "secret treasure trove"—in order to address the esteemed scientists gathered at the Royal Society's headquarters in Somerset House. Their charge that night was to render judgment on whether to offer Roget admission as a fellow. Located next to Covent Garden, near the banks of the Thames, the building stood on the site of a sixteenth-century palace initiated by Protector Somerset. The meeting room featured

Somerset House was home to the Royal Society from 1780 to 1857.

a high ceiling with elaborate gold chandeliers and walls festooned with portraits of past Society presidents, including Bishop Wilkins, Samuel Pepys, Isaac Newton, and Hans Sloane. Behind the president's table, upon which was placed the mace, sat botanist Joseph Banks, who had by then held the top spot for nearly four decades.

Roget's paper was titled "Description of a New Instrument for Performing Mechanically the Involution and Evolution of Numbers." (In this context, "involution" refers to multiplication, and "evolution" to taking the root of. In the 1852 edition of the *Thesaurus*, Roget put these two mathematical terms next to one another under "Numeration," 85.) Roget, as Wollaston communicated to the attentive Royal Society fellows who surrounded him, was interested in making the slide rule more useful: "The machine invented by Pascal, and others constructed on the same principle, were, strictly speaking, limited to the simpler operations of addition and subtraction." Providing a brief history of the slide rule, Roget's paper explained how the scale developed by the seventeenth-century astronomer Edmund Gunter, which was based on logarithms, made it possible to multiply and divide large numbers. Roget sought to build on other recent attempts to broaden its use, and Wollaston was soon speaking of himself in the third person:

> The instrument has been variously modified with a view of enlarging its scale. . . . The Society has recently witnessed its successful application by Dr. WOLLASTON, to another science, in his synoptic scale of chemical equivalents, for the invention of which every practical as well as philosophical chemist must acknowledge to him their deep obligation.

What Wollaston unveiled to the world that November night was Roget's new scale—also based on logarithms—that could ascertain the powers and roots of numbers. What Roget had invented was the log-log scale, the centerpiece of the modern slide rule, which remained in wide use until the rise of the pocket calculator in the 1970s.

Based on the enthusiastic reaction to this paper, Roget was elected as a Fellow of the Royal Society on March 16, 1815. That same year, his slide-rule paper would be published in the Royal Society's house organ, *Philosophical Transactions*.

Roughly a decade later, the London engraver John Rooker would mass-produce Roget's "New Sliding Rule of Involution." Roget gave Rooker's invention his full endorsement, noting he was "quite satisfied with its correctness."

· · ·

The suicide of Sir Samuel Romilly on November 2, 1818, was not just a tragedy for Roget and his family. All of England was reeling from shock and despair. In the words of one periodical:

> Since the day when the public was made acquainted with the fall of the immortal [Horatio] Nelson, we do not recollect one, in which the mourning was so deep and universal as on the death of Sir Samuel Romilly; and never was there an occasion when there was a more general expression of profound sorrow in all ranks of the people.

Upon reading a newspaper account of Romilly's suicide at breakfast on the following day, November 3, one man, later identified only as "Mr. Elliott," suddenly grabbed a razor and ended his own life, too. Romilly was widely eulogzied as a man of uncommon virtue, as well as a model husband and father. For example, one obituary put it, "To such a distinguished citizen, Rome would have erected altars, Greece statues." Romilly's death also made news in France. In a memorial service held at the Royal Athenaeum in Paris at the end of 1818, Benjamin Constant—he had stopped pining for Madame de Staël years earlier, as she had married a young Swiss officer in 1811—had eulogized him as "an illustrious foreigner who belongs to all nations because he . . . [has] defended the cause of humanity, of Liberty and of Justice." Talk of Romilly faded from the news after a few months, but Roget was shaken for years and his mother was never the same.

Perhaps the only Englishman left unfazed was the poet Lord Byron, who had long been enraged with Romilly for helping his wife, Annabella, secure her separation agreement in 1816. That November, Byron wrote a mean-spirited letter to Lady Byron in which he accused Romilly of "poisoning my life at its sources. . . . Perhaps, previous to his annihilation, he felt a portion of what he contributed his legal mite to make me feel; but I have lived—lived to see him a Sexagenary Suicide." Bryon also later poeticized his feelings in his legendary autobiographical poem *Don Juan*:

> *Like the lamented late Sir Samuel Romilly,*
> *The Law's expounder, and the State's corrector,*
> *Whose suicide was almost an anomaly—*
> *One sad example more, that "All is vanity"*
> *(The jury brought their verdict in "Insanity").*

Since the jury convened by the coroner reached this verdict—and not *felo-de-se* (premeditated suicide)—the family did not have to forfeit his estate to the crown. Romilly received a proper burial at a private family service, on November 11, in Herefordshire, where his late wife had grown up. Roget had been too agitated to attend.

The next few years were perhaps the most trying period in Roget's life. Just two weeks after Romilly's suicide—while Roget was still sequestered in his crepe-lined bedroom—Alexander Marcet, who had provided so much support in the days immediately following the tragedy, left London. Having recently inherited half a million pounds from his father-in-law, Marcet decided to resign from Guy's Hospital. Giving up his clinical responsibilities, Marcet wanted to return to his native Geneva to conduct research. On November 18, he wrote Roget:

> It is with great regret that I quit England without bidding you adieu. . . . I hope that you are far advanced in your recovery. . . . I

have taken the liberty, my dear Sir, of desiring a French clock which has long been used in our family to be sent to you, hoping it may sometimes remind you of those whom you have so kindly and carefully attended.

Roget felt completely abandoned. As he wrote Dumont the following summer: "[Marcet's] departure gives me a lot of grief; and makes me experience a feeling of sadness, which associates itself too much with what I have already felt by the loss of so many friends. . . ." Roget was here also indirectly alluding to Romilly's suicide, an event so traumatic that he rarely spoke of it directly.

Roget and Marcet did manage to keep their friendship alive through frequent letters. From Switzerland, Marcet did what he could for his beleaguered friend. He recommended Roget to all his former patients and also helped him land a valuable medical post: in 1820, Roget replaced Marcet as physician to the Spanish Embassy, a lucrative sinecure. Partly to repay these many kindnesses, Roget provided some valuable assistance to Alexander's wife, Jane—then a highly successful author of popular books on academic subjects. Her first book, *Conversations on Chemistry*, completed in 1805, would eventually sell hundreds of thousands of copies. In 1820, Roget worked directly with Longmans, helping to prepare the second edition of her second book, *Conversations on Political Economy* (first published in 1816).

For the most part, however, Roget's career was floundering. In March 1821, he confided to Alexander Marcet: "I think I hear you asking me how I go on professionally—I should answer tolerably. I do not feel that I am advancing; nor perhaps am I receding; unless in as far as that a physician who is not advancing is in fact receding when compared with his contemporaries in the stream." Often feeling depressed and listless, Roget frequently complained to Marcet about how "dull" London was without him. Though by the spring of 1822, Roget was starting to feel like himself again. That spring, he was buoyed by the warm reception of his new course of lectures at the Royal Institution, which, as he observed in late March, "have succeeded beyond my wildest expectations." But his energy level was still low a few months later when he wrote Marcet:

> I have formed no plan whatever with regard to what I shall do the rest of the summer and autumn. I am, indeed, grown rather weary of forming projects, having become less sanguine as to the power of realizing them: and intend, therefore, to trust to the chapter of accidents for what may present itself. . . .

At times, Roget felt like giving up; he couldn't even count on his favorite refuge—his scientific work—to dull his feelings of anxiety and despair.

While Roget would eventually make a complete recovery, not so his mother. For months after Romilly's suicide, Catherine was nearly paralyzed with grief. In the summer of 1819, Roget wrote to Dumont:

> Time has softened the bitterness of the unhappiness that shook us. But it has proved more devastating to my mother than to my sister and me. When the loss of fortune joins itself to that of those one loves, the weight of the blow is doubled. . . . The idea of having been forgotten about in her old age is that which has had the biggest effect on her.

Then in her mid-sixties, Catherine soon lapsed into madness. Spending much of her time in Ilfracombe with Annette, she became increasingly incoherent and paranoid. By August 1823, five years after Romilly's death, Roget noted in his autobiography that "my poor mother's faculties [have] rapidly declined." Catherine Roget was to remain trapped in a psychotic trance for the rest of her life. Roget and his sister considered sending her to an asylum, but they eventually decided against it. In the end, Annette, who never married, assumed the draining task of caring for Catherine in Ilfracombe, where they settled in 1824. Catherine would often wander the streets aimlessly until her death, in 1835. To Roget's cousin, Joseph Romilly, a son of Catherine's older brother, Thomas, she was a real-life version of that staple of nineteenth-century British fiction—the "crazy aunt." In July 1830, while returning to Cambridge—where he was a dean at Trinity College—from a trip to Wales, Romilly tried to look in on her, but to no avail. "After dinner," he recorded in his diary, "dressed and hunted in vain for Aunt Roget, who certainly lives at Ilfracombe."

The strain of coping with Catherine's madness exacerbated Annette's own chronic unhappiness. Ever since being dumped by Mr. Lock in her early twenties, Annette had waged a constant battle with depression. Her abject despair often made her feel like putting an end to her life. To her brother she confided:

> If only the future could present anything agreeable to me, but since there is nothing ahead but misery, I often hope that the sore foot I have would be fatal. The picture that I have in front of me— to live always, for the rest of my miserable life, in furnished apartments in this place worries me so much that I lose all appetite and all repose.

She would remain in Ilfracombe, though she often spent the winter with Roget in London, until her own death in 1866.

In the fall of 1822, just as Roget was starting to get back on his feet, tragedy struck again: another beloved soul mate died unexpectedly in his arms. This time it was Marcet, whose friendship he once called "the biggest blessing of my life."

Early in the morning of October 11, Marcet, who was visiting his brother-in-law at Westcombe Park, near Greenwich, was stricken by a gripping pain in his chest. Rushing from London, Roget gave Marcet some brandy and laudanum, and the pain soon dissipated. But Marcet couldn't shake the fever and weakness that had overcome him. Roget stayed in Westcombe Park for the next several days; he then accompanied Marcet back to his temporary lodgings in Great Coram Street, right near his own Bernard Street home.

On Saturday afternoon, October 19, Marcet, having just got out of bed, collapsed. Jane Marcet called for Roget, but five minutes after Roget came in, Marcet's pulse had stopped. He was gone.

Roget was deeply shaken. In early November, he came down with an inflammation of the cornea that got steadily worse. For most of that month, he stayed in bed to recuperate.

Though Roget was roughly a decade younger than the fifty-two-year-old Marcet, he began to feel that what had happened to his friend might happen to him at any moment. He developed a new appreciation for the fragility of life. In a biographical tribute to Marcet, published the following year, Roget wrote: "He had before him the prospect of a long career of happiness to himself and of usefulness to his friends and country. The sudden dissolution of all these prospects furnished an impressive lesson of the precarious tenure by which we hold every human good." In the years surrounding the deaths of Romilly and Marcet, Roget was to find little comfort.

· · ·

Ahandsome bachelor making his way up the medical ladder, Roget was attracting quite a bit of attention from eligible women. Roget was the only man who made Jane Griffin swoon, and for years she kept strategizing about how to elicit a marriage proposal from the man she deemed "superior to most men." For a while Roget may also have been smitten, but in contrast to the voluble Griffin, he never revealed much, either to his contemporaries or to posterity.

Roget and Griffin seemed to be made for each other. Like the man of her dreams, Jane Griffin also came from pure Huguenot stock. Born in 1791, Jane had been baptized by the French Episcopal pastor at Le Quarré in Soho who had succeeded Roget's father. Like Roget, the man for whom she confessed her deep longing in her copious diaries, Jane Griffin had also endured a difficult childhood, including the loss of a beloved parent; her mother had died when she was just three. The small, dark girl with blue eyes could be painfully shy. She also had an odd nervous condition, which caused her face to redden for no apparent reason. She had nearly been crippled by a deformity of the shoulder at the age of twelve, but she had received some expert medical care from Dr. Thomas Beddoes, Roget's onetime mentor in Bristol. Despite these hardships, Jane grew into a bright and lively young woman with a tender heart.

Like Eleanor Porden and Jane Marcet, Jane Griffin was an intellectual heavyweight. She devoured the books of the seventeenth-century preacher Isaac Watts, including his *Logic, or the Right Use of Reason*. As a teenager, Griffin followed a rigid study regimen, which she formalized in her own private manual called *A Plan for the Employment of Time & Improvement of the Mind, Arranged According to the Nature & Relative Importance of the Studies Necessary to be Daily Pursued*. Self-improvement was what motivated her. On her daily

agenda were hour-long immersions in various subjects, including the
Bible, history, Latin, and geometry. Like Roget, she, too, had an insatiable desire for knowledge:

> It will be an excellent rule for the solid & permanent improvement
> of the mind, to take a daily review of my advances in knowledge, to
> make a mental abstract of the subject of my studies, to trace my re-
> flections, to recall the impressions of my observations, to disentan-
> gle & simplify my thoughts, & treasure up my newly acquired ideas
> in a regular method and proper heads.

Here was a woman who, too, made a treasure chest of her ideas and
had a penchant for classification. What's more, Jane could play a
mean game of chess. She had had a formidable instructor, Davies
Giddy—later the president of the Royal Society during the beginning of Roget's tenure as secretary—who never forgot her "wonder-
ful quickness in learning chess."

Though Jane's towering intellect had its allure for Roget, it may
have also doomed her chance for a lasting relationship with him. In
a wife, he was not necessarily looking for an intellectual equal.

Roget's romance with Jane Griffin followed a circuitous path. The
two first met in 1809 but didn't start spending much time together until nearly a decade later. In 1816, Jane and her older sister, Frances—
known as "Fanny"—spotted Roget occasionally at parties, and during
his lectures at the Royal Institution. By 1817, Jane was infatuated. As
she noted in her diary, she could think of little else: "I grieve to think
how sadly my mind is unhinged and weakened." Jane Griffin was beginning to sense that Roget might make the ideal husband in whom
she could find "the supremest bliss" through her "sanctified affection."

Jane Griffin at age twenty-four. In 1828 she
would marry the Arctic explorer John Franklin,
whose first wife, Eleanor Porden, died in 1825.

Both Jane and Fanny Griffin began examining Roget's every gesture, searching for what it might mean about the state of his feelings
toward her. As Fanny wrote in her diary in June 1817, "Jane thought
she affronted Dr. Roget by shaking hands with Mr. G. Gregory and
talking to Mr. Acton." In August, Fanny noted, "Dr. Roget called after 3 weeks absence & took leave witht. any visible emotion." That
August, as the Griffins were about to depart for the Continent, Jane
also recorded her anxiety:

We have parted not to meet again perhaps for several months—I
shed a few tears at the tranquil, mere acquaintance-like indifference with which the "good-morning" & "a pleasant journey" were
looked as well as uttered, but I wiped them soon. . . . Can it really

be that I am deceived? that *that* manner, those attentions that I
have received for several months past, meant nothing?

Beginning the following year, Roget would figure ever more prominently in her diaries.

In early 1818, the two Griffin sisters invited Roget to be a founding
member of the Book Society they were organizing. It was similar to
Eleanor Porden's Attic Chest Society, but members discussed books:
"literary *conversazione*" was the point, Jane noted in her diary, not their
own work. At the group's second meeting, in February 1818, Jane and
Fanny Griffin decided to solicit new members, and Roget, they understood, would be a primary drawing card. One of the new invitees was
Isaac D'Israeli, the literary critic and historian who had published the
best-selling *Curiosities of Literature*, a collection of anecdotes on literary
topics ranging from bibliomania to seventeenth-century usurers. A
bibliomaniac himself, D'Israeli had a library containing some 25,000
volumes. D'Israeli (whose son, Benjamin, then a teenager, would grow
up to be prime minister) was universally admired; Byron would declare
that very year: "I don't know a living man's books, I take up so often—
or lay down more reluctantly."

In December 1818—at the first meeting of the Book Society after
Romilly's suicide—Jane Griffin paid even more attention to Roget's
behavior than usual. In the spring she had considered "the Romillys
& the Rogets the happiest families in England," and she, too, was
deeply stricken by their sudden reversal of fortune. In late November, she had written in her diary that "it was my consolation to indulge in weeping, & I woke every morning with images of horror
before my eyes." As Jane was well aware, Roget's appearance at the
book group was one of his first attempts at venturing back into the
everyday world.

As 1819 began, Jane appeared to be on the verge of landing her man. That February, Mary, Jane's younger sister, was to have an "at home"—a dinner party with dancing. Knowing that Roget was on the guest list, Jane made elaborate preparations to turn up the heat. First, there was her attire. She would put white ostrich feathers in her hair and wear her thin pink-and-white-striped party dress—*gauze de Chambery*—which she had purchased in Geneva, and which Miss Cork, her handmaid, had modernized. And then, via a few subtle maneuvers—a warm glance here and a kind word there—she would reveal to Roget her fondness for him, which made it difficult for her even to think about dancing with anyone else.

Her preparations worked spectacularly well. After supper, she waltzed exclusively with Roget, and the party didn't break up until after four the next morning. For this one evening, in which Roget responded in kind to her every move, Jane was nearly delirious. She later wrote:

> I felt it to be an eventful evening because I suffered myself to shew my feelings towards that individual in the room who alone occupied my mind & I marked the impression I made upon him & the return of his feelings, my heart thrilled with emotion & my spirit bounded with joy, alas! of how short duration.

This soirée was to be the high point of her romance with Roget.

A few months later, during Jane's "at home," Roget became disgruntled. Another man—one Jane hardly knew—began showering her with attention. And even though Jane did nothing to encourage this other suitor, Roget appeared to experience a wave of jealousy, which immediately alienated him from her. But his sudden change

of heart, in turn, forced Jane to reassess his character. Her rumina-
tions during this "cooling-off" period in 1819 were as follows:

> The individual [Roget] who in Febry. had possessed almost exclu-
> sive influence over it, in June had lost much of his dominion over
> my heart. The sentiments I had cherished for him, tho' not extin-
> guished, were subdued and changed, my undivided respect & at-
> tachment had been wrung from me painfully & with reluctance
> partly by the continuance of his own ungenerous suspicions & his
> extreme cautiousness & selfishness in his conduct toward me. . . . I
> permitted myself to . . . weigh his faults in the balance, & thus the
> *prestige* of imagination was gone.

As the son of the mercurial Catherine, Roget was perpetually insecure around women. He could not trust the constancy of Jane's
affection. At any moment, he felt that Jane might turn on him, or
abandon him. His paranoid streak, however, turned Jane off for
good.

One May evening in 1821, while both were attending a perfor-
mance by a ventriloquist, Roget—much to Jane's surprise—tried to
rekindle the romance. Roget, Jane later recalled, made "an unusual
and most unlooked for tho' I thought an artificial effort to revive
long dormant emotions by renewed assiduities." But feeling "un-
mixed pain," Jane rejected his advances. She later referred to this
event as "a last trial."

Roget never again paid much attention to Jane. But he soon became attracted to a friend of hers by the name of Sophia Pouncy,
about whom little is known. Remarkably, just a few months later, Roget proposed marriage to Sophia—twice. And just like that, Sophia,

too, was out of his life. No evidence remains of Roget's emotional response to being jilted. Most likely, in contrast to his sister Annette, he kept his hurt feelings to himself, assuming that he wrestled with them at all. The only record of the end of this relationship comes from Jane Griffin's diary. Referring to her tête-à-tête with Sophia right after the latter had turned down Roget's second proposal of marriage, Jane noted:

> She mentioned one particular fault she had observed in him which was that very one that more than all his distrust, his suspicions, his want of ardour, more even than his inconstancy weighs with a deadly weight upon my feelings and produces a forced revulsion in them whenever as they too often do, they lead into their original channel.

According to Jane, Sophia later identified the particular fault as "extreme cunning—this strange anomaly in his character."

Since the death of his uncle in 1818, Roget had encountered one personal setback after another. Having lost her mind, his mother had become an invalid; and his overwhelmed sister was gripped by constant despair. In addition to Marcet, another close friend from his Edinburgh days, John Reid, his Bloomsbury neighbor, had died unexpectedly. And his vigorous attempts to find a mate were leading only to repeated heartache.

But suddenly, Roget's fortunes began to change. In the middle of 1824, he would fall in love with a beautiful and charming woman, who came not from the Bloomsbury intellectual elite but from the Liverpool gentry.

7.

Mary

(903) MARRIAGE, matrimony, wedlock, union, match, intermarriage, coverture, vinculum matrimonii.

A married man, a husband, spouse, bridegroom, benedict, neogamist, consort.

A married woman, a wife, bride, mate, helpmate, rib, better half, feme covert.

Mary Hobson was everything that Roget could have hoped for in a wife. She had beauty and brains plus considerable wealth—a noteworthy attribute in an age where the husband automatically assumed control over his new wife's personal property. Mary was from Liverpool, a city that Roget had first gotten to know during his days in neighboring Manchester—just thirty miles away. Roget's medical school colleague John Bostock had known Mary during his childhood in Liverpool, and he may well have introduced the couple. About the early stages of their relationship, little evidence remains.

Born on April 15, 1795, Mary was sixteen years younger than Roget. She had an angular face and long, curly brown hair. Everyone seemed to find her striking and likable. Dumont, for example, once wrote Roget that "her physiognomy and conversation have made an impression, which can't be erased." Jane Griffin described Mary in her journal as "extremely interesting, sensible and elegant." In many

A portrait of twenty-nine-year-old Mary Roget from 1824,
the year of her marriage to Roget.

ways, Mary—later described as "a woman of great beauty" in a family memoir written by Roget's grandson, Samuel Romilly Roget—
was Roget's opposite. Blessed with a lively sense of humor, she
exuded warmth. She was exceedingly humble, and she felt a kinship
with members of the working class. At her family's farm, she would
help the servants milk the cows.

Though well read, Mary wasn't as intellectual as Jane Griffin or
Jane Marcet. But her boundless curiosity suited Roget perfectly, as
she was ever the eager student in search of his guidance. He was delighted to have found a woman happy to spend the evening taking
an algebra lesson from him. For a few weeks in the spring of 1826,

Mary was sitting down with Roget once a day to bone up on her math skills. With Mary looking up to him as a fountain of knowledge, Roget had no trouble feeling appreciated.

Mary's father was Jonathan Hobson, a wealthy merchant, who, like many Liverpudlians in the city's thriving business community, specialized in selling cotton. At the beginning of the nineteenth century, Liverpool did half as much commerce as London, though it was a fraction of the size—its population was just 77,000. Liverpool's streets were, as *Gentleman's Magazine* put it in a profile published in 1820, "clean and neat, and the houses well built." Hobson owned a stately home at 1 Nile Street in the eastern part of the downtown area near the river Mersey—opposite from where the Liverpool Cathedral now stands. In contrast to Manchester's filthy river Irk, Liverpool's Mersey, as Dr. Samuel Heinrich Spiker, the librarian to the king of Prussia observed in his visit in 1816, "gleamed along the horizon like a silver plain." At the time of Mary's marriage to Roget, Hobson also had a counting house (office) at 22 Cook Street—about two miles to the west. Mary's two brothers, her twin, Samuel, and her younger brother, Thomas, worked in the family business and often traveled to the United States to conduct business with large Southern plantations.

The elder Hobson was ambitious and hard-driving. He could also be intimidating and possessed, Mary's mother, Fanny, once conceded, "a hasty temper." By contrast, Fanny Taylor Hobson, though a stickler for propriety—Mary was not allowed to go to dancing parties until she was eighteen—was gentle and affectionate.

On the morning of Thursday, November 18, 1824, Peter Mark Roget and Mary Taylor Hobson were married in St. Philip's Church in Liverpool. Sanctifying the union with his "adored and ever blessed Mary," as Roget referred to his bride decades later in his autobiography, was the Reverend J. Wildig. In attendance were her parents,

Jonathan and Fanny Hobson, and the family friends Ellen Potter
and Dr. John Bostock. Neither Catherine nor Annette made it to
Liverpool. Perhaps sensing that Roget had replaced her, the disori-
ented Catherine would never acknowledge the union.

Roget and his wife would get along well because they helped each
other heal from some of their deep wounds dating back to childhood.
After enduring Catherine's countless intrusions, Roget was thrilled to
be in the company of a woman who gave him the space to talk about
his own hopes and fears. Likewise, for Mary, Roget offered the
prospect of intimacy with an emotionally safe man—the very opposite of her father. Though Roget would always be obtuse with regard
to what others, including his wife, were feeling—he never did grow
into the attentive husband of Jane Griffin's dreams—he was even-
keeled. And his concern for his wife's welfare was heartfelt.

After the wedding, Roget whisked his new bride away—not on a
honeymoon, but right back to 39 Bernard Street. By Monday
morning, November 21, he was back at work. Within days after welcoming Mary into his home, Roget would stumble upon one of the
most far-reaching scientific discoveries of his life. While Mary was
making breakfast in the basement kitchen, Roget stepped toward
the window and looked through the wooden blinds. He soon found
himself staring at the wheels of a horse-drawn cart. Suddenly, he
blurted out, "Mary, I have just noticed something truly remarkable
about human vision."

For the past decade, Roget had been captivated by the field of
optics—the subject of his recent series of lectures at the Royal Institution. And his new finding that morning built directly on his prior
research.

Roget had published a brief scholarly article, "On the Kaleidoscope," in *The Annals of Philosophy* in April 1818. Invented by Sir David Brewster, a Scottish astronomer and mathematician, the kaleidoscope (the word, also invented by Brewster, came from three Greek words meaning "beautiful," "form," and "see") created a sensation upon its initial appearance in 1816. Throughout London, people from all walks of life, including toddlers, could be found peering upward through those cardboard tubes. As Roget observed a couple of months later in *Blackwood's Magazine*:

In the memory of man, no invention, and no work, whether addressed to the imagination or to the understanding ever produced such an effect. A universal mania seized all the classes, from the lowest to the highest . . . and every person not only felt, but expressed that a new pleasure had been added to their existence.

Roget was perhaps overstating the case; but as a lover of gadgets, he, too, was swept up by Brewster's ingenious invention.

In 1820, Roget had also written "On a Voluntary Action of the Iris," a short article that described various optical experiments conducted at his Bernard Street home. Using a mirror, Roget noticed that he possessed the power of dilating the iris, "the fibres of which are usually considered as no more under the dominion of the will than the heart or the bloodvessels." As Roget argued, the iris typically contracts only in response to an environmental stimulus—when, for example, a person, after looking at an object far away, suddenly looks at a near object, assuming there is sufficient light projected onto the retina. Roget was proud of his unique ability to control this part of his body as it bolstered his illusory sense of mastery over the external world.

The insight that Roget had arrived at that late November morning while gazing out of the basement window also concerned the properties of the retina. As he peered through the blinds, the spokes of the cart's moving wheels appeared to be curved. He attributed this optical illusion to the fact that an impression made on the retina can remain even after the object in question has passed from view.

Before Mary could respond to his "Eureka!" moment, Roget rushed out the door, without even bothering to put on his waistcoat. He tracked down the man who was commanding the horse, and asked him to parade the horse and cart back and forth in front of his house several times. Tossing the man a shilling, Roget dashed back down to the basement and made further observations. He then told Mary that he would have to skip breakfast.

Roget spent the afternoon in his study, where he immediately began jotting down his thoughts. Within a couple of weeks, he had completed a paper, "Explanation of an Optical Deception in the Appearance of the Spokes of a Wheel as Seen Through Vertical Apertures." Besides describing in considerable detail the optical phenomenon he had observed, Roget also provided a mathematical analysis. In addition, he explained how different conditions—say, a change in the speed of the wheel or the size of the slits—would affect the appearance of the spokes. On December 9, Roget read his paper at the Royal Society.

What Roget had put his finger on was that the retina typically sees a series of still images as a continuous picture. This theoretical insight would eventually lead to the discovery of the movies.

Roget's paper immediately inspired research by several other leading British scientists. For example, Michael Faraday of the Royal Institution conducted a series of experiments on moving images generated by a pair of revolving wheels and published his findings in its flagship journal in 1831.

In 1832, after learning of Faraday's research, the Belgian physicist Joseph Plateau invented the phenakistoscope ("spindle viewer").
This optical toy consisted of two discs. When viewed in a mirror
through the slits of one disc, the pictures on the second disc would
appear to move. Two years later, the British scientist William George
Horner tweaked Plateau's invention to come up with the zoetrope
("wheel of life"). Unlike Plateau's phenakistoscope, this cylindrical
device required no mirror. Even more significant, more than one
person could view the moving images at the same time. The motion
picture theater had been born.

A hundred years after that skipped breakfast, the Royal Society
commemorated Roget's discovery. Around the same time, the Hollywood elite eagerly embraced Roget, who was then at the height of
his posthumous popularity. With the crossword puzzle craze in full
swing, copies of *Roget's Thesaurus* were flying off the shelves. As Hollywood spin-meisters such as Will Hays, the president of the Motion
Picture Producers and Distributors of America, figured out, invok-
ing Roget's name made for excellent PR. In the Roaring Twenties it
seemed as if Roget had invented the word, so it wasn't much of a
stretch to credit him with inventing the moving picture, too.

In an early (1929) history of the movies by Hays, whose name
later became synonymous with Hollywood's morally upright production code, Roget plays a seminal role. According to Hays, the motion picture, which he called the "epitome of civilization," sprang
Athena-like out of Roget's forehead:

Conscious scientific endeavor, first as a study of the nature of appearances of motion, and later of the synthesis of appearances of
motion, began with the studies of Peter Mark Roget, the same
whose name appears on the classic and authoritative Roget's

Thesaurus—first aid to word mongers—who was in 1824 secretary
of the Royal Society in Great Britain. . . . Out of the labours
started by Roget's studies came a machine which finally became
the familiar toy called Zoetrope, using hand-drawn pictures.

Hays's take has remained the conventional wisdom in Hollywood
ever since.

Roget never lost his enthusiasm for optics. In his *Thesaurus*, he reserved 445 for "Optical Instruments." This concept, which falls under Class III, "Matter," Division II, "Organic Matter," and Section 2,
"Sensation," contains such synonyms as "lens, magnifier, microscope, . . . mirror, . . . kaleidoscope."

For the first time since his infancy on Broad Street, Roget was living in a stable and loving home. After enduring several years of
nearly constant turmoil, including Romilly's suicide and his mother's
descent into madness, life was exhilarating. Mary ran the household
smoothly—the servants, too, were fond of her—and kept the townhouse spotless. She also prepared elaborate meals.

Roget and his wife enjoyed exploring London together. They took
a stroll nearly every evening after dinner and on those Sunday morn-
ings when they went to church. Mary also frequently accompanied
her husband on his medical rounds in Bloomsbury. She recorded
many of these outings in her diary, which she began keeping in April
1826—nearly two years into their marriage. Here's how she captured one Sunday in May 1826: "My dear mother's birthday. Heard
Dr. Blomfield, bishop of Chester, preach a charity sermon at St.
Pancras on the education of poor children—not only taught to read
and have the Bible given to them but with it the *right* interpretation

of its meaning." Though Roget didn't go to church every Sunday, he made it a point to go that day. As someone who was then making a name for himself as a formidable lecturer, Roget couldn't resist the chance to get a glimpse of Bishop Blomfield, whose diction was said to be impeccable. As the American senator Daniel Webster once noted, "In dignity of manner and weight of matter, no speaker in Great Britain was . . . [Blomfield's] equal." A little over a decade later, as the bishop of London, Blomfield would preside over Queen Victoria's coronation.

After his marriage, Roget maintained his busy lecture schedule, and Mary was often in attendance. From 1824 to 1826, Roget taught physiology on Friday afternoons at the London Institution. In May 1826, Mary wrote, "R.'s last lecture at the London Institution—exhibited two drawings we had made together—one a head illustrative of the eyes described by Dr. Wollaston; the other a convex and concave object in drawing made to descend upon the side the light comes from. Great applause and very gratifying." Roget also maintained his long-standing affiliation with the London Institution's rival, the Royal Institution, and he was constantly receiving requests to speak at other prestigious venues, including the newly established London University (now the University of London) and the Royal Liverpool Institution. He was soon turning down all offers except for the most lucrative ones. The teenager who had bored his mother with his scientific lectures had found the proper setting in which to impart his cogitations. Though Roget couldn't always connect with others one on one, he never failed to dazzle his audience.

Roget and his wife maintained a lively circle of friends, which included John Bostock, along with his wife, Anne, and their daughter Elizabeth (later a confidante of Roget's daughter); Elizabeth Jesser-Reid, the widow of his friend and colleague Dr. John Reid; and William Swainson, along with his wife, Mary, and their five children.

Swainson, a prominent naturalist, of whom it was said "he never went to bed without describing a new species," was a classifier extraordinaire, then busy publishing mammoth tomes on all sorts of animals, including insects, birds, and mammals. The Rogets frequently visited the Swainsons at their sumptuous home in Tyttenhanger Green near St. Albans, about twenty miles north of London.

As Mary quickly realized, Roget, despite his scholarly achievements, was a pauper when compared with many of their friends. Elizabeth Jesser-Reid, for example, used her vast fortune to support a variety of philanthropic causes, including women's education and the abolition of slavery. In a letter to her younger brother, Thomas, Mary once confessed to wishing Roget were as well-to-do as a London banker she came across one day while riding in a carriage with her husband. However, such feelings were fleeting. About this incident she would write, "I looked at my best of husbands by my side and all my envy vanished."

Like many London professionals, after the end of the Parliamentary session in July, Roget typically left for the country. The Rogets would spend the bulk of the summer either in Liverpool with the Hobsons on Nile Street, or in a rented house in Hampstead. But even while on vacation, Roget could not entirely abandon his scholarly pursuits. The "dear Doctor," as Mary's friend Charlotte Parks would refer to him, felt compelled to give lectures to his neighbors on astronomy and electricity.

The Rogets had two children: Catherine Mary, known as Kate, born in 1825, and John, born in 1828. Both were christened by the Reverend John Hewlett, a prominent biblical scholar. Then a rector in Hilgay, Hewlett, who had first met Roget at the Royal Institution, where he held a professorship in belles lettres, emerged as a close personal friend. Nearly twenty years older than Roget, Hewlett lived until 1844; his name, too, would be etched onto Roget's "Date of Deaths."

After the birth of each child, Mary was slow to recover, causing Roget considerable worry. On November 30, 1825, more than a month after his daughter's birth, Roget wrote to Dumont, "I have however had to experience a lot of anxiety during the difficult and tardy reemergence of my poor Mary, who regains her strength, even now, only slowly. The child does well; we gave her the name of Catherine, in order to conserve in her the memory of my poor mother." Mary would complete a full recovery both times, but she remained exceedingly frail.

Like his mother before him, Roget—along with his wife—carefully tracked the moral and intellectual development of their children. One of the couple's favorite books was Jean-Jacques Rousseau's *Emile*, a work that had also inspired both Jean Roget and Samuel Romilly a half-century earlier precisely because it addressed methods of child-rearing.

Peter Mark Roget's mind was constantly defining concepts and exploring their relationships with one another. Perhaps because he took such an interest in overseeing the education of Kate and John, at an early age, they, too, began making ingenious discoveries about how the objects in their world related to one another.

Mary recorded many of her children's early musings in "a journal of the progress of my dear babes," which she began keeping in November 1828—about six months after John's birth. The previous spring, Mary noted, "Kate made a comparison we were vastly pleased with." While Roget had been stoking the fire with a pair of bellows, Kate ran into the nursery and fetched her cuckoo—her toy bird—before blurting out, "This is like that, Papa." In the spring of 1829, Kate made another analogy that Mary found noteworthy: "Mama, the arm is like the leg—the hand, the arm and the elbow are like the foot, the leg, and the knee. The fingers are like the toes."

John could also easily get lost in abstractions. When he was little more than three, Mary told him that a person couldn't be in two places at once. "Now, for instance," she said, "you could not be here and upstairs in the nursery at the same time." John wasn't convinced. "But if we brought the nursery downstairs," he offered, "and made this the nursery, then we could be in two places at the same time."

It was July 4, 1830. In a couple of days, the Roget family would be setting off to spend the summer at Hampstead. But on this steamy afternoon, Roget had set aside time to give Kate, then nearing five, her biweekly quiz.

"Now, Kate, I want you to read to me the first paragraph of *Frank*." While Roget was working in Clifton with Lovell Edgeworth in the late 1790s, Lovell's sister, Maria, had been completing *Frank*, a popular tale designed to help children with their lessons.

Putting the book on her lap, Kate began:

> There was a little boy whose name was Frank. He had a father and a mother, who were very kind to him; and he loved them; he liked to talk to them, and he liked to walk with them, and he liked to be with them. He liked to do what they asked him to do; and he took care not to do what they asked not to do.

"That's very good," said Roget, removing the book from her hands. "I can read everything in *Frank* but the very long words, Daddy.

And Mummy has told you that I can now name all the countries in Europe except for the German states," replied Kate.

"You will need to work on those German principalities," responded Roget. "For your quiz today, I want to ask you about the incident with the cheese that takes place at the end of Part Three. Do you remember how Frank ate his cheese?"

"In a funny way," said Kate.

"Be precise," exhorted her father.

"I don't know."

"Fine, then, I'll remind you."

Taking the book from Kate's lap, Roget riffled through it, noting that Frank

> put [the cheese] betwixt his fore finger and his middle finger; then he took a piece of bread, and stuck it betwixt his idle middle and fourth finger, and then he took a large mouthful of the cheese and a larger mouthful of the bread, so that his mouth was filled in a very disagreeable manner.

"And why did Frank eat the cheese in such a disagreeable manner?" Roget asked, peering into Kate's blue eyes.

"Because he saw the little boy in the cottage eat it that way!"

"That's right, but what is the lesson here?"

"The little boy in the cottage, who was excellent at weeding, didn't know how to eat cheese without getting his fingers all sticky!"

"No, Kate. I'm afraid I will have to tell you." And Roget read to her the wise words of Frank's father: "Apes are apt to imitate every thing which they see done, and they cannot, as you can, Frank, distinguish what is useful and agreeable, from what is useless or disagreeable—they imitate everything without reflecting."

"So, Papa, you mean that Frank was an ape."

"No, but that he was acting *like* an ape, as he was imitating the boy in the cottage without reflecting. You will need to read this part again, Kate.

"But that's all right. The process of acquiring knowledge," added Roget, raising his index finger, "is perpetual. It requires constant toil. I'm over fifty, and I still have much to learn."

Saturday, September 4, 1830, was a glorious day for a trip across the Channel. The sun was shining and both wind and tide were favorable. That morning at half past seven, Roget and his wife, having arrived in Southampton the night before, boarded the *George IV* steam packet and headed for Le Havre. Their ultimate destination: Paris.

Roget had been back just once since the days of Napoleon: two Septembers earlier, he had briefly traveled there with John Bostock. A few weeks before that 1828 trip, his close friend William Swainson had also set off for Paris—accompanied by his fellow bird maven, the American naturalist and artist John James Audubon, to visit Baron Cuvier, France's leading naturalist. Roget and Bostock may well have spent time with all these eminent classifiers, but there are no records of their precise whereabouts. But in contrast to that 1828 trip, which was at least partly about business, this time around, with his wife by his side, Roget would take in Paris as a tourist.

After taking on passengers at Portsmouth, the *George IV* steamed past what Mary called in her journal "the beautiful smiling coast of the Isle of Wight." Roget couldn't help but think back a dozen years. In the late summer of 1818, he had rushed to John Nash's coastal villa to see the dying Anne Romilly. As the image of his frail aunt and nearly deranged uncle passed before his eyes, he shed a tear.

"My life has changed so much since then," he thought to himself. "Like my uncle, I have found a beautiful woman who truly loves me."

Roget was now in the prime of his life. He was the patriarch of his own flourishing family. And his scientific career had taken off. On November 30, 1827, he had been elected as one of the two Secretaries of the Royal Society and was in charge of physical sciences. And on March 1, 1829, he had begun the first of two one-year terms as president of the Medical and Chirurgical Society. A few years earlier, he had been selected as a charter member of a prestigious literary society, the Athenaeum Club, cofounded by Sir Walter Scott along with other luminaries. So esteemed was the club that Charles Dickens would regard his own election in the mid–1830s as a major milestone in his career. Roget also had become a prominent member of several other scholarly societies, including the Zoological Society of London, the home of Britain's top-flight naturalists.

The couple settled in different spots on deck. Roget was seated in an armchair where he could dig into some scientific manuscripts. And Mary spent the whole day—from eleven in the morning till ten at night—lying on a mattress propped up on a wooden sofa.

As the steamer approached Le Havre, Mary was struck by the magnificence of the setting. "By that time the moon had risen," she wrote in her journal, "and her dear light beautifully illumined the line of houses on the quay, which, seen through the shipping, had a very picturesque effect." For Mary, as for Roget, nature often proved calming. She, too, tended to see the moon and other celestial bodies as friends she could turn to for comfort.

Once the couple reached Le Havre, Mary became upset. She squirmed as a female customs officer inserted her hands beneath the stays of her corset. Mary also was unhappy with the room that Roget had reserved in a local inn. Her anxiety was so severe that she would lapse into the third person to describe her experience:

> But the dismay of an English lady was considerable to find that this room was but a step raised above the court-yard, a tiled floor without carpet and two very high windows, with very thin muslin curtains half-way up, opening into the court or public entrance, so that it was exactly like sleeping in the street. I did not like the idea of undressing in so exposed a situation.

Like Roget, who had felt the same sort of vulnerability while living in Bentham's house without locks, Mary put a high premium on privacy and propriety.

After spending a couple of days in Le Havre, the Rogets visited Rouen, where they took an extensive tour of the city before moving on to Paris. Little is known about what the Rogets did during their two-week stay in the French capital; Roget did manage to take Mary to his favorite museum—the Louvre—and on their last day there, September 21, they took a stroll in the Palais Royal. Before leaving Paris, Roget also procured a birthday present for Kate: a microscope.

On the morning of Thursday, September 23, the Rogets reached Calais, where they had planned on catching the noon steamer back to Dover. But just as they were boarding, the captain said that he could not advise ladies to make this crossing because he would have to land at Ramsgate, where the disembarking was much less agreeable than at Dover.

Disappointed, the Rogets spent a grim day in Calais, which, Mary noted, was "not an attractive town. . . . We found nothing to entertain us." But later that day, Mary entered into a lively conversation with a Frenchwoman traveling alone to England. The story she told proved deeply moving to Mary. Eight years earlier, while making this same crossing, the Frenchwoman had to throw herself overboard just before reaching Dover because of a ferocious storm. Feeling ill, the woman was unable to swim the three-quarters of a mile to shore. But suddenly a knight in shining armor appeared in the form of an intrepid young Englishman. The young gentleman told her not to despair, for he would save her, if possible. He took off his coat, tied her to his back, and carried her ashore. Mary kept thinking of this heroic Englishman as she drifted off to sleep. At two o'clock in the morning, the Rogets were roused by a message from the captain of the next Dover steamer. An hour later, the couple—along with the Frenchwoman—boarded the boat, which finally set sail for England.

On this rough voyage, Mary's husband provided the chivalry. In her diary she wrote: "The lady with us was so long in dressing that we were the last on board and found the ladies' cabin filled. . . . Roget found me shivering in despair. . . . His berth in the gentlemen's cabin was the only resource I had, and he sat by me till morning, four hours of tossing and sickness." Though Roget was often self-absorbed and aloof, he was capable of occasional gallantry. On that windy morning, Roget, ever the dutiful husband, made Mary feel loved and protected.

The trip would prove to be a high point of their marriage—their long-deferred honeymoon.

In 1826, Roget had become a founding member of the Society for the Diffusion of Useful Knowledge, which aimed to disseminate scientific ideas in nontechnical language to the public. Roget contributed treatises on electricity, galvanism, magnetism, and electromagnetism. In writing these four treatises, Roget was compelled by the same forces that would later give rise to his *Thesaurus*. Here, too, Roget was putting in the immense labor of classifying and arranging specific ideas so as to "supply a deficiency"—in this case, not his own difficulty writing clear prose, but the lack of well organized information on these complicated subjects.

While Roget's linguistic masterpiece organized all of knowledge, each of these treatises organized a different branch of natural philosophy. Just as he later divided up his one thousand concepts into six classes, in his first treatise he subsumed the facts relating to electricity under six headings:

1. Excitation
2. Attraction
3. Repulsion
4. Distribution
5. Induction
6. Transference

Not only did Roget classify and arrange the key ideas of electricity in the 241 numbered paragraphs in his treatise, he also often gave order to the terms mentioned within specific paragraphs. For example, in paragraph 24, Roget provided a complete catalogue of some fifty bodies, including items such as metallic ores and animal fluids, in order of their conducting power. The treatises, like many other texts penned by Roget, were, in part, concatenations of lists.

After completing the fourth and final treatise in December 1831, Roget felt drained. The effort had been massive, as, all told, Roget's output amounted to some one thousand densely packed paragraphs, totaling three hundred pages. In a postscript added that month, Roget

mentioned that when beginning the work four years earlier, he had
had no idea of the extent of the labor involved. He also apologized
to his readers for having "to prosecute the work in a desultory manner and at irregular and uncertain intervals." Although Roget's many
other professional obligations did not allow him to work as consis-
tently on this project as he may have liked, the end result was hardly
irregular or desultory.

After the publication of this volume, Roget never wrote anything
again for the Society for the Diffusion of Useful Knowledge. However, he did continue his heavy load of editorial duties until his resignation in 1844. The Society disbanded a few years later. Its
marketing plan wasn't working. Lay readers found the material too
dull, and intellectuals not meaty enough. As Lucy Aikin, a literary
historian whom Roget saw from time to time in Hampstead—she
was the sister of the scientist Arthur Aikin, whom Roget had first
met in Edinburgh—once complained, "Literature is low indeed—
swamped . . . by the tract makers, with the Useful Knowledge Society at their head." But in contrast to Roget's treatises, his *Thesaurus*
would electrify readers from all walks of life.

On July 3, 1832, Roget was struck by some devastating news:
Mary had cancer. A few days later, the Rogets set off for Net-
ley Cottage in Hampstead as planned. But as Mary's tumor kept
growing, her strength began to fail. Iodine treatments had little effect
besides weakening her still further. Though Roget was heartsick, he
decided not to burden his wife with his despair. Instead, unbeknownst
to Mary, he began confiding in her younger brother, Thomas, whose
wedding they had attended that February in Liverpool. Directly
revealing his innermost fears for one of the few times in his life,

Roget wrote Tom in August, "The future is to me all mist and darkness through which I cannot yet see my way. My poor children, too—what will become of them!"

Shortly after returning to London with Roget in September, Mary went back to Hampstead to stay with Jane Marcet for a couple of weeks. That October, in a departure from their usual pattern, Roget rented a house for the family in Frognal, a section of Hampstead noted for its salubrious breezes. But the "clean air" cure so beloved by generations of Rogets did Mary no good, and a month later, the family was back in Bernard Street. On November 20, 1832, as Roget later noted in his autobiography, "Mary went out for the last time."

In early January, with Mary bedridden, Roget found a governess for the children. Roget selected Miss Agnes Catlow for her expertise not in child-rearing but in classification. A budding amateur botanist then in her mid-twenties and living in Hampstead, Catlow also had considerable talent as a painter and engraver. At the time, she was also beginning an assignment as the illustrator for Roget's comprehensive survey of physiology, his *Bridgewater Treatise*.

Agnes Catlow immediately began instructing Kate and John— then seven and four—in classification. On walks, Catlow would teach the young Rogets the English and Latin names for the plants they encountered. It was as if Catlow were steeping the next generation of Rogets in the word lists that made up Peter Mark Roget's childhood notebook. (A decade later, Catlow would publish *Popular Field Botany*, based on the lessons she had provided to Kate and John, to whom she "most affectionately" dedicated this highly successful book.)

On January 30, 1833, Mary's father, Jonathan Hobson, died after a long illness. Mary was so weak that the family didn't attend the funeral. The surviving family records do not reveal the site or nature of Mary's tumor. But wherever it was, she was suffering from an

inflammation—referred to as "dropsy" at the time—and Roget recommended paracentesis, a common surgical procedure that involved
an incision with a tube to drain accumulated fluid. This tapping often
relieved pain and shortness of breath, but it could be painful, and the
therapeutic effects rarely lasted very long. Mary's first treatment took
place on February 10, and her second one on April 3—a little more
than a week before she took her last breath.

On April 12, 1833, as Roget later put it in his autobiography, his
"adored and angelic wife expired." She was just thirty-eight. The following day, Roget's cousin Joseph Romilly recorded in his diary:
"Poor Mrs. Roget (who we hoped was getting better) is dead. What
a dreadful loss to poor Dr. Roget!"

On April 17, Mary Roget's remains were deposited in the inner
vaults of St. George's Church in Bloomsbury.

Roget's immediate reaction to Mary's death was the same as the
one that followed his uncle's suicide: emotional paralysis. For the
next few months, he often voiced a desire to end his life. His in-
laws—Mary's brothers and her mother, Fanny—invited him to Liverpool, where they nursed him back to health. Roget would remain
close to the Hobsons, frequently seeing them either in London or
Liverpool. He would, however, lose the financial subsidy that he had
been receiving regularly from his in-laws since his marriage in 1824.
Decades later, Roget still remembered the date of April 22, 1833,
when, as he wrote in his autobiography, "The house of Jonathan
Hobson and sons stopped payment."

Though by the fall of 1833 Roget was back in London, where he
resumed his hectic professional life, a huge part of him died with
Mary.

Roget's life took an increasingly religious turn. Despite his strict
scientific bent, Roget, like the rest of his social circle, had always held
a traditional worldview, in which Heaven was accepted as a given. In

a letter to an ailing Mary Roget in 1832, Jane Marcet spelled out
these cosmological assumptions:

> Bear this in mind, my dear friend, and look forward to it with hope
> and security; for it is the certain reward of those who deserve it;
> and if not always in this world in another where happiness is much
> more stable than it is here. But for our sakes, I hope that happiness
> will be long deferred.

After Mary's death, Roget began to think even more about his relationship to God and the next life.

Roget also looked forward to "a heavenly reunion" with Mary—
one of the major comforts that Christianity offered to the grief-
stricken at the dawn of the Victorian era. Spending eternity with
departed loved ones was a common fantasy. Upon the loss of her sister Fanny in 1832, Emma Wedgwood (later the wife of Charles Darwin) made the following prayer: "What exquisite happiness it will be
to be with her again, to tell her how much I loved her."

That spring, Roget found a letter that Mary had written to him
right before the birth of Kate and sealed up—with the stipulation
that it be opened only after her death. Included were the following
words:

> These few lines then will be seen by you alone. They are to repeat
> to you, my precious, how dearly I love you, and to thank you for
> the sweet tenderness and kindness which have made the last year
> of my life so *very, very* happy. Do not, love, think of me in sorrow,
> for God will let us be happy again where we need not fear to be

separated any more. If I leave you a sweet infant, it will comfort you and you will cherish it for my sake. But more than all, you will be comforted by that firm confidence in the goodness and Mercy of our Heavenly Parent, which we have so often talked of together as the dearest hold of our consoling religion. . . . And God will keep you and bless you till he wills that we may meet again.

As Roget sought to recover from yet another devastating loss, he would read Mary's loving words over and over again. And he would also soothe himself by producing a steady stream of new words of his own.

8.

Mourning, Scholarly Triumph, and a Secret New Love

(357) ORGANIZATION, the organized world, organized nature, living nature, animated nature, living beings.

The science of living beings; Biology: Natural History, Organic Chemistry.

As Roget settled back into the house on Bernard Street at the end of 1833, he was desperate to temper his overwhelming grief. Fortunately, he had recently been assigned a monumental project that would provide an ideal outlet for his emotional distress.

A couple of years before Mary's death, Roget had begun work on a massive survey of physiology—one of eight scientific tomes funded by the estate of the late Earl of Bridgewater, who had died in 1829. Roget, who was then in his early fifties, was no longer up-to-date on the most recent developments in the field. To catch up, he regularly attended lectures at the Royal College of Surgeons and at the University of London.

But bogged down as he was by all his other scientific duties, as well as by the tragic turn of events in his family, Roget hadn't made much progress with the writing. On February 27, 1834, he shipped Miss Agnes Catlow and the two children off to Hampstead, where they would remain until October. He then devoted his attention to his *Bridgewater Treatise*, which he completed on May 6. Finishing the book would take every last ounce of his energy. A week later, Roget showed off his new manuscript and its many illustrations to his cousin Joseph Romilly, who noted in his diary: "Dr. Roget looking very poorly."

From the vantage point of the early twenty-first century one might be tempted to dub Roget's scientific magnum opus a manifesto of "intelligent design." Roget belonged to the last generation of scientists who failed to take evolutionary biology into account. In the early 1830s, Darwinism was barely a dot on the horizon—*On the Origin of Species* would not hit the shelves until 1859. Like most of his contemporaries, Roget adhered to the reigning paradigm of "natural theology," the view that one should use the tools of science to discover evidence of God's infinite wisdom.

Natural theology was a cause that the eighth (and final) Earl of Bridgewater, the Reverend Francis Henry Egerton, wanted to champion. Though eccentric—Egerton clothed his cats in fashionable attire and fed them at his table—this wealthy aristocrat was also a deeply religious man profoundly influenced by the philosopher William Paley. In 1802, Paley had published the highly regarded *Natural Theology, or Evidences of the Existence and Attributes of the Deity*, which made the case that God had designed the universe for man and continued to supervise its operations. Egerton had written his own study on Paley, but it had had little impact.

To spread Paley's doctrine, Egerton realized he would have to rely on more able scientific minds than his own. In his will, written in 1825, Egerton bequeathed 8,000 pounds to the president of the Royal Society to commission eight comprehensive works by leading scientists "on the power, wisdom and goodness of God, as manifested in the Creation; including . . . the variety and formation of God's creatures in the animal, vegetable and mineral kingdoms."

At the time of the earl's death, Davies Gilbert (known as Davies Giddy in the days when he taught Jane Griffin chess) had recently succeeded Humphry Davy as the head of the Royal Society. Gilbert, in turn, enlisted both the archbishop of Canterbury, William Howley, and the bishop of London, Charles Blomfield, whose exquisite oratory Roget had admired a few years earlier at St. Pancras, in the search for authors. By 1830, Gilbert had settled on his final list. In addition to Roget, the authors included such academic legends as Thomas Chalmers, chair of theology in Edinburgh, William Whewell, the polymath of Trinity College who was a close colleague of Roget's cousin Joseph Romilly, and Sir Charles Bell, a former head of the Great Windmill Street School of Anatomy (later famous for identifying several neurological conditions, such as Bell's palsy). Shortly after selecting his roster, Gilbert was forced out of his leadership post, and the task of searching for a publisher fell to the Royal Society's secretary—Peter Mark Roget.

Ever since he had nailed down his first job, as a tutor to the Philips boys, Roget had demonstrated a knack for financial negotiations. Approaching two publishing houses—Longmans and John Murray—Roget sought to get them bidding against each other. But after two years of haggling, Roget was back to square one. On October 8, 1832, he wrote his fellow authors: "I am persuaded we might easily find a respectable publisher who would consent to limit his agreement with us to a single edition, and would gladly give us half the net profits, taking upon himself all risks." By the end of 1832, Roget settled on Mr. William Pickering of Chancery Lane, who agreed to print lavish editions with calf covers and gold lettering emblazoned across the binding.

Roget's efforts paid off. All eight volumes, which were published between 1833 and 1836, went through several editions. In the case of Roget's *Animal and Vegetable Physiology Considered with Reference to Natural Theology*—the fifth in the series, it was first published in 1834—the original one thousand copies sold out right away. Three additional editions came out over the next thirty-three years. Roget's earnings were significant: a thousand guineas (more than $100,000 today) upon publication—and then an additional hundred guineas a year in royalties. As would later be the case with his *Thesaurus*, it was a book that Roget would continue to fine-tune until his death.

With the British intelligentsia well aware that Roget was constantly updating this famous treatise, he became the public face of physiology in Victorian England. Those who spotted a rare species of plant or animal felt a compulsion to contact him. When, for example, in the late 1840s, Charles Kingsley—the well-known author of historical novels—noticed some remarkable flowers called *Comatula rosacea* on the rocks of Ilfracombe, he immediately wrote to a friend in London: "Just send a note to Dr. Roget, to ask him if he has found them here, and to say I shall be happy to preserve some for him." Likewise, Alfred Lord Tennyson carefully perused both volumes of Roget's *Bridgewater Treatise* during the decade and a half that he spent composing *In Memoriam*, published in 1850. In this long poem mourning the loss of his friend, Arthur Hallam, Tennyson focused on the differences between scientific and poetic knowledge. Tennyson's understanding of how scientists organized the world was based largely on his reading of Roget.

Most of Roget's contemporaries assumed that if he was to be remembered for one work, it would be his *Bridgewater Treatise*, not his *Thesaurus*. The former, which firmly established his reputation as an important author, received universal plaudits. Despite—or perhaps because of—his inner turmoil, Roget was at the height of his creative powers. Roget's *Bridgewater Treatise*, Maria Edgeworth observed, was "full of facts the most curious, arranged in the most beautifully luminous manner . . . [and] admirable in every way, scientific, moral and religious." For the first time, Roget also made his mark on the other side of the Atlantic. In Concord, Massachusetts, the philosopher Ralph Waldo Emerson was impressed, calling Roget's treatise "the only good one . . . in the series." And writing in the *Southern Literary Messenger*, a periodical based in Richmond, Virginia, an unknown twentysomething book reviewer by the name of Edgar Allan Poe remarked: "The talents of Dr. Roget, however, are a sufficient guarantee that he has furnished no ordinary work. We are grieved to learn from the Preface that his progress has been greatly impeded by 'long protracted anxieties and afflictions, and by the almost overwhelming pressure of domestic calamity.'" America's soon-to-be literary sensation could fully appreciate how Roget had transformed his personal loss into scholarly triumph.

Roget's 250,000-word treatise was the culmination of his lifelong pursuit, begun in his childhood notebook, to organize the animate world. Incorporating the research of countless specialists in zoology, physiology, and anatomy, Roget had produced a work whose comprehensiveness was breathtaking. He divided his treatise into four parts. Each part covered one of the four classes of physiology—Mechanical Functions, Vital Functions, Sensorial Functions, and Reproductive

Functions (the same four classes Roget had first identified in his Manchester syllabus in 1806). Roget's *Bridgewater Treatise* constituted his intellectual autobiography, as it incorporated the various academic interests that had intrigued him since his university days in Edinburgh.

Roget's introductory chapter, titled "Final Causes," provided a theoretical overview. As Roget saw it, though the animate world was much more complex and varied than the inanimate world, it, too, conformed to God's laws. According to the pre-Darwinian view held by Roget and his contemporaries, God was like a "great watchmaker," and His "intelligent design" was the "final cause" that determined why various creatures responded to the ecosystem in the way that they do. Roget claimed:

> The study of . . . final causes is . . . forced upon our attention by even the most superficial survey of nature. It is impossible not to recognize the character of intention, which is so indelibly impressed upon every part of the structure both of vegetable and animal beings and which marks the whole series of phenomena connected with their history.

In his ensuing discussion of plants and animals of every stripe that comprised the remainder of the first volume, Roget proceeded from the assumption that God has designed all their features in an ingenious way. Roget conceived of God as an artist; and his job as a natural historian was to discover and reveal the order in the work of art known as the universe. In the second volume, Roget described the inner workings of plants and animals—namely, their respiratory, nervous, and reproductive systems. Here he was also able to recycle much of his prior scholarship. For example, in his 1822 spring lectures at the Royal Institution, Roget had addressed slices on this material in talks with titles such as "Respiration," "Introduction to Perception and Feeling in Animals," and "Vision."

A t noon on Monday, October 23, 1837, Roget arrived in Cambridge. Roget had just spent two weeks in Hilgay with his good friend the Reverend John Hewlett. Heading south back to London, he stopped off to meet his cousin Joseph Romilly, recently appointed Registrar of the University, a position he would hold for more than thirty years. Roget had not seen his cousin for three years. Like Roget, Romilly had found a line of work that involved classifying and arranging. The registrar would himself produce a well-regarded book of lists, *Graduati cantabrigienses*, which contained four hundred pages of information on a century's worth of Cambridge graduates.

During the thirty-mile trek south from Hilgay, Roget had been seated in the post chaise between his daughter, Kate, then a few days shy of her twelfth birthday, and his new governess, Miss Margaret Spowers. John, then nine, didn't make the trip to Cambridge, as he was attending boarding school in Hampstead.

Roget had hired the thirty-one-year-old Spowers because Miss Catlow had left the family to set up a school in Regent Square, where Kate was then enrolled. Spowers's profile deviated from the norm, as the vast majority of Victorian governesses tended to fit into two categories. Many had clergyman fathers—as in the case of the famous Brontë sisters. And others came from respectable families that had suddenly come on hard times. By contrast, Spowers had grown up in Hampstead, the daughter of George Spowers, a wealthy businessman. Thus, although Roget was Spowers's employer, they were not divided by social class.

Of Joseph Romilly, his Cambridge colleague the geologist Adam Sedgwick once remarked, "He has a great deal of French blood in his veins, which makes him a merry, genial man."

No photos or descriptions of Margaret Spowers survive. Of her physical appearance, the only clue is the number 142—that's how much she weighed, in pounds. This factoid appears in a brief list at the beginning of Roget's autobiography, in which Roget also noted his own weight in a few isolated years (it veered from a high of 137 pounds in 1808 to a low of 121 pounds in 1858) and that of his two children at a few points in their childhood. Spowers's presence on this list suggests that Roget eventually considered her a member of the family.

Roget's post chaise reached its destination—the Sun, a Cambridge inn—precisely on time. When Romilly was nowhere to be found, Roget became antsy. At one in the afternoon, Romilly finally appeared. After shaking Romilly's hand, Roget introduced the new woman of the house, "This is Margaret Spowers who came to us in the middle of July."

Romilly proceeded to give his three guests a brief tour of Trinity College, where he was a fellow. They walked through the chapel as well as the spectacular library, which had been designed by Christopher Wren in the 1670s. Noticing how well-spoken Spowers was—like Agnes Catlow, she, too, possessed a wide-ranging intellect—Romilly made a point of introducing her to Trinity College's two reigning scholars, William Whewell, the author of the *Bridgewater Treatise* on astronomy and general physics, and George Peacock, a renowned mathematician.

Romilly then suggested that the group take a short stroll around Cambridge. "I want to show all of you the site of what will be the new Fitzwilliam Museum. About twenty years ago, the seventh Viscount of Fitzwilliam bequeathed his art collection, which features the work of several Dutch masters, including Rembrandt and Titian. Next Thursday, November 2, there will be a procession to lay the first stone. I will be carrying the copper-plate inscription." The Fitzwilliam, which first opened its doors to the public in 1848, is now considered one of Europe's finest small art museums.

As they walked back through the Great Gate and out of Trinity College, Roget turned to Romilly. "You know, Kate is quite a talented amateur botanist."

Sidling up to Romilly, Kate said, "I have learned so much from

Miss Catlow, who was our first governess. She used to say, 'Through botany, one can learn fresh instances of the wisdom and goodness of God.' I have memorized all twenty-four of the classes that make up Linnaeus's 'Artificial System.' And I can also tell you about the 'Natural System,' devised by his successor, Augustin-Pyramus de Candolle, who, like my father, is from Geneva."

"What have we here?" Romilly asked, noticing a flower at their feet. Soon Kate began rattling off the names of dozens of flowers, in both Latin and English, as they made their way across town.

As Kate kept peppering Romilly with botanical information, Miss Spowers and Roget trailed farther and farther behind. Roget confessed to Spowers that he wasn't all that interested in art museums, but thought it impolite to say so to Romilly.

That night, when he got around to recording his daily diary entry, Romilly's mind turned to Roget's precocious daughter: "I went to . . . meet Dr. Roget, Katy and her governess Miss Spowers (what an odd name!). . . . Thought Katy an agreeable intelligent Maedchen."

In Roget's recollection of that day, Spowers figured most prominently. After enduring the despair of losing Mary, his heart was starting to open up again.

Sometime between that afternoon in Cambridge and Roget's trip to the Continent with Spowers and the children in the summer of 1844—his first since his excursion to Paris with Mary in 1830—Roget and his onetime governess began living as man and wife. Due to the social mores, Roget and his heirs would do everything they could to cover up the true nature of their relationship. Unlike Roget's unpublished diary, the published account of this European trip, edited by his grandson, failed to mention Spowers at all.

In the census of 1851, Roget would list her as a "visitor," not as a "governess," as he had ten years earlier. But in truth, Roget's home would be Spowers's sole residence for the rest of her life.

. . .

In October 1846, Roget escorted his son, John, to Cambridge to begin his undergraduate studies. Roget figured Trinity College was a wise choice because Joseph Romilly could keep an eye on his son. But unlike Roget, who had imbibed Latin as a schoolboy, John's Latin was shaky. Based on an impromptu examination conducted before John started Cambridge, Romilly determined that the young Roget "made a very poor display in classics." John eventually focused his attention on mathematics, the subject in which he earned a bachelor's degree in 1850. At Cambridge, John also pursued a variety of other interests: he joined both a drawing club and a literary society called the "Honourable Fraternity of the Rummy Cockatoos."

Just as John was entering Cambridge, Roget's own academic career was winding down. Though his health remained robust—apart from his increasing deafness—he had already closed his medical practice in 1840, and in the spring of the following year he had withdrawn from the Medical and Chirurgical Society. In early 1842, Roget resigned from his post as an examiner in physiology at the University of London. The university was suddenly cutting its fees by one fifth, and Roget no longer felt it paid enough. Roget still held the powerful position of secretary of the Royal Society, but he was coming under heavy fire for a variety of alleged missteps.

One controversy revolved around the charge that in his *Bridgewater Treatise*, Roget had plundered the work of Robert Grant, a prominent doctor and marine biologist whom Charles Darwin had also consulted before setting off aboard the *Beagle* in 1831. Grant, a professor of comparative anatomy and zoology at the University of London, made the charge of plagiarism himself. In a letter to *The Lancet* published on April 18, 1846, Grant complained that Roget had taken advantage of his generosity. Noting that Roget had attended all sixty-four of his lectures in the spring of 1832 and all forty-eight of his lectures that fall, Grant charged that "[Roget's] pen was never at rest; after each lecture, extended explanations were cheerfully given him, and innumerable references to books, plates, and diagrams, were carefully communicated to him." But what most galled Grant was that Roget appeared to have no compunction about his behavior. Grant reported that Roget had written to him just before the publication of his treatise, claiming that he had "the full right to make whatever use I please of the information I may derive from my attendance as regular pupil on the lectures of a public professor."

Roget tried to defuse the uproar by responding to Grant right away. Roget had *The Lancet* reprint, the following week, his entire correspondence with Grant from a decade earlier. Back in 1833, Roget had told Grant that he planned to include a brief acknowledgment in his *Bridgewater Treatise*—a promise that he had kept. As he had also informed Grant then, he would have gladly added additional references to Grant's work had Grant ever made any such request.

Many scholars agreed that Grant had overstated his case. By the mid-1840s, Grant's own career was in decline, largely because of the meager wages doled out by the University of London, which, after 1831, no longer provided "guarantee money" (a minimum of 300 pounds a year) to its lecturers. Reduced to living in a slum, Grant was prone to ranting about his sad fate. He reportedly told one colleague, "I have found the world to be chiefly composed of knaves and harlots."

However, Roget's reputation did not escape untarnished. If nothing else, Grant's charges revealed how much Roget had had to brush up on physiology to write his treatise. And in the same issue in which *The Lancet* published Roget's defense, its editors included a five-page commentary on the recent turns in his scientific career. Siding with Grant, they dubbed Roget "a literary pilferer."

The Lancet's editors also went after Roget for what they termed his "disgraceful treatment" of the scientist Marshall Hall. In the 1830s, the Royal Society kept refusing to publish Hall's groundbreaking papers on the nervous system. As its secretary, Roget, the journal concluded, had been complicit in a plot to deprive Hall of his due. Roget had, for example, slighted Hall by writing disparaging abstracts of his papers. Under the headline "Subterfuges of the Secretary of the Royal Society," appeared the editors' opinion: "Most assuredly the name of Dr. Roget will remain in disreputable connexion with these transactions [regarding Dr. Hall] as long as the Royal Society or physiology itself shall continue." On the basis of his egregious behavior toward both Grant and Hall, the editors concluded Roget should be sacked.

The following year, Roget was also embroiled in the fall-out from the so-called "Beck-Lee affair." This conflict involved the Royal Society's Committee of Zoology and Physiology, which Roget headed, and two scientists: Robert Lee, a lecturer in midwifery at St. George's Hospital, and Thomas Snow Beck, a prominent surgeon. In 1845, Beck received the Society's Royal Medal for research on the gravid uterus, even though Lee was widely considered the authority on the topic. What's more, Beck's paper, "On the Nerves of the Uterus," had never even been read to the Society—a requirement for the award. Roget's committee, The Lancet concluded, had "caused the Society to stink in the nostrils of all decent people."

On February 11, 1847, a special general meeting of the Royal Society was held to examine the situation. Thomas Wharton Jones, a prominent physiologist and ophthalmologist, made a motion to rescind Beck's award. Roget—along with the president of the Royal Society, the Marquis of Northampton—conceded that errors had been made, but he refused to take any action. Though the old guard of the Royal Society had won this battle, they had lost the war: both Roget and the Marquis would soon be forced out of the corridors of power.

On November 30, 1847, at the Royal Society's annual meeting, Roget announced his resignation as secretary, effective the following year. As he stated, he had been forced to endure "malignant attacks." Unwilling to back down, Roget refused to take responsibility for any of his questionable behavior. Looking forward, Roget expressed the hope "that I may dedicate the remaining term of life that may yet be spared me to those pursuits of science to which I have always been warmly attached and with which the labours and cares of office have seriously interfered." Though Roget was nearly seventy, he found himself, once again, at a crossroads. He had no idea what to do next, and wasn't sure whether he still had the energy to tackle another major scientific project.

During his final year at the Royal Society, Roget kept thinking about his legacy. "Will I be remembered," he asked himself, "simply as someone who had classified and arranged the work of others in my elegant treatises? Will I ever be able to distinguish myself by producing a groundbreaking work of my own?"

After the publication of his *Bridgewater Treatise*, Roget's scholarship had come to almost a complete halt. He had been reduced to menial tasks such as drafting an alphabetical index to the first volume of printed minutes of the Council of the Royal Society for the years 1832 to 1845. "The copious Index," Roget complained to John Lubbock, the society's vice president in 1846, "has cost me a vast deal of time and trouble and I only hope it may be useful in proportion." During the 1840s, his only bona fide publications were the abstracts for Royal Society papers that he had produced as secretary.

By the time of his retirement, some British academics saw Roget not only as well past his prime, but also as a popularizer rather than a scientist. He was just a book physiologist—not a bona fide researcher like Robert Grant, the University of London lecturer from whom he had borrowed so heavily. Though Roget had written hundreds of thousands of words in his clear and useful prose, so went the lament, he never really had had anything original or profound to say. "What," the editors of *The Lancet* had asked in 1846, had Roget "done to advance . . . the sciences of anatomy or physiology?"

Unbeknownst to Roget, a few people who knew him well went even further in their denunciations. To Mary Clarke, a family acquaintance, who, after her marriage to the orientalist Julius Mohl, would maintain a celebrated literary salon in Paris, Roget lacked substance. After reading *The Memoirs of the Life of Sir Samuel Romilly*, first published in 1840, Clarke was struck by how poorly Roget stacked up against Romilly, not to mention his own father, Jean Roget. Clarke wrote the philanthropist Elizabeth Reid, who had long been close to both Roget and his wife: "Is it not grievous that the nephew of such a man and the son of such another should have so little of the soul of them both for you will own that Dr. Roget is very well and clever and learned, etc. He is like an empty bag compared to his uncle and . . . his father." For Clarke, Roget's scholarship was too disconnected from his heart to amount to much.

As the curtain fell on his academic career at the end of 1848, Roget wasn't quite ready to pack it in. His mind was as sharp as ever, and he was still teeming with ambition.

PART THREE

Wordsmith in Retirement

(1849–1869)

(128) AGE, old age, senility, senescence, oldness, years, anility, decline of life, grey hairs, climacteric, decrepitude, hoary age, caducity, the sere and yellow leaf, wane of life, crow's feet, superannuation, dotage, vale of years, seniority, green old age, eldership, elders.

9.

Back
to the
Thesaurus

(562) WORD, term, vocable, monogram, cypher, terminology, etymon.

Word similarly pronounced, homonym.

A dictionary, vocabulary, lexicon, index, polyglot, glossary, thesaurus, gradus; lexicography; a lexicographer.

It was a cold evening at the end of January. The year was 1849. Roget, who had just turned seventy, was in his home at 18 Upper Bedford Place. Having just finished dinner, he got up from the table and sat down on his favorite ottoman, upholstered in the same crimson fabric used for the drapes. Immediately, Margaret Spowers, Kate, and John, who was to go back to Cambridge the following week, as well as Annette, who was visiting from Ilfracombe for the winter holidays, all followed his lead.

Roget suddenly stood up and declared, "I was just reading the current issue of *Gentleman's Magazine*. I am at a loss for words. Hester Lynch Piozzi is making a return."

"I thought she had been dead for years, Papa," said Kate.

"Yes, she died in 1821. And then *Piozziana*—that small book of scattered recollections by the writer Edward Mangin, who knew her toward the end of her life—appeared in 1833. I thought she would then fade into history. But listen to this."

Roget picked up the magazine and read aloud the following:

The purpose of this and a few following papers will be to add to [Mangin's] recollections of that celebrated and clever lady by extracts from one of her publications which is but little known—we mean her *British Synonymy*. They will contain anecdotes of literature, mention of her contemporaries, criticisms and miscellaneous information that has not been incorporated into other works. Mrs. Piozzi deserves to be known by her own writings.

"If they really want to revive her writings, let them bring back her anecdotes about Dr. Johnson," said Roget. "Her synonym book is nothing but a collection of irregularities."

"Your unpublished manuscript is so much more useful," said Spowers.

"I know it is. Piozzi is so vague and unscientific. Consider her entry for 'dull.'" Grabbing the magazine, he continued to read aloud:

DULL, STUPID, HEAVY.

Of the first upon this flat and insipid list, Mr. Pope has greatly enlarged the signification and taught us to call every thing *dull* that was not indubitably and pointedly witty. This is too much, surely.

Spowers then left the room and went into Roget's study. Roget said, "Piozzi is right to point to Pope's lapse, but her work is so disorganized. The opposite of dull is cheerful, not witty or intelligent."

Just then Spowers reappeared, holding Roget's 1805 manuscript in her hand. "And here are the synonyms you list next to 'dull': 'flat, spiritless, sad, mournful.'"

"Yes, 'dull' is more closely related to that class of words," said Roget.

"Perhaps it is time that you publish your book, Papa," said Kate.

Two months after officially stepping down from his post at the Royal Society, Roget hadn't yet decided what he was going to work on next. Now he knew. He had to pick up the fight against Piozzi.

Roget was not the only Englishman upset by Piozzi's reemergence. Though *Gentleman's Magazine* would continue to fawn over her, sprinkling excerpts from her *Synonymy* in several issues over the next couple of years, *Fraser's* would take her on. Alluding to her "evil genius," and her "slip-shod" manner, an unidentified writer concluded:

> Mrs. Piozzi runs in amongst words like a child at romps, and tosses them about apparently more in sport than earnest. The want of earnestedness is in her . . . simply the want of sense and information. Shallow people can never be in earnest; and Mrs. Piozzi is a shining illustration of shallowness.

To those critics who considered his *Bridgewater Treatise* second-rate, Roget would show the stuff of which he was made. Roget felt compelled to put sense back into synonymy. He knew how indispensable his little book of lists had been to him over the last half-century. Now he would put it into a form so that English-speakers all around the globe could also express themselves clearly and precisely. He would make one last effort to restore order to the world.

B ut just as Roget started reimmersing himself in his word lists, a family crisis was brewing. His daughter, Kate, was rapidly descending into madness.

In early October 1849, Kate Roget, then nearing her twenty-fourth birthday, began feeling sad and listless. For most of the month, Kate remained bedridden with a brain fever. Worried about the state of her soul, Kate kept referring to her "religious despondence." In mid-October, Roget took her to Hampstead along with John. At times, his daughter could barely move. She also appeared to be plagued by obsessions of a sexual nature; no one, however, could make sense of her behavior. Having already watched both his mother and his uncle go mad, Roget was terrified. At the end of the month, John confessed to his uncle Joseph Romilly that he and his father saw "no prospect of her recovering her senses."

Just when Roget had nearly lost all hope, Kate made a sudden turnaround. As the fever went away, she was no longer so preoccupied with her obsessions about sex and religion. In early November, she sent John, who was back at Cambridge, a letter in which she spoke of herself as being no more "Kate the crazed." She was, she wrote, "clothed and in her right mind." (A close reader of the Bible, Kate was alluding to the description of the demon-possessed man whom Christ comes upon in the Gospel of Mark.)

Elizabeth Bostock—known as Eliza—the daughter of Roget's former neighbor, the late Dr. John Bostock, had known Kate since she had been a little girl and tried to assume the role of Kate's protector. As Eliza Bostock, then in her early thirties, observed in 1849, "I feel as if dear Kate were a sort of charge of mine, as she was commended to my friendship both by her mother and grandmother and how I wish it were in my power to be of more use to her." After her father's death in 1844, an event which would later make it onto Roget's "Dates of Deaths," Bostock had moved to Mayfair.

Eliza initially thought Kate might have consumption, so she was greatly relieved to discover that Kate was back on her feet. After visiting the Rogets on December 9, Bostock reported to their mutual friend Elizabeth Jesser-Reid: "I was delighted to find Kate so cheerful. I wish I could also add that she is looking well. Her manner to her father is quite touching, so affectionate and tender; the Doctor himself is radiant with good spirits." Underneath her cheerful demeanor, however, Kate was still struggling with intense feelings of anxiety and despair.

In 1850, Kate Roget hit rock bottom. That spring, Eliza reported to Mrs. Reid that Kate was "very sad" and had lost interest in doing much of anything. What had led to Kate's incapacitating depression is not entirely clear. Like her aunt Annette some four decades earlier, Kate appears to have been rocked by the sudden loss of a suitor. In one letter to Mrs. Reid, Eliza linked Kate with a tale of two lovers who couldn't marry. Kate's surge of sexual and religious mania may well have had its roots in an illicit affair. Whatever the ultimate source of Kate's nervous collapse, her tense relationship with Margaret Spowers made matters only worse. Victorian governesses were supposed to help the young women of the house make their entrance into society, but Spowers was interested solely in Roget. And Kate felt nothing but resentment.

Roget sent Kate to see two of his friends—the doctors Richard Bright and Charles Locock, both of whom were then attending to Queen Victoria. While Bright, who had opened a private practice on Oxford Street after retiring from Guy's Hospital, was the monarch's personal physician, Locock, a physician at Westminster Lying-In Hospital, was her midwife and gynecologist. Locock appeared particularly ill-suited to the emotionally distraught Kate; one colleague described

him as "undemonstrative . . . to the point of coldness." Treatment records do not exist, so it's not clear what exactly either Bright or Locock
did for Kate. But as Eliza reported, Bright—today considered "the father of nephrology"—did make a constructive suggestion, encourag-
ing her to leave the Roget home and get a job as a governess.

While Kate awaited a change of scene, she languished. She managed to take a brief trip with Eliza in April to Wales to visit Eliza's eld-
erly mother. Eliza began to worry that something was fundamentally
wrong with Kate. She wrote Reid that Roget's daughter seemed to
lack the emotional wherewithal to deal with the ups and downs of life:

> There is reason in her present state of mind, but also some disease.
> Most people's minds possess a power of righting themselves
> notwithstanding . . . the hard mysteries of life which are enough to
> bewilder the wisest of us . . . but this poor Kate cannot do. If you
> could see her in her depressed mood, you would not doubt there
> being disease.

Roget kept trying to place Kate with a family, but none could be
found. Frantic, he took a drastic step. On May 18 he sent Kate away
to the suburb of Blackheath, along with just a maidservant and a
companion. Kate had become a pariah. Her brother, John, like the
rest of the family, was aghast. In June 1850, Joseph Romilly went to
a family gathering at the West End home of his cousin Edward
Romilly—a son of Samuel Romilly. Kate was the topic du jour, and
the Romillys all condemned Roget's treatment of his daughter as
brutal. As the Cambridge dean reported in his diary, "All the windows [in Kate's temporary abode] are barred up, & he [Roget] will
not give anyone her address—he has taken away from her her bible

and all religious books. It's a most melancholy case!" Roget, who had survived his own bouts of despair by shutting out the world, had prescribed the sensory-deprivation cure. Kate was permitted to do little else but to request to be read to.

Eliza Bostock was one of those family friends kept in the dark about Kate's whereabouts. Remarkably, despite Roget's draconian measures, later that summer Kate was on the mend. John reported to Eliza that she was writing lively letters and was once again interested in the family's activities. Realizing that, wherever Kate was, sooner or later she would have to go back to Upper Bedford Place, Eliza was worried. She pleaded with Mrs. Reid to intercede on Kate's behalf: "But now to avoid a relapse! How difficult that will be! If the place could but be cleared of Miss Spowers before Kate returns. If you have still kept in favour with Dr. Roget, . . . use it in this direction." But Roget would never agree to part ways with his mistress.

Kate first came back home on a trial basis for a few weeks in December 1850. In April of the following year, she returned from Blackheath for good. Her disabling symptoms had subsided, and life was back to normal at 18 Upper Bedford Place. However, Kate's relationship with Spowers remained frosty, so she decided to get away as much as she could. That fall, Kate escaped to the lodgings of her former governess, Miss Agnes Catlow, then living twenty-five miles north of London, in Beaconsfield.

Though Kate never became quite so depressed again, like her aunt Annette, she would resign herself to a lonely life. She would eventually return to live full-time with Roget, but only after Spowers's early death a couple of years later. Kate would then replace Spowers as her father's constant companion. Never marrying, Kate would remain fiercely devoted to her father until his death.

. . . .

The breakdown of a cherished adult daughter right before one's eyes might have nearly incapacitated another septuagenarian father, but not Roget. He managed to carry on more or less as usual. After all, he had the perfect refuge—the manuscript of his emerging *Thesaurus*, which required his constant attention.

As Roget began to rework his dusty 1805 draft, he first had to reacquaint himself with the new synonym books that had appeared over the last half-century.

By far the most popular contribution to the genre, in both England and America, was *English Synonymes Explained*, published by George Crabb in 1816. A lawyer and writer, Crabb had no academic credentials; he had started out in medicine, but had quit the field after fainting during dissections. Like both Trusler and Piozzi, Crabb also drafted short articles on groups of words relating not to physical objects but to behavioral phenomena. But Crabb's text was much more comprehensive, consisting of roughly 2,400 alphabetically arranged articles comprising more than 1,000 pages. While Crabb acknowledged "profiting by everything which has been written in any language on the subject" and referred directly to the works of his famous predecessors, he also engaged in some literary piracy. *The Quarterly Review* pointed out that Crabb had lifted about 150 of his articles nearly verbatim from William Taylor's little-read 1813 contribution, *English Synonyms Discriminated*.

Roget also took a look at *A Selection of English Synonyms*, published by Richard Whately, the archbishop of Dublin, in 1851. Divided into four sections corresponding to different parts of speech—adverbs, pronouns and particles, verbs, and adjectives and nouns—Whately's slender book of just 170 pages featured short articles that elucidated the meanings of closely related words. Its tone was moralistic. Whately admitted to being a dilettante. As the archbishop once confessed, "I know nothing thoroughly. Elementary studies are most to my taste." Roget looked down upon Whately, considering him a subpar scholar. On one crucial point, however, Roget did agree with Whately. Whately argued in his synonym book—the only one Roget would footnote in his *Thesaurus*—there really was no such thing as a synonym, because no two words can mean exactly the same thing.

Roget felt so strongly about this common misuse of the word "synonym" that he ended up changing the title of his new book; unlike his 1805 manuscript, it would not be "Collection of English Synonyms" but *Thesaurus of Words and Phrases*. For Roget, a synonym was not another word for the same thing but the same word for the same thing. In the 1852 edition, he stuck "synonym" next to "namesake" under "Nomenclature" 564.

Though Roget studied carefully all the previous synonym books, going back to Abbé Girard's early-eighteenth-century masterpiece, he would chart an entirely new direction in lexicography. Unlike Girard and his successors, Roget aimed not to explain or prescribe the use of words. Rather, he felt he just needed to list all the options. He would write in the introduction, "My object . . . is not to regulate the use of words, but simply to supply and to suggest such as may be wanted on occasion, leaving the proper selection entirely to the discretion and taste of the employer." The closest analogue to *Roget's* was not a synonym book but a dictionary. In 1805, William Perry, an Edinburgh schoolteacher and onetime surgeon in the Royal Navy, had come out with *The Synonymous, Etymological, and Pronouncing English Dictionary*. Based on Samuel Johnson's *Dictionary*, Perry's word book contained some 24,000 alphabetically arranged lists such as the following:

Abbreviation, ABRIDGEMENT

For just about every entry, Perry designated one synonym a root word—which he referred to as a "radical"—under which he listed numerous other synonyms. For example, the above entry continues as follows:

ABRIDGEMENT, contraction, reduction, diminution

His goal, Perry noted, was to help the reader "select terms to express his ideas with greater clearness and precision."

To organize his ideas, Roget turned to numbers. In his 1805 manuscript, Roget had identified a few hundred concepts, about three per page. For example, the first page contained the ideas "existence, state, mode, and relation." He mined this turf to come up with his first two ideas: "Existence" 1 and "Relation" 2. Greatly expanding his 1805 lists, Roget eventually came up with an even one thousand ideas, including those last-minute add-ons 450a and 465a.

Roget ended up categorizing each idea according by class, division, and section, just as natural historians like Linnaeus had catalogued animals according to phylum, class, and order. For example, the idea "PERFECTION" falls under Class V, "Words Relating to the Voluntary Powers," Division I, "Individual Volition," and Section i, "Volition in General." (The Roman numerals V. I. i. are written at the top of the page where the entry, "Perfection" appears, thus giving the book the feel of scripture.)

As Roget envisioned it, the *Thesaurus* would be a reverse dictionary. In his introduction, he explained how it worked: "The idea being given, to find the word, or words by which that idea may be most fitly and aptly expressed." Here's the beginning of the entry for "perfection":

(650) PERFECTION, perfectness, bestness, indefectibility, impeccability, beau ideal (210).

Master-piece, chef d'oeuvre, model, pattern, mirror, phoenix, rara avis, paragon, prime, flower, cream, none such, non-pareil, elite.

Gem, bijou, jewel, pearl, diamond, ruby, brilliant.

The entry then continued with the verb and adjectival forms of "perfect"—"to be perfect" and "perfect"—and listed several synonyms for each.

As in Roget's draft from 1805, each page was divided into two columns. The "correlative word" (Roget's term for "antonym," which still had not yet been coined) for each entry listed in the left column was printed in the right column. For this "correlative word," Roget then listed numerous synonymous words. On the right side of the page, across from "(650) PERFECTION" was the following entry:

(651) IMPERFECTION, imperfectness, unsoundness, faultiness, deficiency, drawback, inadequacy, inadequateness.

Fault, defect, flaw, crack, twist, taint, peccancy.

Mediocrity, mean (29), indifference, inferiority.

For Roget, the careful use of language depended on understanding not only the meanings of individual words but also the relations between them. These neighboring lists of opposing ideas, he believed, opened up all kinds of new vistas for readers. Roget noted in his introduction, "The inquirer may often discover forms of expression, of which he may avail himself advantageously, to diversify and infuse vigor into his phraseology."

Initially Roget thought that readers would find the words they were looking for by first immersing themselves in his classification system. But at the last minute, he realized that this process could be cumbersome. To ensure that readers could easily locate where a given word appears, he supplied an alphabetical index in the back. For example, under "defect," one finds: "incomplete," 53, "imperfect," 651, and "failing," 945. Although Roget's work had a philosophical bent, his audience was the man in the street, not scholars.

Roget also had a social agenda that was consistent with his firm belief in historical progress. Like his Edinburgh mentor, Dugald Stewart, and his uncle Sir Samuel Romilly, Roget sought to improve the welfare of the nation. "Specious phraseology," Roget asserted, could disseminate "the seeds of prejudice and error." If the masses could learn to use language better, he emphasized, perhaps they might be able to right much of what was wrong with the world.

Roget's hopes for improving the lot of mankind were, in turn, firmly rooted in his religious faith. By organizing not just all words, but all ideas—that is, all knowledge—Roget believed that he was highlighting God's creative achievements. As Roget saw it, his *Thesaurus*, like his *Bridgewater Treatise*, was a tribute to God, who alone was responsible for the order in the universe.

The thousand copies of the first edition published in May 1852, priced at fourteen shillings apiece, sold out quickly. Roget felt immense pride when he began reading the glowing reviews. On July 8, 1852, *The Times* noted, "There cannot be the slightest doubt that, upon the whole, it is one of the most learned as well as one of the most admirable contributions that have been made to philology since . . . the *Diversions of Purley* by Horne Tooke." Likewise, *The Literary Examiner* referred to "its great value." However, a few reviewers had a quibble. As *The Athenaeum* stressed in September 1852, good writers really didn't need a "crutch." However, no one raised any doubt about the quality of his finished product. Roget had redeemed his reputation.

It was a bright, sunny morning; the date was Thursday, November 18, 1852, and the biggest funeral the world had ever seen was about to begin.

Some two months after his death, at the age of eighty-three, the first Duke of Wellington, who had conquered Napoleon before dominating British politics for a generation, was to take his final ride. The man born Arthur Wellesley was, Queen Victoria declared, "the greatest man this country ever produced."

It had been pouring all night long, and puddles pervaded the streets of London. Perhaps this was fitting because, as many commentators recalled, it had also rained the night before Wellington's greatest triumph—the Battle of Waterloo.

Along with some one and a half million of his fellow countrymen, Roget was eager to view the procession that would take Wellington's twenty-seven-foot-long funeral carriage from Horse Guards—the headquarters of the British army's general staff—via Constitution Hill to St. Paul's Cathedral.

Standing just outside of the cathedral, Roget spotted the French delegation. Even Wellington's most bitter enemies could now acknowledge his greatness. As it turned out, all the major European countries—with the exception of Austria—had sent representatives to the funeral.

Accompanying Roget to St. Paul's was Samuel Hobson, the twin of his long-departed wife—then in his late fifties—who had come in from Liverpool on the 16th just for the occasion. John was also with him, and so was Kate, who had returned home for good a month earlier.

Kate had ended her peripatetic existence soon after the chief obstacle to her residence at 18 Upper Bedford Place had been removed. On September 20, less than a week after the death of Wellington, Margaret Spowers had died. Roget, who had supervised her medical care, had been at her bedside.

Spowers's death from breast cancer had been sudden. Just two weeks before her death, she had finalized her will, which Roget and his son signed as witnesses. Spowers left her considerable holdings to various relatives; Roget, then well-to-do, but not as wealthy as he would soon become on account of the brisk sales of the *Thesaurus*, received nothing.

As Roget entered St. Paul's, he was feeling angry. Though his ticket had a number, there were no numbers on the seats. The ensuing scramble for a spot proved particularly unsettling. Eventually, he and the rest of the family found a pew toward the front. Once settled, Roget noticed his cousin Joseph Romilly, sitting by himself in the second row, buried in a book. Romilly, who had brought along a copy of *She Stoops to Conquer*—a comedy by the eighteenth-century writer Oliver Goldsmith—to keep himself entertained, saw Roget out of the corner of his eye and put his hand to his hat.

While Wellington was buried under the dome next to Nelson, everyone in the cathedral sat transfixed. As Romilly later recorded in his diary, "The rehearsal of the long list of titles by the Herald, the breaking his wand and throwing it into the Grave, & the discharge of a single cannon concluded the sublime ceremonial."

As Roget walked out of St. Paul's, he was overcome by sadness. Observing a tear streaming down his cheek, Samuel Hobson asked, "The loss of the great man moves you so?"

Seeing Wellington's coffin up close, Roget told his onetime

brother-in-law, he had been flooded with memories of Napoleon; he felt so grateful that Wellington had saved his country from that awful tyrant.

But in truth, Roget was also grieving the loss of Spowers, and that was something he had to keep from both Samuel Hobson and his children—particularly Kate. What Spowers had meant to him, he would tell no one.

Five years later, however, when he got around to compiling his "Dates of Deaths," he could hardly omit her name. He would always remember Spowers.

B ut Roget didn't have much time to grieve, because he had work to do. He had recently signed a new contract with Longmans to bring out a second edition of the *Thesaurus* (consisting of 1,500 copies) in March 1853. This time around, Roget would receive two-thirds—rather than one-half—of the profits. The following year, an American edition of his *Thesaurus* appeared.

Though the *Thesaurus* would emerge as a huge hit in America, the first overseas edition was a disaster. The responsibility lay not with Roget but with the American editor, Dr. Barnas Sears, a religious educator who had imposed his own priggish sensibility on Roget's text. Sears, who became president of Brown University in 1855, wrote in his preface, "The greatest fault of the work is that of incorporating so many objectionable words and phrases, which ought never to meet the eye or tempt the tongue." To combat what he perceived to be an oversight on Roget's part, Sears excised this so-called "objectionable" material from the *Thesaurus*. But in point of fact, Roget himself was rather prudish, and most of the "vulgar" words and phrases that Sears suppressed—such as "aria" and "fugue," as well as "the ups and downs of life"—were hardly scatological.

In response to the fierce criticism in the American press of his first edition, Sears tried a slightly different tack. In the second edition, published the following year, Sears banished the words and phrases that he did not consider "classical" to an appendix. The reviewer in *Putnam's Monthly* considered this strategy even more ridiculous, since the so-called objectionable words "are more likely to catch the eye of 'students and younger readers' as they are now placed, than they are in Roget's original arrangement." Sears, the reviewer concluded, should stop "meddling with Prof. Roget's book." (In later editions published after Roget's death, Sears acquiesced and restored Roget's original arrangement.)

Though Roget was disheartened by the American *Thesaurus*, he was delighted by its French incarnation, called *Dictionnaire idéologique*, which came out in 1859 under the editorship of Theodore Robertson. In his preface, Robertson, a language instructor, long a resident of Paris, who had written a popular English textbook for French speakers, admitted that he had spent years trying to come up with his own classification system. Amazed by the utility of the *Thesaurus*, Robertson heaped praise on Roget, calling him "not only an erudite man, but a philosopher and a scholar."

Roget, who had personally authorized Robertson's replication, felt vindicated. While a Frenchman—Abbé Girard—had launched the synonym book in the early eighteenth century, the French were now imitating him. Roget had created the gold standard. No lexicographer in any language would ever be able to think about writing one without first consulting *Roget's*.

10.

Vibrant Until the Last Breath

(360) DEATH, decease, dissolution, demise, departure, obit, expiration, termination, close or extinction of life, existence, &c., sideration, mortality, fall, doom, fate, release, rest, quietus, loss.

Last breath, last gasp, last agonies, dying breath, agonies of death.

I n 1833, when Roget was in his mid-fifties, he had written an article, "Age," in which he detailed the physiological mechanisms of the aging process for *The Cyclopaedia of Practical Medicine*, a popular magazine that published contributions from England's best medical writers. Summing up his thoughts on old age, Roget had mused:

Old age steals upon us by slow and imperceptible degrees, which, even when obvious to others, are often unknown to ourselves. . . . But the number of those who thus gently glide along the stream of years is small indeed, when compared with those whose declining age is withered by infirmities or embittered by disease.

Roget, pictured at age eighty-eight, frequently dressed in black.

Little did Roget then know that he, in contrast to his mother and sister, would later evolve into one of those rare human beings who aged gracefully.

As he began his eighties, Roget seemed indestructible. Even after a botched surgery in 1861 to remove a polyp from his right nostril (he hemorrhaged for nineteen hours), Roget quickly rebounded. Right after this mishap, Joseph Romilly recorded in his diary: "[Dr.

Roget] is in that vigorous state of health that he was none the worse." After he ran into Roget a few years later at a dinner party, the publisher Charles Knight made a similar remark, observing that Roget was "full of animation—with undimmed intelligence—his age was 'as a lusty winter, frosty, but kindly.'"

Roget could still do everything that he had always done, including traveling and hiking. Eliza Bostock, who spent part of the summer of 1862 with the Rogets in Ilfracombe, noted that August, "The Doctor walked eight miles one day—no symptoms of decay there!"

As Roget continued to tinker with the new editions of the *Thesaurus*, his mind was still as sharp as ever; both his short-term and long-term memory remained entirely intact. At the age of eighty-eight, Roget reported that he could still remember the face of the legendary leader of the French Revolution, the Comte de Mirabeau, whom he had met eight decades earlier through Dumont: "I have a perfect recollection of having seen this remarkable man, when I was quite a child and when he was paying a visit at the house where I was staying."

Retirement also left Roget time to pursue such hobbies as chess, book collecting, and word games. Letting his guard down late in life, Roget developed a dry sense of humor. He began writing riddles such as the following:

> *What is that which is under you?*
> *Take one letter from it and it is over you?*
> *Take two letters from it and it is round you?*
> *(Answers—chair, hair, air.)*

Roget also wrote witty maxims. For example, maxim 41: "When an old man complains that he is weary of the world, we may be pretty sure that the world has already been weary of him."

. . .

It was Saturday morning, June 30, 1860. The site was the Natural History Museum at Oxford University. The debate of the century was about to take place, and Roget, then eighty-one, was there to witness it.

Roget had arrived in Oxford by train on Wednesday—the day before the start of the thirtieth annual meeting of the British Association for the Advancement of Science. He had attended nearly every annual meeting of the society since its founding in 1831. Especially after his retirement from the Royal Society, the conferences, which typically lasted several days, held enormous significance for him, constituting his one remaining link to academia. In his "List of Principal Events," the telegraphic summary of his life written in 1857, he kept a list of every British Association meeting and its locale (it circulated among Britain's major cities), including those planned well into the 1860s.

Roget had initially been wary of the British Association because it had sprung up to protest the goings-on at his beloved Royal Society. Cofounded a generation earlier by Roget's good friend Sir David Brewster, the inventor of the kaleidoscope, and Charles Babbage, the grandfather of the modern calculator, this group of elite scientists aimed to keep Britain in the vanguard of international scientific research. Back in 1830, both Brewster and Babbage had been convinced that the Royal Society lacked the necessary vitality. "The society once justly famed as the focus of talent and genius," Babbage had written then, "is now reduced [to] . . . a medical advertising office, a very puff-shop for the chaff of medical-scribblers." Though unlike Babbage and Brewster, Roget never turned his back on the Royal Society, he quickly embraced the new association, serving as a council member throughout most of its first decade.

But after the events that were to unfold that June day in 1860, Roget would suddenly change his opinion about the activities of the British Association. The annual meeting would no longer be a fixture on his schedule—not because of his advancing age, but because of its new direction.

This was to be the first conference since the publication of Darwin's *Origin of Species*, which was provoking fierce debate throughout England. All 1,250 copies of the first edition, which had come out half a year earlier, on November 24, 1859, had sold out in a day. Though Darwin himself was not in attendance, he was foremost on everyone's mind.

Roget was one of about seven hundred people packed into the long west room of the museum to attend a session organized by the Association's Zoology and Botany section. On the left side, near the window, were scores of ladies waving white handkerchiefs to combat the suffocating heat. On the right side was the platform where the speaker, Dr. John William Draper, a chemist from Liverpool who headed the new medical school at the University of New York (today New York University), slowly rose. Draper then began to read his paper, "On the Intellectual Development of Europe Considered with Reference to the Views of Mr. Darwin."

Roget was looking forward to hearing Draper's remarks. He had glanced at Draper's most recent book, a survey of human physiology, and had been impressed. Though Roget was upset that Draper had failed to cite his *Bridgewater Treatise*, Draper, he thought, seemed an eminently reasonable chap. But Roget was soon crestfallen. "The motion of the earth round the sun, the antiquity of the globe, the origin of species," Draper began, "are doctrines which have had to force their way not against philosophical opposition, but against opposition of a totally different nature."

"Oh no," Roget thought to himself. "Draper has it wrong. Darwin is no Copernicus!" Copernicus had been a hero to Roget ever since he put pen to paper and created his diagrams of the solar system in his childhood notebook. By contrast, for Roget, Darwin posed a threat to his belief in God's infinite wisdom.

An hour later, Draper finished, and a hush came over the throng. The members of the clergy, seated in a mass at the center of the room, were aghast at Dr. Draper's repeated assertions of the need to value science over theology.

After a few brief outcries against Darwin, calls were made for Samuel Wilberforce, the bishop of Oxford, to give his reply. As Wilberforce, who was known as one of the country's most eloquent speakers, began to fill the room with his melodic tones, Roget's mind suddenly wandered.

For a moment, he was back at another British Association meeting, this one in Cambridge in 1845, when he had slept in Joseph Romilly's bed at Trinity College. On Friday, June 20 of that year, he had dined with Wilberforce, then the new dean of Westminster. Two days later, Roget had heard Wilberforce give a charity sermon before a packed audience at St. Mary's Church. Though his manner had been charming, Wilberforce had occasionally lapsed into vigorous rhetoric. "The chamber of voluptuousness," he had declared, "is the antechamber of hell." And on the following Monday, while Roget and Romilly were having tea at the Observatory, Wilberforce had given what Romilly later called "a memorable speech vindicating science from the charge of irreligion."

Sitting in the overheated room in Oxford, Roget was eager to hear Wilberforce deliver similarly noble sentiments.

Roget was well aware of Wilberforce's distinguished lineage. His father had also been a crusader. Four decades before—on the night of February 23, 1807—William Wilberforce, the longtime MP from Yorkshire—had brought forth his motion in the House of Commons to put an end to the slave trade. On that occasion, Roget's uncle Samuel Romilly, then England's solicitor general, had made a memorable speech in support of Wilberforce. Romilly's words immediately had an almost magical impact. After three rousing hurrahs, during which Wilberforce shed many a tear, the MPs voted to abolish the slave trade by a vote of 283 to 16.

Roget sensed that another major turning point was at hand. As Roget knew, the bishop, who had just completed a critique of Darwin's *Origin*, to be published the next month in *The Quarterly Review*, was about to defend the word of God from the onslaught of evolution.

For half an hour, Wilberforce dug into the new theory. "Rock pigeons," he stated with a slight smile on his face, "were what rock pigeons had always been." After he finished his peroration, he suddenly turned to Thomas Huxley, the biologist seated next to him who had recently published several scholarly articles in defense of Darwin. Wilberforce then asked that scientist—known as "Darwin's bulldog"—whether it was through his grandfather or his grandmother that he claimed his descent from a monkey.

Before responding, the tall and thin Huxley looked over at Sir Benjamin Brodie, the physiologist and surgeon, who was also seated on the platform. Roget had known Brodie, then the royal physician, for more than half a century. Brodie had also recently operated on Roget, removing some polyps from his nose. Roget's heart sank when he heard Huxley sidle up to Brodie and say, "The Lord hath delivered him into mine hands."

Huxley then retorted: "If there were an ancestor whom I should feel shame in recalling it would rather be a man—a man of restless and versatile intellect—who, not content with an equivocal success in his own sphere of activity, plunges into scientific questions with which he has no real acquaintance."

After Huxley was finished, a man got up and raised a Bible over his head. His name was Robert FitzRoy, and though he was still in his mid-fifties, he looked old and decrepit.

"I was captain of the ship—the *Beagle*—on which Darwin did his preliminary research nearly thirty years ago. Huxley is wrong to say that Darwin's book is a logical arrangement of the facts."

Roget nodded his assent.

He was soon to lose interest in keeping up with science. He simply could not abide by the new paradigm in which God was becoming increasingly irrelevant. For Roget, natural history had to be reconciled with William Paley's *Natural Theology*. Yet although Roget didn't think it worth his while to study Darwin, Darwin was not through with Roget.

After all, Darwin was following in Roget's footsteps. According to Darwin's personal notebooks, back in December 1847 when he was beginning the research for *Origin*, he had pored over Roget's *Bridgewater Treatise*. And Roget's masterpiece was a book to which Darwin would constantly refer. On February 16, 1863, Darwin wrote to Huxley, asking him to double-check a fact maintained by his predecessor: "I am told that Roget (no good authority) says in his *Bridgewater Treatise* that in Frogs or Toads there is a rudiment of a sixth digit." Darwin may not have thought much of Roget's theoretical perspective, but he was forced to acknowledge his thoroughness. On June 27, 1863, he wrote Huxley a follow-up note: "You will remember my telling you that Roget says a frog has a rudiment of a 6th toe. I caught one yesterday (it is *rarissima avis* [a most rare bird])."

Though Roget didn't allow himself to be consumed by the heartache of Margaret Spowers's early death, he turned increasingly to Kate for emotional support. In June 1862, to lighten Kate's load and help him manage the household, he decided to hire a professional companion, a young woman named Julia Roe. Unlike Spowers, Roe didn't alienate anyone in the family. As Eliza Bostock reported from Ilfracombe, where she was vacationing along with the Rogets in August: "[Kate] says . . . Miss Roe is an excellent conscientious person. . . . Under her influence the whole [family] including the Aunt [Annette], is in a better state than it has been for years." Throughout the early 1860s, Roget continued to spend his summers in Ilfracombe, where he could see Annette, who still maintained her own home there. However, by 1862, Annette had become quite frail and required two live-in nursemaids. She would die a few years later, at the age of eighty-three.

But Julia Roe couldn't entirely alleviate the pressure Roget put on his daughter. Though Kate's severest bouts of depression were behind her, she still felt suffocated by her father's emotional neediness. In August 1862, Kate wanted to go with Eliza Bostock to Morte Bay—a Devon beach town not far from Ilfracombe—but Kate's duties at home took precedence. Miss Roe had taken the month off, and Roget insisted that Kate stay by his side. As Bostock confided to Mrs. Reid, "It is very difficult to manage a holiday for her. I am truly glad to have come to be near her [Kate], as her life here is most irksome."

The following year, Roget spent both April and August in Ilfracombe with Kate. In early September, Eliza Bostock, attentive as always to Kate's mental state, took Roget's two children, both now in their mid-thirties, with her on a month-long trip to Cornwall. As Bostock realized, Roget's worn-out daughter was much in need of a vacation of her own. Bostock's scheme worked. From Cornwall, she wrote Mrs. Reid, "We three get on capitally together. I am sure Kate is already better and enjoying all enthusiastically."

. . . .

At Ilfracombe in the summer of 1864, John became engaged to Frances Ditchfield, the daughter of a London doctor, James Butterworth Ditchfield. The marriage took place on February 28, 1865, at St. Pancras Church in Bloomsbury. After a five-month honeymoon on the Continent, the couple eventually settled in Paddington. In 1868, their daughter Elinor was born. At eighty-nine, Roget finally had a grandchild. John Lewis Roget went on to have two more children: Isobel, born in 1870, and Samuel Romilly—whose namesake, as John understood, had been like a father to Roget—born in 1875.

Roget was also delighted by the exciting developments in his son's professional life. After getting a master's degree from Cambridge in 1853, John began working as a lawyer in London. In 1864, he changed course, deciding to focus solely on his artistic and literary endeavors.

Ever since his Cambridge days, John had shown remarkable talent for pencil sketches. During summers in Ilfracombe in the 1850s, he had also started painting watercolors of landscape scenes. And by his early twenties, he was contributing decorative illustrations—along with short articles—to *The Pixie*, an Ilfracombe periodical. In 1859, he wrote *A Cambridge Scrap-Book*, a collection of humorous illustrations about university life. For example, John Roget made fun of mathematics—and perhaps indirectly of his father, the author of that famous paper on the "involution of numbers"—in his depiction of a nervous student in a dentist's chair, with the caption: "Extraction of a Root." A year later, Macmillan published a sequel, *A Volunteer's Scrap-Book*, in which John similarly spoofed military life.

John was also a budding art critic. In the early 1860s, Roget proudly attended John's occasional lectures on aesthetics at the Russell Institution, where he himself had spoken on physiology nearly half a century earlier. In 1864, John transformed the materials from these lectures into an article, "On the Study of Nature as a Guide to Art," for *Macmillan's Magazine*. In distinguishing the qualities of the naturalist from those of the artist, John was carving out his own identity vis-à-vis his legendary father, the perennial student of natural history. "The possession of a facile hand and a correct eye," John wrote in these aesthetic musings, "is not . . . enough to convert a learned naturalist into a good painter." In John's view, unlike the naturalist, the artist was duty-bound not only to observe all natural objects but also to pay special attention to those that inspired him with delight. For John, creating beauty involved feeling the world rather than simply reproducing it mechanically. In contrast to his father, John was not the prototypical repressed Victorian. "As for John," Eliza Bostock once observed, "I do most thoroughly appreciate his good feeling, as in these days when it is the fashion to have or to express no feeling—for men at least."

Yet despite his artistic sensibility, John, like his father, was a "classifying and arranging" machine. He spent many years working on a massive two-volume history of the Royal Society of Painters in Water-Colors, a survey of the careers of all the leading English watercolorists of the nineteenth century. In an effort to be of the utmost use to his readers, John introduced his short biographies of Royal Society members by listing the highlights of their lives in short phrases—say, Published Works—which then became the headings for the write-ups that followed. Sounding much like his father, John announced in his preface that he had "classified, to some extent, on a uniform system, under the names of several artists, the facts referred to in their respective biographies."

After leaving the law, John also began helping his father with new editions of the *Thesaurus*. After Roget's death in 1869, John would

John Roget and his family in 1882, in front of the summer house he owned at 13 The Beach, Walmer, in Kent.

take over as editor. In 1879, John produced a well-received enlarged edition of the *Thesaurus*, which his father had been preparing upon his death. As John Roget wrote in the introduction (Longmans printed 4,000 copies, twice as many as for any previous edition): "It became my duty, as his son, to attempt to carry the design into execution." One innovation was a greatly expanded index, which now included not only words, but also phrases—for example, "Neck, break one's." The new index would be almost the same length as the main body of the text.

After Annette's death, Roget began spending his summers in West Malvern rather than in Ilfracombe. He enjoyed hiking on the lush farmland overlooking the river Severn and felt at home in this town high up in the Worcestershire Hills, which, like Ilfracombe, typically had a soothing effect on its visitors. In 1842, neighboring Great Malvern had established itself as the English capital of hydrotherapy, then considered a valuable tool to combat nervous afflictions. Legions of distraught Victorian intellectuals—among them Charles Darwin, Charles Dickens, and Samuel Wilberforce—would make pilgrimages to obtain a prolonged course of treatment. The "water cure" typically consisted of lots of well water and cold showers, combined with daily immersion in wet sheets.

On September 12, 1869, the nearly ninety-one-year-old Roget died while on vacation with Kate in West Malvern. He was laid to rest in the graveyard of St. James Church. Kate would be buried under the same tombstone as her father when she died, thirty-six years later.

Roget's peaceful death at the age of ninety is reminiscent of the gentle slumber that the narrator falls into at the beginning of the famous fourteenth-century poem *Piers Plowman*. In the immortal words of the poet William Langland, an area native:

But on a May morning on Malvern hills . . .
Being tired of wandering, I took a rest
Under a broad bank by a bourne's side,
And as I lay down, leaned over and looked into the water.
I fell into a sleep for it sounded so merry.

Once asleep, the poet has the dream-visions that make up the heart of this Middle English epic. By contrast, Roget, having already created his literary masterpiece, was ready for his eternal rest. He had few regrets. As *The New York Times* obituary observed, "At the ripe old age of nearly a century he was enabled to look back through the years that had passed, and calmly awaiting the approach of death, feel that his life had not been wasted, but that all his energies and his best years had been freely given for the benefit of mankind."

But *Roget's* was not a project that Peter Mark Roget ever chose—his obsessions and compulsions hardly gave him the latitude *not* to work on it. Ever since childhood, burying himself in words was the only survival strategy available to him. Ultimately, *Roget's*—along with all the decades of prepatory work—did much more for its creator than it has done for its hundreds of millions of users across the centuries; it enabled Roget to live a vibrant life in the face of overwhelming loss, anxiety, and despair. This personal feat was an equally impressive achievement.

The *Thesaurus* Through the Years

(65) SEQUEL, after-part, suffix, successor, tail, queue, train, wake, trail, rear, retinue, appendix, postscript, epilogue, after-piece, after-thought.

Yes, I'm the guy who put 'masturbation' into *Roget's*," says George Davidson, the current British editor of the *Thesaurus*, now published by Penguin Books. In 2002, Davidson, a freelance lexicographer who lives in Edinburgh, spearheaded Penguin's 150th-anniversary edition of *Roget's*. He is the sixth person to succeed Peter Mark Roget. First came Roget's two heirs: his son, John, and his grandson, Samuel. Shortly before his death in 1952, Samuel Romilly Roget sold off the copyright of the family heirloom to Longmans for 4,500 pounds. In 1962, Longmans put out an edition edited by Robert Dutch, and from there, Penguin took over.

Over the last century and a half, *Roget's* has lost ten concepts—it's down to 990—but it has gained a couple hundred thousand new words. In fact, Penguin's 2002 *Thesaurus* contains about twenty-five times as many words as Roget's original 1805 manuscript. Even Penguin's concise edition, also edited by Davidson, is considerably longer than Roget's original 1852 edition. "The main change since Roget's day," emphasizes Davidson, "has been the huge increase in its vocabulary." As an example, Davidson cites his decision to include dozens of specific phobias—from acaraphobia (fear of mites and small insects) to xenophobia—under "Fear" *854*.

And as the person entrusted by Penguin to update *Roget's*, adding new words is the main part of Davidson's job. An inveterate list maker himself, Davidson locates about a hundred new words a month. For the anniversary edition, he stuck in tens of thousands of new finds, while subtracting only seven. And one of the cuts—"cabbage patch doll"—listed under both "Image" *551* and "Plaything" *837*—he now regrets. "I thought it was history, but it has made a comeback."

The addition of each new word involves a complicated set of lexicographical challenges. Take "masturbation," for example. Explains Davidson:

Sexual intercourse is covered under "Junction" *45* along with other words denoting "joining." So where should masturbation go? Along with other words for privacy and solitude at "Unsociability" *883*? It just didn't seem to fit in anywhere. In the end, I added a completely new "sexual pleasure" paragraph under "Physical pleasure" *376* to cover all aspects including masturbation, and added a brief cross-reference to it in the "illicit love" paragraph at "Impurity" *951*.

This new "sexual pleasure" paragraph does indeed take *Roget's* into the twenty-first century, as it also features several words and phrases that could not possibly have entered into Peter Roget's head: "sex addiction or sexual addiction," "Viagra (tdmk)," and "cybersex."

The explosion of new words led Davidson's predecessor, Robert Dutch, to ax the two-column format, which placed "correlative terms" side by side with the main entries. In other words, *Roget's* no longer includes antonyms. Davidson sees this change as inevitable: "What was a good idea for a relatively small book in 1852 just doesn't work for the immense tome that the *Thesaurus* has now become."

The British edition is just the trunk of the tree planted by Peter Mark Roget. In the late nineteenth century, two different German versions appeared; in the mid-twentieth century, a Spanish version, one which continues to be reprinted. And of course, Roget's 1852 masterpiece has also spawned a swarm of American thesauruses (or thesauri—to use the official but stiff Latin plural Roget himself preferred). Particularly over the last twenty-five years, the production of new versions of *Roget's* has evolved into a virtual American cottage industry. Most have little connection to Roget himself or his original classification scheme; his name is simply invoked as a marketing tool. As one recent American editor acknowledges, "*Roget* has become a generic term for any book that supplies synonyms and antonyms."

Though nearly every major American publishing house now prints its own *Roget's*, Peter Mark Roget's legacy suffered two big hits in the early twenty-first century. One threat to his preeminence came from Bill Gates: for many members of Generation Y, the word "thesaurus" refers merely to a feature on Microsoft Word. Though this word-finder typically offers just a handful of choices, not the dozens offered in just about any printed *Roget's*—some Microsoft users aren't even aware that *Thesaurus* also happens to be the name of a famous book.

The other assault came in the form of an article, "Roget and His Brilliant, Unrivaled, Malign and Detestable Thesaurus," by British journalist Simon Winchester, published in *The Atlantic Monthly* in 2001. According to Winchester, *Roget's Thesaurus* is single-handedly responsible for the "dumbing-down" of Western culture. Though Winchester praises Roget the man as an ingenious polymath, he has nothing but scorn for his oft-used text. As he argues, "To put it more forcefully: Roget's *Thesaurus* no longer merits the unvarnished adoration it has over the years almost invariably received. It should be roundly condemned as a crucial part of the engine work that has transported us to our current state of linguistic and intellectual mediocrity."

Citing numerous examples—such as his undergraduate student who tried to pass off Roget's big words as his own profound cogitations—Winchester is convinced that *Roget's* invariably has a noxious effect. His proposed remedy can only be described as extreme. "Might it not," concludes Winchester in an angry apostrophe to Peter Mark Roget himself, "be best for your book simply to vanish and for [your] name . . . to be banished from the lexicon for all time?"

The fault, however, lies not with *Roget's* but with the mind-set of some of its users. Roget assumed that the reader would play an active role in selecting the right word. Back in 1852, he stressed that "amidst the many objects [words] thus brought within the realm of our contemplation . . . some excursive flight or brilliant conception may flash on the mind . . . awakening a responsive chord in the imagination or sensibility of the reader." *Roget's* has always been an interactive tool whose usefulness ultimately depends on both the thoughtfulness and industry of the reader.

ACKNOWLEDGMENTS

(916) GRATITUDE, thankfulness, feeling of obligation. Acknowledgement, recognition, thanksgiving, giving thanks, benediction.

Though Roget himself never crossed the pond, California is today home to the world's most illuminating Rogetiana. I could not have written this book without the generosity of two Roget enthusiasts from the Golden State, Donald Emblen and David Karpeles. A retired professor of English at Santa Rosa College, Don wrote the first full-scale Roget biography, *Peter Mark Roget: The Word and the Man* (Thomas Crowell, 1970); David is founder of the Karpeles Manuscript Library in Santa Barbara.

Don Emblen invited me to spend several days at his home in Santa Rosa, combing through his Roget files. I ended up obtaining copies of hundreds of letters written by members of the Roget family not yet available in any library. In addition, Don also shared with me the sixty-five letters that Etienne Dumont wrote to Peter and his mother (in French) between 1782 and 1825. I also benefited from several delightful dinner conversations with Don about Roget's strengths and foibles.

David Karpeles was equally gracious, showering me with Rogetiana at his magnificent home in Montecito. His extensive Roget archive features the 1805 manuscript, his "List of Principal Events," and his "autobiography"—manuscripts that had long been considered lost. David acquired all his Roget holdings at an auction held in

London in 1992 by Philips (now Bonham). I managed to track down a few other items from that sale at various libraries—such as Roget's account of his 1795 trip through the Scottish Highlands, in the National Library of Scotland, and some early correspondence of Catherine Romilly, in the archives of the Huguenot Society of London.

For providing access to Roget manuscripts, I am also grateful to archivists at the following institutions: the Houghton Library at Harvard, the Beinecke Library at Yale, the British Library, the Huntington Library, the Morgan Library, the Royal Society, the Royal College of Physicians, the University of Edinburgh, the Wren Library at Trinity College, the Wellcome Library, the University of London, the municipal archives of Geneva, the Berlin State library, the Manchester Public Library, the Liverpool Record Office, and Royal Holloway College. Special thanks go to Emma Marigliano of the Portico Library in Manchester, who showed me Roget's handwritten minutes dating back to his stint as the library's secretary.

In London I had the pleasure of meeting with several members of the Roget and Romilly families—including Mimi Romilly and Mary Bain, descendants of Sir Samuel; and Ursula Roget, Peter Mark Roget's great-granddaughter. I am especially grateful to Ursula for taking the time to talk about her illustrious forebears and for showing me her own "tatty" copy of the *Thesaurus* over tea in her Sloane Avenue apartment. I also appreciate the efforts of Victorine Martineau of the Huguenot Society of London, who shared with me her solid grounding in the history of the Romillys.

One of the joys of working on this book was the chance to spend many hours in the elegant surroundings of my home institution, the Boston Athenaeum, poring over rare eighteenth- and nineteenth-century books such as the first edition of the *Thesaurus*. The library's entire reference department—especially Stephen Nonack and Mary Warnement—proved exceedingly helpful. For providing access to rare books, I also want to thank the staff at the Countway Library at the Harvard Medical School and the Boston Public Library.

Despite my exhaustive research, which included the careful examination of many newly discovered Roget manuscripts, this book is not meant to be a scholarly biography. Though all the scenes are based on actual events, in several instances, where primary source material was lacking, I offered my best approximation of specific details. For example, though Roget's diary indicates that he took Dugald Stewart's course in moral philosophy, in June 1796, no transcripts of Stewart's actual lectures remain. Stewart's words in that section in chapter two come from his *Outlines of Moral Philosophy* published in 1793. Likewise, in the case of Matthew Baillie's final lecture at the Great Windmill School, covered in chapter three, Baillie's words are quoted from his *Morbid Anatomy*, published in 1793. Another scene for which I didn't have access to the complete historical record is the meeting of the Attic Chest Society in 1812. The published diary of the journalist Henry Crabb Robinson provides evidence of who was there that night, but not what they talked about. However, my account of Eleanor Porden's borrowings from Roget's lectures is taken directly from the footnotes in her mock-epic poem *The Veils*.

I owe a particular debt to my agent, Lane Zachary, for suggesting the topic and for her careful editing of the proposal. I would also like to thank Putnam's president, Ivan Held, for his enthusiastic support of this project. At Putnam, I would also like to acknowledge the hard work of my editors, Sarah Landis, Dan Conaway, and especially Rachel Holtzman, who were always willing to go the extra mile. I'm also grateful for the savvy of Doug Jones and Chris Nelson in the marketing department and Marilyn Ducksworth, Stephanie Sorensen, and Matthew Venzon in publicity.

Thanks go also to Rachel Youdelman for her expert photo research. I'm also appreciative of those historians and literary critics who responded to my various queries—in particular, Rosemarie Bodenheimer, Ann Gardiner, Neil Hertz, John Pickles, Penny Russell, Harriet Rivo, and A. J. Wright. For help with lexicographical matters, I am grateful to Werner Hullen, the author of numerous books and articles on the *Thesaurus*, and George Davidson, the British editor of *Roget's*.

Thanks also to a grant from the Virginia Center for the Creative Arts. My colleagues at VCCA—especially Marianne Hofmann—provided helpful feedback to a draft of the prologue, which I happened to read on November 2, 2006—188 years to the day after the events therein described.

INDEX

A freelance writer and journalist, Joshua Kendall has written for numerous publications, including *BusinessWeek*, *The Boston Globe*, and *The Washington Post*. For his outstanding reporting on psychiatry, he has won national journalism awards from both the National Mental Health Association and the American Psychoanalytic Association. He is also the coauthor of three academic psychology books. Kendall, who lives in Boston, received his B.A. in comparative literature summa cum laude from Yale College. He also did graduate work in comparative literature at Johns Hopkins.

To arrange a speaking engagement for Joshua Kendall, please contact the Penguin Speakers Bureau at speakersbureau@us.penguingroup.com.